BULLETPROOF
BOOK PROPOSALS

WRITER'S DIGEST BOOKS
Cincinnati, Ohio
www.writersdigest.com

BULLETPROOF

BOOK PROPOSALS

- 12 real-life proposals that were accepted
- agent-editor-author viewpoints on each proposal
- simple 10-step plan for writing your proposal

PAM BRODOWSKY AND ERIC NEUHAUS

Distributed in Canada by Fraser Direct, 100 Armstrong Avenue, Georgetown, ON, Canada L7G 5S4, Tel: (905) 877-4411. Distributed in the U.K. and Europe by David & Charles, Brunel House, Newton Abbot, Devon, TQ12 4PU, England, Tel: (+44) 1626 323200, Fax: (+44) 1626 323319, E-mail: mail@davidandcharles.co.uk. Distributed in Australia by Capricorn Link, P.O. Box 704, Windsor, NSW 2756 Australia, Tel: (02) 4577-3555.

Visit our Web sites at www.writersdigest.com and www.wdeditors.com for information on more resources for writers.

To receive a free weekly e-mail newsletter delivering tips and updates about writing and about Writer's Digest products, register directly at our Web site at http://newsletters.fwpublications.com.

11 10 09 08 07   5 4 3 2 1

Library of Congress Cataloging-in-Publication Data
Brodowsky, Pamela K.
  Bulletproof book proposal / by Pam Brodowsky and Eric Neuhaus.
    p. cm.
  Includes index.
  "13 real-life proposals that were accepted--agent, editor, and author viewpoints on each proposal--simple 10-step plan for writing your proposal."
  ISBN-13: 978-1-58297-367-8 (pbk. : alk. paper)
  ISBN-10: 1-58297-367-9
  1. Book proposals. I. Neuhaus, Eric. II. Title.
  PN161.B73 2007
  070.5'2--dc22   2006022617

Edited by Michelle Ehrhard
Designed by Grace Ring
Production coordinated by Mark Griffin

ABOUT THE AUTHORS

Pamela K. Brodowsky is an experienced literary agent, co-author of The Staying Sane Series (Da Capo Press, November 2005) and *Girl's Night Out: A Ladies Guide to Beginners Poker* (Citadel, (January 2007) She is the founder of International Literary Arts, a full-service literary agency.

Eric Neuhaus is a writer, journalist and award-winning television producer. He is the co-author of *The World's Fittest You: Four Weeks to Total Fitness* (Dutton, January 2004) and *Iron Yoga* (Rodale, 2005) He has written for numerous magazines including *Body & Soul*, *Experience Life* and *Clublife*. He is also an adjunct professor at New York University in the division of Film, Video and Broadcasting where he teaches news writing. He started his career as a story editor and producer at *ABC News 20/20* and has worked for Martha Stewart Living Omnimedia and Court TV. Visit him at his Web iste www.ericneuhaus.com.

ACKNOWLEDGMENTS

First of all the authors would like to acknowledge our editors, Michelle Ehrhard, and Jane Friedman, for all their hard work in the making of this book. You are both truly a pleasure to work with. Next we wish to thank Daniel Zitin and Dana Mirman for their invaluable help and contributions in the making of this project.

As well as Peter Neuhaus, Sylvia Neuhaus, Shana Neuhaus, and Callie Neuhaus.

We also wish to thank all the editors and agents who took the time out of their busy schedules to contribute their comments to our project.

Finally, and most important, we wish to thank all the authors who contributed their book proposals. Without their help and contributions there wouldn't be a book.

DEDICATION

All it takes to sell your book is a superior book proposal. We dedicate this book to all the up and coming new authors. We wish you much success.

To my husband, Edward, and our children, Sarah and Jacob.
With love.
—PKB

PERMISSIONS

Permission to print the sample proposals in this book were granted by:

William G. Ramroth, Jr. for *Pragmatism and Modern Architecture* and *Project Management for Design Professionals*

Leonard Saffir for *PR on a Budget*

Tom Philbin and Michael Philbin for *The Killer Book of True Crime Trivia*

Sandy Trupp and Maureen Chase for *Emails That Click*

Steve Greenberg for *Gadget Nation*

Suzan St. Maur for *Powerwriting*

Sheri Colberg, Ph.D. for *Diabetes-Free Kids*

Jan Cannon, Ph.D. for *Now What Do I Do?*

Amy Weintraub for *Yoga for Depression*

Rena Greenberg for *The Right Weigh*

Jerry R. Day, Ed.D. for *How to Raise Children You Want to Keep*

Table of Contents

Introduction

Have you ever walked down the aisle in your local bookstore and said to yourself, "Wow, I could have written that book"? The truth of the matter is you can, and we'll show you how. After following the steps in this book and reading through the twelve sample proposals, you'll have all the inside knowledge you need to get your nonfiction book on the shelf of that same bookstore.

What most aspiring writers, like yourself, might not consider is that book publishing is a business. Like any business, editors and publishers want to make money—lots of money. So do the agents who sell books to publishing houses. And so do you! When it comes to nonfiction, editors are in the business, for the most part, of buying book proposals, not books. That's right—you don't have to write the entire book before a publisher pays you an advance to publish your book! All you have to do is write a blockbuster book proposal.

Nonfiction book proposals are more like business plans than books. Like any other business, the ultimate goal of a book proposal is to sell your idea. In order to accomplish that goal, you need a systematic way to organize and present your idea to editors and agents. Let's be clear: The presentation of your idea—in the form of a book proposal—needs to stand out from the crowd. Agents and editors receive hundreds, perhaps thousands, of proposals each year. To make your proposal rise from the mounds of paper and e-mail that circulate through the publishing world, you'll need inside information and tools from authors who have sold book proposals and from agents and editors who ultimately decide whether to publish your work.

Here you'll find a unique method for writing a nonfiction book. First, we've broken down the writing process into ten simple steps. Each step of the process is a chapter in the first section of the book. We suggest you read through the chapters and try the exercises at the end of each before attempting to sit down and write the entire proposal. Book proposals take time. Some say that writing the book proposal is harder than writing the actual book. We agree. That's why you'll need to think through all the elements of the proposal before tackling the project as a whole.

But the real heart of this book is the twelve book proposals that writers like you have sold. We believe that one of the best ways to learn how to write an effective book proposal is by example. If you're writing a novel, you'll certainly want to read other novels that have been published. Nonfiction book proposals are no different.

We've gathered together a wide variety of proposals and formats covering topics from health to humor. Then, we've critiqued each proposal from a unique three-point perspective of all those involved in the process of publishing nonfiction books, from writer to agent to editor. In some cases you'll only find the author and editor perspective. The reason: These authors decided to bypass the agent and submit directly to the publisher. We'll explain more about this later in the book. For now, this three-point perspective gives you an insider's edge that you won't find in any other book. We've also inclued comments throughout the proposal section that point out why each proposal worked and how you can emulate its success. We believe that your exposure to and understanding of why each of these proposals sold will ultimately help you sell your nonfiction book.

In the first section (chapters one through ten) we give you the basic understanding of each element of the proposal in a step-by-step format. In the next section we show you how to apply that knowledge using real-life examples of successful proposals. Finally, we give you Web sites and resources to jump-start your entry into the world of publishing. Let's get started!

Part I
Writing Your Proposal

Follow the steps in these ten chapters to learn how to write an effective book proposal that will sell. You'll learn everything you need to know to create a book proposal that will sell your project to an agent or editor. If you follow these proposal-writing guidelines, from finding an idea to packaging your proposal, you will put yourself in a great position to find success.

Chapter 1
Defining Your Idea

GREAT IDEAS TAKE SHAPE

Everyone has a book idea. Some are good, and some seem pretty silly. How do you tell the difference? How can you determine whether your idea is a good one? And then, how do you express that idea in just the words that will sell it to an editor?

The Idea

We think we know a bad idea when we hear one. It's been done. It's old hat. It's boring. It's far-fetched. It's silly. No one cares. It's too small—an article but not a book. On the other hand, it's probably a good enough idea if you can write a substantial and interesting book about it. So how do you make that assessment?

- Is it something you would want to read? Frequently, book ideas are generated because someone was looking for some information he couldn't find anywhere. On the assumption that others might be looking for the same information, he writes a book about it. A good book idea is one that fills a gap.
- Is it something you want to spend six months or a year or two years writing? Is the idea interesting enough to keep you engaged for the time it will take to research and write it? And, if it's going to take a trip to Indonesia to research the book, are you in a position to take that trip? These practical questions are of great importance. Even if the idea is a brilliant one that intrigues and excites you, if it may be difficult or

impossible for you to actually do a good job of bringing it to life, it's not a workable idea.

- Is the research within your grasp? This is another practical matter. Are you familiar with and capable of using the resources you will need to research and write the book? If you need to interview people for the book, are you likely to be able to gain access to the number of people or the particular people you need to speak to?
- Do you have something important or significant or new or very funny or definitive to say? Is what you want to tell people something they need or want to know? Is it something that hasn't been done before? Is your take on the subject fresh, new, unusual, more complete, exhaustive? Is it more concise? Do you have new information, a new discovery, something based on new science?
- Is it something you can write about well, authoritatively, based on a broad or at least sufficient knowledge of the subject area? You would love to write the definitive history of the war in Iraq. Unfortunately, you've never served in the military, never worked as a journalist, don't understand the language of Iraq, and don't even know the name of their language. The history of the war in Iraq is a good idea—for somebody else to write.
- Is it big, complex, or extensive enough to be worth an entire book? Not every idea is worth an article, and not every article can be expanded into a book. "Brad and Angelina's Wedding" is an article. A self-help book about how to keep your celebrity marriage alive might be a book, albeit one with a limited audience. Is there enough material to justify a complete book, rather than just an article?

If you can't answer a passionate *Yes!* to all the questions asked above, you're not on firm ground with your idea. It's not the idea for you, or you're not the writer for it.

Let's sum up the attributes of a good idea.

- **It's interesting.** Obviously, it's interesting to you, but is it interesting to others? Run it by friends and family, and see if you can extract honest reactions. See whether people respond to the idea by engaging in conversation about it. It's a good sign if people have a lot to say, even if they are critical. Negative responses can help you focus your idea. If people have nothing to say about it beyond general praise, you may not have a very interesting idea.

- **It presents new content or a fresh approach to old content.** If the last biography of Fidel Castro was published ten years ago, your biography will include ten years never written about before in a book. If the last biography of Fidel was written by a Florida exile who hates Castro's regime and you are a leftist who finds much to admire, your approach to the same biographical facts will be fresh.

- **It's the first, best, or only.** The great publisher Alfred A. Knopf famously used these three words to sum up what he required of any book. The first book about the development of the iPod might have been a candidate for the Knopf list. The best book—the most comprehensive and complete book—about the disputed 2000 presidential election would also qualify. A book about how to build a healthy life if suffering from lactose intolerance—if it's going to be the only book out there that addresses this niche market—would also have good potential.

- **It's worth a whole book.** Sometimes the difference between an article and a book is how you focus and develop your idea. Sometimes the more you try to expand an idea, the thinner it gets. In that case maybe it's never going to be more than an article. If you can enrich your idea and keep it interesting, you may have a book.

- **It links ideas in a new way.** This is another way of talking about "point of view." It's what you personally bring to the subject, whether it's your expertise, your extensive research, your particular take on the subject, your style of writing, or the depth and quality of your thinking. John Gray's *Men Are From Mars, Women Are From Venus* was a brilliant success based not on new ideas but on familiar ideas focused and presented in a fresh, exciting way.

- **It resembles previously successful books in its general outline.** You're on the right track if your book looks, in general, like recent successful titles. For instance, both *The Tipping Point* by Malcolm Gladwell and *Freakonomics* by Steven D. Levitt and Stephen J. Dubner are made up of chapters on separate topics that, when looked at together, seem to demonstrate the basic premise of the book. So books that take a basic premise and gather far-flung examples to illustrate it could not be rejected on the grounds that the form isn't commercial. In fact, it's a proven form. Of course, it will help if your book, like those, is filled with fresh ideas, presented in a lively prose style. It's the same, but different. A paradox? Not really. There are other books out there like it, which tells you there's a market, but yours is different enough to separate itself from the crowd. If your idea is better than the others, that's really a plus!

- **It deals with subjects that have previously attracted a demonstrable audience.** World War II, the Knights Templar, dieting—these are subjects people have shown in the past they are interested in reading about. Subjects are cyclical. There's nothing new under the sun, but there are always trends. Some years back, it seemed that any book about Jacqueline Kennedy Onassis was a good idea. There was a period when anything anyone wrote about Howard Hughes seemed to be successful. Not every new diet book is really new; there are probably only a few basic ideas in weight control and diet planning. But each new book is constructed around a fresh aspect of dieting, and the demand for new ideas in diets is apparently limitless. Today's fresh idea can get stale fast, but there always seems to be a new way to capture the attention of constant dieters, who tend to need fresh approaches that will help them maintain their focus on weight loss. In other words, there's a big market for books with fresh ideas on trendy issues.
- **It deals with something that hasn't been written about for a popular audience, but has been hot lately in scholarly or intellectual circles.** This is called "popularizing," and it's the general name for a kind of book that's always a good idea—if you have the knowledge and the writing skill to do a good job. Brian Greene's books take the most obscure contemporary theories of physics and present them in a way that the general reader can understand. The latest "hot" diet book is usually a popularization of the latest scientific developments in nutrition research.
- **It's about something that's always there but has been taken for granted.** It could be rats, salt, truly tasteless jokes—information hidden in plain sight, illumination cast on the obvious. It's something of a current trend to focus on the small and investigate it to uncover its significance. Abraham Lincoln is a ripe subject for scholars and popularizers; Abraham Lincoln's stovepipe hat might be the hook for a fresh, trendy look at Lincoln.
- **It's about neglected historical or scientific developments that might have a particular relevance to contemporary situations.** The Crusades, for example, probably have special relevance today in light of current western relations with the Muslim world. Recently Dava Sobel's book, *Longitude: The True Story of a Lone Genius Who Solved the*

Greatest Scientific Problem of His Time, was a great success. The idea here is well expressed in the title and subtitle—a flashback that explains something we take for granted today, something abstract personalized in a character: a lone genius. So history here is personalized (there are more readers of *People* than there are of *American Heritage*) and simplified. It's a good idea, well executed and well presented.

The Hook

Now that you have a good idea, let's take a look at how to present it. You may have a good idea, but if you can't hook your audience, all is for naught. Let's separate the idea from the hook. The *idea* is what you want to write about, what you have to tell, or sell, or teach, or explain. The *hook* is how you put the idea into words that immediately interest your potential readers. It's a cue, a neon sign, a shortcut to the bottom line of the idea. It's got to click instantly. The idea will grow into the book's content. The hook will lead off the overview that opens your proposal, and it will grow into a blueprint for how the book is marketed. The hook should be brief, if possible just a paragraph. It should not be more than half a page. It's the essence of your proposal, and every key selling point that you will detail later in your proposal must be present in the hook.

Creating the right hook means:

- **You must understand the rhetoric, the different ways you may present something to different people.** The audience for your proposal is, first of all, an editor, so it's important to understand her business needs in assessing an idea; your rhetoric must speak a language that she will understand and respond to. At the same time you must make the idea sound interesting to readers who might be interested in the idea. There are many markets to which books can be directed; editors will try to determine whether your idea will appeal to readers who like ideas similar to yours. It sounds circular, but it means that you're not trying to sell your idea to people who are not its audience, only to those who are.
- **The hook is an accurate image of the content.** You don't want to lie, deceive, or trick the reader into thinking he's going to get something he's not going to get.
- **The hook is brief; it's sharp; it's accurate.** Every word counts in the hook. Say everything you need to say once. Do not repeat yourself.

- **The hook presents a powerful reader benefit.** John Gottman's *Why Marriages Succeed or Fail: And How You Can Make Yours Last* popularizes research Gottman and his associates did to identify behaviors that are correlated with successful marriages and behaviors that are correlated with unsuccessful marriages. It is presented in a form that readers can use to assess the potential of their own marriages, and more important, can then apply to changing marital habits from potentially ruinous ones to those more likely to succeed. Whenever possible, personalize your material and present it as something that can directly benefit the reader. "The reader will learn ...," "The reader will be able to ...," and "The reader will discover ..." are phrases that emphasize this key element.

Sometimes the difference between a good idea and a weak one will be the hook itself. By answering the tough questions and refining your idea, you may find that your idea is evolving into something different from what you started with. The process of narrowing and focusing your idea may become the process of developing a different and better idea. You may have started out with an article, but by thinking more deeply about the idea, you may work the basic idea into something worthy of a book. Or you may start out with an idea that would take years to write, but by focusing the idea you may develop something that can be written more efficiently. Or you may start out with an idea that's interesting to you—but only to you. The process of focusing—of trying to come up with the right angle and the right point of view and the right hook—might lead you to a different idea, one that has a greater general interest because of a slightly different slant. The process of developing your idea is the beginning of your proposal, and writing the proposal is the beginning of writing your book.

An idea isn't a good one unless it can be expressed in a strong hook. The processes of developing your idea and developing your hook are linked. These two elements are like the roadmap for a long journey: You can't leave home without them. When you have your idea and your hook, you're on your way to a strong proposal and a strong book.

It all comes down to this:

A. A good idea is one you can write well.
B. A good idea is one whose value can be easily conveyed to its market.
C. A good hook concisely and convincingly expresses A and B.

EXERCISE: Clearly Identify Your Idea in Twenty-Five Words or Less

This is your crucial first exercise. You need to clearly condense and state the idea for your project in this short summary. Don't be surprised if it takes you several rewrites to get all your points across in this concise statement. When you're finished, hand this summary off to your friends, family, and colleagues—without any further explanation than you are preparing to write a book on the subject. If, after reading it, even one person comes up with questions as to what your book is about, you haven't done your job. Remember, you need to clearly define your idea and hook your reader. Agents and editors will not be speaking with you until *after* the proposal has gotten their attention. Your writing needs to speak for you.

Chapter 2
Choosing a Title

CREATING THE TELL-AND-SELL TITLE

The most critical element that's going to sell your idea is the title. That title is the first thing your audience is going to consider when they come across your book in a bookstore or online. Think of all the titles you see when walking up and down the aisle of your local bookstore. How much time do you spend looking at a book before you pick it up and browse through it? Probably just a few seconds, if that much. Yes, maybe some catchy cover art will grab your attention, but cover art is more of an attention getter when it comes to fiction rather than nonfiction. Yet if the book's title means something to you and connects to something in your life that you want or need, "*BAM!*"—that author has got you in the tent for at least a pickup, browse, and glance at the table of contents.

In some cases after a publisher buys your book, the title may change. Your editor as well as the marketing and publicity departments may decide that another title may be better at selling your book. That's okay. In the end, the publisher's goal—and yours, too—is to sell as many books as you can. Take this book as an example. Our original title was *10 Secret Steps to Write a Superior Book Proposal*. After consultation with the editor and sales team at the publishing house, we revised the title to better reflect the scope and focus of the book. And the new title sounds catchier. So even if your title changes in the publishing process, you still need to launch your project with a title that will hook everyone.

But even before your proposal can be sold to a buying public in the bookstore, your book's title must first attract the attention of an agent and publisher. The title is the first thing a literary agent is going to see. Most likely, if you're e-mailing an agent with a query letter (we'll get to that in chapter ten), the title will be the subject line of the e-mail. Taking it a step further, once you have an agent, the title is the first thing a publisher is going to read—and yes, it will probably be the same subject line of an e-mail that your agent will send to the publisher to introduce your book. And so on and so on until a customer comes across your title and is motivated to buy it.

WHAT MAKES A GOOD TITLE?

Think about what kind of titles get your attention when you're browsing through a bookstore. Consider the thousands of books that are published each year. Clever titles go a long way in this crowded market. And the more clever your title is, the more likely you are to get someone to reach out and pick up your book. Let's be clear: Publishers want to be wowed by titles. If your proposal has a title that grabs the publisher's attention, congratulations—you've gotten over the first hurdle.

The other aspect of a good title is often an even better subtitle. A great subtitle can really help your book stand out from the crowd. When creating a subtitle, consider some of the tips we offer later in this section. A subtitle can help clarify your topic, express a benefit of the book, or be clever and amusing. Only use a subtitle if it really offers some type of selling hook and a way to differentiate your book from others.

Consider some of these best-selling titles. *Bad Cat: 244 Not-So-Pretty Kitties and Cats Gone Bad* says it all. The minute you hear that title and subtitle you chuckle to yourself and can relate to the concept. The author delivers on this clever title with a simple execution. He compiles photographs of "bad cats" juxtaposed with witty and amusing captions. A great title and clever execution launched *Bad Cat* onto the best-seller lists shortly after its publication and led to another book by with the same concept, entitled *Bad Dog: 278 Outspoken, Indecent, and Overdressed Dogs.*

Now consider another best-selling title: *He's Just Not That Into You.* This title originated from an episode of *Sex and the City* and delivered some funny advice for the single girl trying to figure out why the guy she's dating suddenly dumps her. The answer, according to the authors of the book, is quite simple—and it's right there in the title—*he's just not that into you.* The marketing buzz surrounding the book was huge, in part because the title was so catchy. Everyone loved saying it. When the authors appeared on *The Oprah Winfrey Show*, Oprah Winfrey herself kept repeating the title of the book every time she tried to explain why some guy isn't returning her guest's calls. What better publicity could there be than Oprah Winfrey shouting the title of your book on national television and the studio audience repeating after her in call-and-response fashion? The result: an instant bestseller.

Oprah shouting the title of your book on national television is something of a long shot. However, you can follow these simple rules to create a title that will sell your proposal—and your book.

A NEW TWIST ON AN OLD IDEA

Diet books rely on titles to make something old sound new. Every year hundreds of diet books are published, yet there's generally little new information about losing weight, so you need a title to make your diet or weight-loss program sound new and different. Jorge Cruise wrote the best-selling *The 3-Hour Diet* based on the premise that you can lose weight by eating five or six small meals a day. While this is not necessarily a new concept or theory, the great title makes something old new again, with best-selling results. Here you'll find some useful ways to help you generate the "tell-and-sell title." Notice how these examples that take old ideas and give them a new twist (which they also do with their titles):

- *The Little Red Book of Selling: 12.5 Principles of Sales Greatness* by Jeffrey Gitomer takes the basic concept of sales to a whole new level.
- *The Dog Whisperer: A Compassionate, Nonviolent Approach to Dog Training* by Paul Owens and Norma Eckroate offers a new approach to the old problem of training your dog.
- *Nothing to Wear? A Five-Step Cure for the Common Closet* by Joe Lupo and Jesse Garza gives some new ways to add style to your wardrobe.

TIES INTO SOMETHING POPULAR

A title that connects to something in current events or popular culture is an easy way to get people's attention. With *He's Just Not That Into You,* authors Greg Behrendt and Liz Tucillo were able to capitalize on the popularity of *Sex and the City.* Try hooking your title to some idea that everyone is talking about. For example:

- As a tie-in to the "new" Superman movies, consider *The Physics of Superheroes* by James Kakalios.

- *Everything Bad Is Good for You: How Today's Popular Culture Is Actually Making Us Smarter* by Steven Johnson takes on popular beliefs about pop culture.
- If you've ever thought about getting on one of the popular reality shows, you may want to consider *The Ultimate Reality Show: How Far Would You Go to Win $10 Million?* By Clay Jacobsen.

GIVES YOU THE PROMISE

If you're writing a proposal that is prescriptive, you might want to consider putting the benefit the reader is going to get right in the title or subtitle. This is very common for health, diet, and fitness books: "Lose seven pounds in seven days," "Four weeks to a better body," and "Five minutes to boost your memory." But time isn't the only way to deliver a prescriptive promise. Here are ten other ways to help you figure out the promise of your book:

- **New and revolutionary.** If your book really promises something different and new, make that clear in the subtitle. For instance, the title of Lee Eisenberg's *The Number: A Completely Different Way to Think About the Rest of Your Life* makes it very clear that this book is offering you a new way of thinking.
- **Transformational.** Many books promise that their text will do nothing short of change your life. Dr. Laura Schlessinger, for instance, makes that promise in the subheading of her book, *Woman Power: Transform Your Man, Your Marriage, Your Life.*
- **Mastery.** Will your book offer the reader mastery of a topic? The bestselling book *Secrets of the Millionaire Mind: Mastering the Inner Game of Wealth*, by T. Harv Eker, makes this promise, a promise that helped turn the book into a bestseller.
- **Power.** Who wouldn't want more power in any area of their lives? Take, for instance, *The Automatic Millionaire Homeowner: A Powerful Plan to Finish Rich in Real Estate* by David Bach. This title promises the reader more power in the area of wealth creation. In what area of your reader's life can you offer him more power?
- **Extraordinary.** Promise the reader something beyond the ordinary. Frank Warren's *PostSecret: Extraordinary Confessions From Ordinary Lives,* for example, is a book that compiles people's confessions, thereby giving the reader a look at the lives of strangers, which is beyond the usual scope of daily life.

- **Secret.** Readers want to be let in on inside information they may not otherwise encounter in their everyday lives. One title that promises to let the reader in on a secret is *The Millionaire Next Door: The Surprising Secrets of America's Wealthy* by Thomas J. Stanley and William D. Danko.
- **Simple.** When it comes to solving a problem in their lives, readers would love to find a simple solution. Perhaps you can promise your reader simplicity, like Nicholas Perricone's *The Perricone Weight-Loss Diet: A Simple 3-Part Plan to Help You Lose the Fat, the Wrinkles, and the Years*.
- **Results.** For many readers, the bottom line may be whether your book can help them produce results in an area of their lives they wish to improve. For example, Oprah's personal trainer, Bob Greene, gives the reader the promise of results in the subhead of his book, *Bob Greene's Total Body Makeover: An Accelerated Program of Exercise and Nutrition for Maximum Results in Minimum Time*.
- **Step-by-step.** You may choose to have your title let readers know that your book will guide them through a process every step of the way. One title that makes such a promise is Jeanine Cox's *The Perfect Name: A Step-by-Step Guide to Naming Your Baby*.

THE BENEFIT OF TIME

Publishers are always trying to capitalize on how busy everyone is. Your title can reflect this by emphasizing that the promise of your book is going to be quick and easy. We call that "the benefit of time." Many readers want to know that by buying this book they won't need a lot of time to execute the action plan. For instance, you'll find a lot of cookbook titles that promise recipes that are simple and easy to follow. Likewise, to capitalize on the benefit of time in your title, you can also offer simple take-away information. The most basic form of take-away information is the "tip." Magazines use this technique all the time. On the cover you'll notice enticing headlines like "585 Ways to Satisfy Your Lover" or "1001 Ways to Make Yourself Look 10 Years Younger." These types of headlines can be turned into attention-grabbing titles for books, too.

FUNNY OR A PLAY ON WORDS

Any time you can play on a word or phrase, give it try. A diet book title I just love is *Portion Tellers*. The premise is simple—use portion size to control your food—but the title is blockbuster. You may think it's trite, but if you can figure out a way to work a pun into your title, try it. Publishers and agents love wordplay, and the more clever the better. If you can get a publisher to chuckle when reading your title, she's more apt to read on. Remember, wordplay titles are not easy, and you don't want to be too cutesy. There's a fine line between pun and overdone, so try not to cross it. You may want to test out your puns on your friends and family first and see what reaction you get.

One of the masters of clever titles is humor writer Mark Leyner. One of his most well-known titles quickly jumped to *The New York Times* best-seller list. *Why Do Men Have Nipples? Hundreds of Questions You'd Only Ask a Doctor After Your Third Martini* is written with the help of an emergency room physician. The title is definitely an attention grabber. What's more, the author really delivers on that funny title with hilarious stories and anecdotes.

So the question is, how do you think of a funny title for your book? It's not easy. One thing to do is keep a pen and paper with you at all times. When you hear something or see something that might be good fodder for your clever title, write it down. You might come up with a brilliant title in the middle of the night. Even if you're not sure, write it down; you never know if it's something that may turn out to be viable. The other way to jump-start your wordplay title is to see how others have done it. This may spark your own creative juices. Here are some we found particularly clever:

- *Behind Every Great Woman There's a Fabulous Gay Man: Advice From a Guy Who Gives It to You Straight* by Dave Singleton
- *A Special Education: One Family's Journey Through the Maze of Learning Disabilities*, by fashion designer Dana Buchman, offers advice for parents with learning-disabled kids, based on her own experiences with her daughter.
- By titling her book about the art of obituary writing *The Dead Beat: Lost Souls, Lucky Stiffs, and the Perverse Pleasure of Obituaries*, author Marilyn Johnson creates a catchy, upbeat pun out of a morbid topic.
- *The Daily Show With Jon Stewart Presents America (the Book): A Citizen's Guide to Democracy Inaction*. Here, the comedian makes a clever play on the term "democracy in action" to bring a smile to the reader's face and catch his attention.
- *Take the Bully by the Horns: Stop Unethical, Uncooperative, or Unpleasant People From Running or Ruining Your Life* by Sam Horn
- *It Takes a Prophet to Make a Profit: 15 Trends That Are Reshaping American Business* by C. Britt Beemer and Robert L. Shook

- *The Right Nation: Conservative Power in America,* by John Micklethwait and Adrian Wooldridge, catches the reader's attention to this book about the Republican Party.
- *The I of the Storm: Embracing Conflict, Creating Peace* by Gary Simmons
- *Stress for Success: The Proven Program for Transforming Stress Into Positive Energy at Work* by James E. Loehr
- *Tails of Devotion: A Look at the Bond Between People and Their Pets* by Emily Scott Pottruck

OFFER SECRET ADVICE AND INSIDER KNOWLEDGE

One of the best "secret advice" titles is one that is surprisingly simple: the *What Your Doctor Won't Tell You...* series of books. Readers often buy a book to get information they don't think they can get elsewhere. They want inside information. They want to be surprised by the information in the book, but first you're going to have to surprise them with a clever title. Take a look at some of these examples. All of these titles show you how to package your information so readers know right away they are getting a unique and insider's perspective to the information.

- *The Girlfriends' Guide to Pregnancy*, by Vicki Iovine, promises to provide the reader with the kind of "secret" information she can only get from other women.
- Bernard Goldberg had a bestseller with *Bias: A CBS Insider Exposes How the Media Distort the News* by promising the reader a "whistle-blower's" inside account of TV news.
- Another title that promises to bring the reader in on "inside information" about the wealthy is Barbara Stanny's *Secrets of Six-Figure Women: Surprising Strategies to Up Your Earnings and Change Your Life.*
- The title of Joel Greenblatt's *You Can Be a Stock Market Genius: Uncover the Secret Hiding Places of Stock Market Profits* promises the average investor a pro's inside knowledge.
- For the parents who are wondering what's going on inside their teenager's mind, Jennifer Marshall Lippincott and Robin M. Deutsch offer the inside scoop on teens in *7 Things Your Teenager Won't Tell You: And How to Talk to Them Anyway.*
- Car shopping? Then surely you'd want to pick up *What Car Dealers Won't Tell You: The Insider's Guide to Buying or Leasing a New or Used Car* by Bob Ford.

- Author John Perkins had a bestseller with *Confessions of an Economic Hit Man,* his exposé about his former career as an economic planner for an international consulting firm.
- Kevin Trudeau's *Natural Cures "They" Don't Want You to Know About* promises to reveal to the reader information that Trudeau claims is obscured by traditional health care providers.
- Since Michael F. Roizen and Mehmet C. Oz, the authors of *YOU: The Smart Patient: An Insider's Handbook for Getting the Best Treatment*, are doctors, they can promise the reader a physician's "inside" look at how to get great health care.

FILL A SPECIFIC NEED OR PROBLEM—SELL A SOLUTION

Readers buy nonfiction self-help books for a reason—to find a solution to a problem. Don't be coy in your title if your proposal has a solution to a major life problem. Dean Ornish gets right to the point with the title of his bestseller *Reversing Heart Disease*. To help women navigate the problems of pregnancy, the authors of *What to Expect When You're Expecting* didn't waste any time telling prospective readers how their book would help women get though pregnancy.

We've come up with ten basic needs to show you how to transform a solution to a need into a blockbuster title. There are certainly many more needs out there—and solutions to needs, too. We can't fit them all in this book. If the topic for your book falls outside one of the needs listed here, that's okay. As we did with this book, you'll first need to identify what that need is and how the title of your book can offer the solution. These examples will show you how other authors transformed a need into a successful title.

- **Love:** Everyone's looking for love in their lives, and Alexander Avila's book, *LoveTypes*, gets right to the point and promises to fulfill the need for love in its subheading: *Discover Your Romantic Style and Find Your Soul Mate.*
- **Money:** Who wouldn't say they want and need more money? Best-selling author Suze Orman gets right to the point, promising to help readers find *The Road to Wealth: A Comprehensive Guide to Your Money.*
- **Sex:** One writer who has found a niche in helping readers solve their problems about sex is gynecologist Dr. Hilda Hutcherson. One of her books specifically addresses women's need for sex in its title, *Pleasure: A Woman's Guide to Getting the Sex You Want, Need, and Deserve.*

- **Health:** Good health is an obvious basic need, and one example of a title that promises to help readers meet that need is Dr. Andrew Weil's *8 Weeks to Optimum Health: A Proven Program for Taking Full Advantage of Your Body's Natural Healing Power.*
- **Power:** A sense of power is an important need, and one book that addresses this concern is David J. Lieberman's *Get Anyone to Do Anything: Never Feel Powerless Again—Psychological Secrets to Predict, Control and Influence Every Situation.*
- **Freedom:** People need to feel a sense of freedom in their lives, and *The Four Agreements: A Practical Guide to Personal Freedom,* by Don Miguel Ruiz, is one book looking to answer that need.
- **Communication:** Communication is a basic need, yet self-expression is not always obvious or intuitive for people. One book that tries to meet readers' communication needs is Margaret Shepherd's *The Art of Civilized Conversation: A Guide to Expressing Yourself With Style and Grace.*
- **Recognition:** Whatever their chosen field, people want and need to be acknowledged. Larry A. Thompson's *Shine: A Powerful 4-Step Plan to Becoming a Star in Anything You Do* promises to help readers get recognition.
- **Happiness:** For people seeking to meet their need to be happy, Dr. Dan Baker and Cameron Stauth's *What Happy People Know: How the New Science of Happiness Can Change Your Life for the Better* is one book that strives to meet that need.
- **Family:** People need harmony in the home, and TV's Dr. Phil McGraw seeks to answer that need with his book *Family First: Your Step-by-Step Plan for Creating a Phenomenal Family.*

DON'T SOUND TOO ACADEMIC

You might be familiar with a certain best-selling book with a rather unusual title. In fact, the title can't even be said on television or listed on *The New York Times* best-seller list without being masked. *On Bullshit* is an academic treatise on the philosophy of lying written by a noted Princeton philosophy professor, Harry G. Frankfurt. If the title reflected the academic nature of the book—something like *The Philosophy of Lying in Modern Culture*—it's doubtful the book would have landed on the best-seller list.

Now consider *Freakonomics: A Rogue Economist Explores the Hidden Side of Everything.* We believe it's a surprising book for the best-seller list, too, because its concept is very academic. *Freakonomics* tackles a rather lofty subject—economic theory—in a way that is accessible, relevant, and entertaining. The authors, Steven D. Levitt, an economic professor, and Stephen J. Dubner, a journalist, deliver and package the information in a fun and lively way, not at all like an academic economics textbook.

How do the authors of *Freakonomics* accomplish this task? First, the title of the book piques people's curiosity. By having an interesting, fun title, it helps readers see that the authors aren't going to take a dry approach to an academic topic. The title probably also helped the authors shape the tone and direction of their book. They show how economics, a subject that may seem remote and irrelevant to readers' daily lives, can actually tell us a lot about human behavior and motivation. Now, the average reader might not be interested in economic theory as a concept, but readers are surely interested in learning what motivates people! Thus, the *Freakonomics* authors have turned a seemingly academic subject into a very practical guide to the human psyche.

How do you turn your academic topic into a commercial title? See how others have done it. Here are some other book titles that turn an academic subject into something more popular and commercial:

- *The Tipping Point: How Little Things Can Make a Big Difference* by Malcolm Gladwell. The term "tipping point" is used by epidemiologists to describe the moment when a virus reaches critical mass and turns into an epidemic. Borrowing from epidemiology and other fields, the author analyzes various social issues. Sounds like a rather academic topic, doesn't it? Yet the author was able to produce a best-selling book by applying this theory to issues that affect readers' everyday lives, such as crime rates.

- *Blink: The Power of Thinking Without Thinking,* also by Malcolm Gladwell, is another example of a book that takes an academic subject and turns it into a bestseller. Again the author takes on a seemingly esoteric topic—this time, a theory from psychology called "rapid cognition," which is how people arrive at snap judgments.

- *The World Is Flat: A Brief History of the Twenty-First Century*, a book about globalization by *New York Times* columnist Thomas L. Friedman, hit the best-seller list, perhaps in part due to its interesting title.

- *The Informant* by Kurt Eichenwald. This book about price fixing was a best-seller partly because of the author's compelling, crime-dramalike writing style.

- *Conspiracy of Fools* by Kurt Eichenwald. Here, the author turns a business report about the collapse of Enron into a page turner.
- *Collapse: How Societies Choose to Fail or Succeed* by Jared Diamond. Diamond, an evolutionary biologist, analyzes broad patterns in human history.
- *Guns, Germs, and Steel: The Fates of Human Societies* by Jared Diamond. In this bestseller, Diamond again explores wide patterns of history in a way that appeals to the masses.
- *Why Is Sex Fun? The Evolution of Human Sexuality* by Jared Diamond. The catchy title of this book helps attain the reader's interest in this book about evolution and sexuality.
- *The Wisdom of Crowds: Why the Many Are Smarter Than the Few and How Collective Wisdom Shapes Business, Economies, Societies and Nations* by James Surowiecki. The author of this book takes sophisticated ideas about the wisdom of groups and presents them in an entertaining manner.

HYPE SELLS

Readers want to know they're getting something better than what is already on the market. If it's the "best" or "most comprehensive," say so. Magazines, television news, and newspapers know how to hype a story with a splashy headline or promo. If they can do it, why can't you? Don't be afraid to add a little splash or hype to your title. Phrases like "World's Best" or "Most Extreme" added to your title can really add some punch. Consider these ten titles that use hyperbole to sell the concept:

- Remember our earlier example, *Freakonomics?* The subheading of that book is *A Rogue Economist Explores the Hidden Side of Everything.* Now clearly an approximately 250-page book cannot possibly explore "everything," but the hyperbole is sure to capture a reader's attention.
- Joel Osteen's motivational *Your Best Life Now: 7 Steps to Living at Your Full Potential*
- Brandith Irwin and Mark McPherson's *Your Best Face: Looking Your Best Without Plastic Surgery* is a skincare advice book
- Another pair of authors who know the value of superlatives is Dr. Steven Pratt and Kathy Matthews, whose book *Superfoods Rx* is subtitled *Fourteen Foods That Will Change Your Life.* This book stands out from the crowded field of health and nutrition books by promising nothing short of a revolutionary effect on readers' lives.

EXERCISE: Create Your Own Title

Now it's your turn. Wander through the bookstore and find some titles you like. See if you can analyze why that particular title caught your eye. Is it a pun? Is it connected to a popular event? Generate three titles for your book and do an informal market test with your friends and family.

Chapter 3
Crafting the Opener

CREATING THE POWERFUL AND PERSUASIVE HIGH-POINT SUMMARY

The editor is your conduit to the publishing apparatus for which she works. She may be burning with enthusiasm for your project and feel certain that your book will sell. She must still prove to the editorial director that your book will have the quality to meet the standards the house sets for its list. To the marketing director she must prove that the book can be packaged effectively to reach a certain designated market. To the sales director she must prove that there is an answer to every objection the buyers at the major chains will raise against the efforts of the sales reps who are trying to get them to stock your book in marketable quantities in their stores. The editor will cover your proposal with a memo, but she will use the proposal itself as her main tool to answer all the objections of the editorial board, soothe all their worries, and perhaps even arouse some enthusiasm in their jaded hearts.

The task of enlisting all these allies begins with the proposal overview, or high-point summary—a carefully crafted presentation of exactly what your book is about. As with any introduction or opening, it's essential that this part of your proposal hook the attention of the reader, be accurate, and make your book sound like it will be terrific. The trick is to do this without overhyping the book; you should avoid words like "super" or "fabulous." You will have ample chance in the rest of your proposal to demonstrate the brilliance of your idea. In the overview, the idea must stand up by itself when viewed in a clear spotlight. Extravagant language is not the key; overheated prose is likely to be a turnoff. Editors are experts at analyzing proposals, and overstatement smells to them like a lack of confidence. Better to tell concisely and clearly what you intend to write—if the idea is good, its virtue will shine forth. Assemble your facts and rely on them to sell your idea.

Just as the proposal is a particular version of the book itself—a summary designed to convince—the overview is a condensed version of the introduction to the book. In fact, it may grow into the introduction to the book. This proposal overview is a development of the book's hook, telling what the book is about and why there is a need for the book in the marketplace. It should be well thought out, upbeat, informative, and written in the style in which the book is to be written. The overview is usually between five and twenty pages in length. It starts with the hook and then develops the content of the book and the book's strong selling points.

Your proposal is a test of the power of your idea. If you can sell a short version of your book to an editor, you can sell the complete book to an audience. When the editor reads your proposal, he is sitting in for the audience, representing them, as he uses his experience and judgment to assess whether your book will appeal to its target audience. Do hunters want to read your book *Deer Calls of the Wild: How to Determine Your Quarry's Weight From Shooting Range Before You Pull the Trigger?* Is this something a hunter wants or needs to know? Perhaps not. The first paragraph of your proposal has to convince the editor that it is, and the best way to start is with numbers.

Organize your opener as follows:

- **A strong hook.** This might be a question or series of questions. It might be an intriguing example or anecdote. It might be a paragraph that contrasts your idea to the conventional wisdom. The hook depends on your material, but however it's constructed, it must immediately catch the reader's interest.
- **An exciting presentation of what the book is about.** This is the condensed version of your thesis or theme.
- **A convincing argument that the book is important, or revolutionary, or desperately needed,** or whatever your key selling points are.
- **A condensed presentation of the argument you're making that your book will sell,** based on the best, most concrete evidence you have.

Contrary to the usual view that editors are English majors who flunked math, the fact is editors are in love with numbers. When an editor wants to acquire a book, she has to believe and convince her boss, her board, the marketing department, and the sales department that the book really will sell. Hard numbers will be your best evidence. They exist outside the world of opinion and bridge the gap between an editorial approach and a sales approach; they are persuasive.

It's not easy to get sales figures. Everyone in a sales department has them at their fingertips, and every bookstore buyer can access them instantly, but you can't. You have to do the best you can. Try the following methods:

- The copyright page of a competitive book will tell you how many printings that book has gone through since its original publication. Printings may be small, but a high number of printings over a few years indicates a strong selling title.
- If the sales have been good, the cover copy of a paperback will usually feature sales claims by the publisher. You may read that the title you hold in your hands has "sold over a million copies." This may be an exaggeration, but it's fair for you to refer to it.
- The cover copy may also trumpet how many weeks the title has spent on *The New York Times* best-seller list. Success is measured by this standard. Any time on the *Times* list is a real plus, and an extended number of weeks is a very strong selling point not just for the competitive title but for any book that can be compared to it.
- Both Amazon.com and Barnes & Noble list their current sales ranking on titles they warehouse. This information is online and readily available. But keep in mind this does not reflect the total number of book sales but only sales that pertain to that particular bookseller.

USING WHAT YOU LEARN THROUGH THE PROCESS

Everything you do in writing the proposal is a useful step in writing the book. When you write the proposal you are not just writing a sales tool for the book; you are writing an outline for the book. You are refining your focus. You are gaining an understanding of the essence of the book, what belongs inside the circle of your particular subject and what's outside it. You are narrowing and defining the special approach you intend to take in your book—the special qualities of thought or the unique gathering of information that will make your book something the audience needs to have.

The overview is constructed around the high points of the book. High points are the most important features of your book, those that communicate its value to potential readers—its selling points. Consider the following when thinking about the potential high points of your book:

- In a how-to book the high points refer to the main things the book will tell the reader how to do.
- In a biography, mention the high points of the subject's life and why the life is relevant to today's world.
- For a humor book, front load your funniest stuff.
- For a self-help book, squeeze into the overview what the problem is that the book will help people solve and what the approach is to solving that problem. Sometimes questions will work here. *Do you wake up in the middle of the night afraid of getting up in the morning? The reason for this may be work-based anxiety syndrome. The cure for this syndrome is cognitive affirmation therapy. This book will teach you, in ten easy steps, a program to cure your syndrome and get you back to sleeping through the night.*

Bullet points are good. It's always useful, when your material lends itself to being itemized and highlighted, to present the material as items rather than in large blocks of type. Bullet points are brief, and using them will require you to trim your points to the bare minimum number of words.

Don't hem and haw; try not to overelaborate; don't make the same point several times in the same portion of the presentation; be concise. Don't say: *This book will teach readers how to make a schedule, give order to their lives, organize their time more effectively.* Choose the phrase that best expresses your point, modify for optimal effect, and drop the repetitive words. *This book will teach readers how to organize their lives by effectively scheduling their time.*

The process of writing the high-point summary will help you outline your book because it will force you to define your subject and focus your approach.

PUTTING IT ALL TOGETHER

STEP I: Pour your thoughts about your idea onto the page. State as many ways as you can what it is, in one to three sentences. Do it again. Write several pages. Take as long as you want and use as many words as you need to explain your idea. Imagine you are simply telling someone about it and trying to make your explanation as clear and accurate as possible.

STEP II: Now get it organized. Your introduction/overview must:

- state clearly what the book will be about
- state convincingly why there's a need for the book

- suggest why you know the book will sell
- show that the book you intend to write can compete against the existing titles in your subject area by being fresh or exhaustive or unique in its approach to the material

The introductory overview must do all these things in brief. The details will follow in the balance of the proposal.

The main point of the overview is to describe the book—its content, its argument, and its point of view—in a way that makes it sound interesting and exciting. The lead of the overview gives a few reasons why the book will sell, but the bulk of this argument comes later. Beware at all times of arguments like this: *Fifty million people in America go bowling at least ten times a year. Therefore, there's a huge market for my book about the psychology of bowling.* What's wrong with this logic? Editors are looking for book-based demographics. There's no reason to believe that any of those fifty million bowlers are also readers of psychology. There's no reason to believe they are readers at all, let alone book buyers. The information you'd want to provide to the editor is that previous books about the psychology of bowling have sold well. That's a statistic that will interest an editor.

And remember Abraham Lincoln's answer to the question, *How long should a man's legs be? Long enough to reach the ground.*

Here's how we crafted the overview in the proposal for this book:

OVERVIEW

What does it take to get your book proposal crafted, written, and ultimately sold? Yes, you need to know the basic elements of a book proposal. But to stand out from the crowd you need an edge—you need to know the publishing secrets that will propel your proposal to the top of the pile. For the first time ever, *10 Secret Steps: Crafting the Superior Book Proposal* brings together three unique perspectives in the publishing process: Agent, Author, and Publisher. Not only will you get insider publishing trade secrets but you will learn a simple and easy-to-follow ten-step game plan to transform your book idea into a blockbuster proposal. You'll also see for yourself why twelve actual proposals succeeded with point-of-view comments from Agent, Author, and Publisher.

SCOPE & FOCUS

With a 98 percent average rejection rate, the odds are not in favor of the up-and-coming author. Writers are often "misled" into preparing book proposals that rarely, if ever, make the cut due to lack of inside knowledge not found in published materials providing the "standard" format. Many would-be qualified writers know little, if any, information relating to the crowded marketplace and consequently have no idea of the need for their proposed project to stand out above and beyond the other submissions in that same running.

10 Secret Steps fills the need for these writers by revealing and going more in-depth into the structure of developing a successful proposal. By offering our original three-point-of-view system, the reader receives insider views into what makes a proposal successful from three key professionals: Agent, Author, and Publisher. By inclusion of many successful examples, along with positive detailed comments, writers will understand with clarity what it means to go that extra step in crafting a proposal that will attract attention and ultimately get sold.

As the most complete insider's guide on nonfiction book proposals, *10 Secret Steps* features an easy-to-follow ten-step instructional program to create and master proposal writing. With an added advantage, utilizing a cutting-edge developmental angle, the authors have chosen to include the proposal for this book, *10 Secret Steps*, in full—showing the reader in more depth the evolution and inside secrets of creating a sensational and standout proposal.

Co-authored by literary agent/author Pamela K. Brodowsky and author/journalist and Emmy Award-winning producer Eric Neuhaus, *10 Secret Steps: Crafting the Superior Book Proposal* makes writing and clarifying the true components of a salable proposal easy for the inexperienced writer—one seeking improvement on his proposal writing skills. *10 Secret Steps* will ultimately leave its reader with a complete knowledge of **what** it takes to write a successful proposal and the **know-how** to do it effectively.

EXERCISE: Draft a High-Point Summary

It's time to get down to business. Using your completed exercise from chapter one, which clearly defined your idea, begin the process of writing the first-draft high-point summary or overview. Include your hook, a summarized presentation of your entire project, and the underlying reasons as to why this book differs from what is out there and why it is going to sell.

Chapter 4
Defining Your Market

ANALYZING WHO AND HOW MANY WILL BUY YOUR BOOK

Keep in mind that one of the main purposes of your proposal is convincing an editor or publisher that your book will sell, and, for that matter, sell lots of copies over a long period of time. Let's not forget that publishers have a bottom line. If you're not an established author like John Gray, author of *Men Are from Mars ...* and over a dozen other best-sellers, you're going to have to make certain there's an audience out there that's going to be motivated to buy your book. To do that you need to investigate and research the potential market for your book. If you're writing a book on back pain, you're surely going to need to know how many people suffer from back pain. What age groups suffer the most? Are men or women more likely to suffer back pain? If you're writing a book about dog training, you'll need to know how many dog owners are out there.

WHO IS YOUR AUDIENCE?

If you're self-publishing your memoirs or family history, generally your audience will be friends and family. But when you're writing a proposal that you want to sell to a major publishing house, you need to think bigger than just your immediate circle of contacts. You need to figure out who is really going to be interested in—and ultimately buy—your book.

At first you might be tempted to think that everyone is your audience. It's only natural to think everyone one is going to want to buy your book. Generally, fiction books like the best-selling *The Da Vinci Code* can appeal to a huge mass market of readers. However, when it comes to nonfiction, your audience needs to be much more targeted and specific. To help you get started identifying your target market, we've identified five very broad categories as examples. Of course there are many more out there, and yours may fall outside one of these categories. To give you an idea of how this works we've identified some common markets and how published authors have positioned their books to tap into those markets.

1. **Age:** Young people don't want the same information as older people. You might even want to target a generation (like Generation X) or specific age group (like the thirties).

   - *The 7 Habits of Highly Effective Teens* by Sean Covey
   - *Chicken Soup for the Preteen Soul: 101 Stories of Changes, Choices and Growing Up for Kids Ages 9–13* by Jack Canfield, et al.
   - *The Complete Idiot's Guide to Personal Finance in Your 20s & 30s* by Sarah Young Fisher and Susan Shelly
   - *Fit Over Forty: The Winning Way to Lifetime Fitness* by Sherri McMillan
   - *The Savvy Senior: The Ultimate Guide to Health, Family, and Finances for Senior Citizens* by Jim Miller

2. **Religion:** Authors have successfully targeted and addressed the specific interests of different religious denominations.

   - *No More Christian Nice Guy: When Being Nice—Instead of Good—Hurts Men, Women and Children* by Paul Coughlin
   - *How to Stay Christian in College* by J. Budziszewski
   - *Lead Like Jesus: Lessons From the Greatest Leadership Role Model of All Time* by Ken Blanchard and Phil Hodges
   - *The Blessing of a Skinned Knee: Using Jewish Teachings to Raise Self-Reliant Children* by Wendy Mogel
   - *Radical Acceptance: Embracing Your Life With the Heart of a Buddha* by Tara Brach

3. **Gender:** Men and women want different information, and authors can address the genders specifically.

   - *The Guy's Guide to Surviving Pregnancy, Childbirth, and the First Year of Fatherhood* by Michael Crider
   - *Younger Next Year for Women* by Chris Crowley and Henry S. Lodge
   - *Totally Me: The Teenage Girl's Survival Guide* by Yvonne Collins and Sandy Rideout

- *For Women Only: What You Need to Know About the Inner Lives of Men* by Shaunti Feldhahn
- *A Guy's Guide to Being a Man's Man* by Frank Vincent and Steven Priggé

4. **Sexual Orientation:** This is a large niche market with its own interests that authors and publishers can fulfill.

   - *A Legal Guide for Lesbian & Gay Couples* by Hayden Curry, Denis Clifford, and Frederick Hertz
   - *The New Essential Guide to Lesbian Conception, Pregnancy, and Birth* by Stephanie Brill
   - *Keeping Mr. Right: The Gay Man's Guide to Lasting Relationships* by Kenneth D. George
   - *The Gay Man's Guide to Growing Older* by John Lockhart
   - *For Lesbian Parents: Your Guide to Helping Your Family Grow Up Happy, Healthy and Proud* by Suzanne M. Johnson and Elizabeth O'Connor

5. **Economic Level:** Personal finances are a big factor in people's lives, and people from different economic levels are looking for different information in books; authors can appeal to a specific subset of the population.

   - *Rich Dad, Poor Dad: What the Rich Teach Their Kids About Money— That the Poor and Middle Class Do Not!* by Robert T. Kiyosaki
   - *Choking on the Silver Spoon: Keeping Your Kids Healthy, Wealthy and Wise in a Land of Plenty* by Gary W. Buffone
   - *Millionaire From Being Poor: A Reasonable Way for Average People to Become Wealthy and Become Healthy Lasting Until Your 90s* by Thomas J. Rundquist
   - *How Not to Get Rich, or Why Being Bad Off Isn't So Bad* by Robert Sullivan
   - *Everybody Wants Your Money: The Straight-Talking Guide to Protecting (and Growing) the Wealth You Worked So Hard to Earn* by David W. Latko

NICHE MARKETS

The latest buzz word in publishing is *niche*. A niche market targets a very specific demographic group. Consider Pamela Peeke's best-seller *Fight Fat After*

Forty. Rather than write a book targeting everyone who is trying to lose weight, the author chose a target group with specific how-to advice for women over forty. General dieting books do sell to large mass audiences like the huge percentage of Americans who are overweight—take Arthur Agatston's *The South Beach Diet*— but if you can identify a specific group or groups in your proposal, you'll have a better case for selling it. Dieting isn't the only niche market subject. Financial books can also be tailored to specific niche markets. There's Suze Orman's *The Money Book for the Young, Fabulous & Broke* for twenty-somethings and *You're Retired, Now What?* by Ronald and Murray Yolles for the older market. So rather than go for the huge market, try for the targeted niche market.

KNOWING YOUR MARKET EXISTS

So now you have some basic understanding of the different types of markets and some examples of how other authors have targeted a specific market. But how do you identify and narrow down your market? What's more, how do you even know your market exists? How do you determine when niche is too niche?

The most convincing way to show editors that there's an audience for your book is through statistics. While editors love words, they also can't resist numbers that indicate consumers are going to want to buy what you write. If you're not a number cruncher, don't fret—and don't skip the rest of this chapter. The Internet and online research have made it easy to get a hold of some convincing statistics to prove your audience is out there. Following are some good resources for gathering statistics.

Google It

One of the easiest places to start your research is with a simple online search. Type your audience—"dog owner" if it's a book targeting that market—into the search engine and see what kind of hits you get. It will probably lead you to the American Dog Owners Association. That's a great start. You can explore their Web site for statistics about numbers of dog owners. If you don't find it there, don't be afraid to pick up the phone and give the press office a call. When you call, tell them you're working on a book proposal targeting dog owners. Chances are they'll be happy to help you with your research and might even give you some information you never thought about.

One note of caution about online searches: Make sure you verify where the numbers are coming from—don't just copy and paste them into your proposal. If your statistics are from the American Dog Owners Association, that's great—specify that in your proposal. Ultimately, make sure the source of your information is reputable. Since these numbers will help publishers make a decision to publish your book, they should be verifiable and attributed to a well-known source.

Census Data (or other government data)

Specificity is key when it comes to the size of your potential market. The U.S. Census Bureau (www.census.gov) is a great place to search. Here you can get national figures broken down by age, race, income, and all sorts of variables. For instance, if you're working on a book for new single mothers, you're going to need to know how many are out there each year. If your book is related to work and employment, The U.S. Department of Labor (http://dol .gov) also has resources to help you determine the size of your market. For health figures, the Centers for Disease Control and Prevention (www.cdc.gov) have great statistics. If you get frustrated with navigating the information on the Web, don't be embarrassed to call. Each government agency has a public information office designed to field calls from journalists and writers. Give them a call and ask them to help you find what you're looking for.

Polls and Market Research Data

There are many companies that constantly generate statistics and data based on polls and market research. One of the most well known is Harris Interactive, Inc. (www.harrisinteractive.com), which generates the Harris Poll (www.harrispollonline.com), but there are many others you may want to consider. With Harris Interactive, you can visit the Web site, search for your topic, and turn up a list of surveys or polls that can support your claims for an audience for your book. Market research is also a great way to highlight a trend or growing interest in your topic (more reason for people to want to buy your book).

Anecdotal Data

Some market data is not so easy to quantify with hard numbers, but that doesn't mean you should leave it out of your proposal. For instance, if you have a blog or Web site that promotes what you do and relates to the content of the proposal, by all means highlight how many visitor hits the site gets each day or month. This will give the publisher an indication that there's a market interested in what you have to say. If you receive e-mail or letters from fans or customers, quote from those sources, too. If you have a mailing list, whether it's e-mail or regular mail, it can help you get the word out about your book.

Whether it's a primary or secondary market, here's one note of caution about your target audience: Be sure your audience is not too small. If you narrow your audience too much, you run the risk of selling yourself short.

PRIMARY AND SECONDARY MARKETS

Whether it's a broad audience category or a niche one, now that you've identified who will buy your book, you'll need to understand two important ways your audience can actually purchase your book—through *primary* and *secondary markets*. Let's look at each in more detail so you can determine how to identify some of the "hidden" markets for your book. When you've identified *all* of the markets for your potential book, list them in your proposal.

The *primary market* is the traditional means by which consumers will buy your book, such as brick-and-mortar bookstores (Barnes & Noble, Borders) and online bookstores (Amazon.com). Books are also sold in airports, drugstores, and even big chains like Wal-Mart, Sam's Club, and Target. In your proposal, you don't need to say that your book will be sold in Barnes & Noble or through Amazon.com; that's a given. For the primary market, all you need to do is show through the statistics and anecdotal evidence you collected that there is a market out there willing to buy your product.

For example, let's say your book is about organic food. In addition to showing how many people currently eat organic food, highlight how this trend has increased over time. Publishers like to know that your book will have a shelf life. A trend that's declining indicates the market for your book has reached its peak. It may come back, but for now, a publisher wants to get on trend that's growing, not waning. Pointing out a growing trend tells the publisher your book will sell over a long period of time.

There are other markets for your book, ones that most nonfiction proposal writers don't immediately think about. *Secondary markets* are not a direct pipeline to consumers. Rather, they are markets of organizations, institutions, or specialty stores. Publishers love it when you can identify a secondary market that will buy your book because usually this means a bulk sale. Let's take the organic food proposal again. Some secondary markets that might be interested in selling a book on organic food are health food stores, yoga studios, and alternative health care centers.

The following are some of the types of secondary markets you should consider as potential buyers for your book. In your proposal, clearly explain how and why each secondary market can propel sales of your book.

Libraries and Educational Courses

Public, private, college, and corporate libraries buy books to maintain a current collection. Librarians generally buy books after reading a favorable review in one of many trade publications such as *Library Journal*. However, if your book can fill a specific gap in the library market, specify this in your proposal. If not, there's no need to mention it since this is an obvious market for the publisher.

What's less obvious is a course adaptation for a class. If you think your book is particularly relevant for inclusion in a high school or college course, by all means mention it. You might even want to get a letter from a few college professors who would commit to using your book if published. Those letters will show publishers that potentially there's a bigger market for your book in the education arena.

Promotional Gifts

Can your book be included with the purchase of a product? Think about the number of kitchen appliances that are sold each year. Would you ever have thought that a slow cooker book would be a top seller? That's right: *Not Your Mother's Slow Cooker Cookbook*, by Beth Hensperger and Julie Kaufmann, is a big seller on Amazon.com. If you can manage to get your cookbook packaged with one of those products and show the publisher you have a guaranteed order, highlight this potential market as a special sale. Here are some other books that lend themselves to promotional tie-ins with products:

- *The iPod Book: Doing Cool Stuff With the iPod and the iTunes Music Store,* by Scott Kelby, gives readers exciting ideas on how to use their iPods.
- *The New Nikon Compendium: Cameras, Lenses & Accessories Since 1917,* by Simon Stafford, Hillebrand, and Hauschild, is a Nikon camera user's reference guide, with tips on how to make the most of the Nikon equipment and shoot a great picture.
- *How to Do Everything With Your Palm Handheld,* by Dave Johnson and Rick Broida, helps readers get maximum value out of using their PDAs.

Large Institutional Sales

If your book has a tie-in to a corporate program, you might want to see if you can get a company to commit to sell your book as part of that program. It's best to approach companies once you have a proposal but before you submit your proposal to agents or editors. Start by brainstorming a list of potential tie-ins. Think about how and why a company might want to use your book. If it's a book about gay and lesbian rights in the workplace, think about how human resource departments at large corporations could use it to promote the goal of workplace diversity. Once you've identified some potential tie-ins, write a query letter to the head of the marketing departments. In the letter, spell out how and why your proposed book will be helpful to their corporate goals. If there's interest from a company, get some form of commitment letter spelling out their interest in using your book. Companies might be hesitant to give you an actual commitment, but see if you can obtain some confirmation of their interest in your project. If you get positive feedback, include that information in your proposal.

Many companies, for instance, promote fitness for their employees. A company might want to buy large quantities of your book on exercise and diet and give it to their employees to help them get in shape. Remember, corporations want to keep their workforce healthy in order to increase productivity and lower health insurance premiums. Any book that can help companies achieve this goal can translate into a huge bulk sale.

Specialty Stores

Books aren't just sold in bookstores anymore. The national housewares store Williams-Sonoma carries a wide variety of cookbooks. Museums sell art books. Research other types of stores where your book can be prominently featured. Health food stores sell books on vitamins, fitness, and alternative health. There are many gift stores that sell quirky and "gifty" types of books. Your book may not have a direct tie to a product but might fit in to the overall theme of the store.

The best way to see which specialty stores might want to sell your book is to visit them. Make a list of the stores in your area that tie in to your topic. Go to the stores and look around at the types of books that are sold. You may also want to speak with the manger of the store and mention your book proposal to her. Ask her if it is the kind of book she would stock in the store. If not, ask her for recommendations on stores she thinks might want to sell your book.

Here's how we defined the market when we put together the proposal for this book:

TARGET MARKET ANALYSIS

In recent years, publishing professionals have witnessed a surge of submissions in the marketplace warranting their undivided attention. People from all walks of life are trying their hand at their dream career: becoming a published author.

With over 300,000 writers subscribing to trade magazines and an estimated 500,000 proposed projects filtering through various publishing venues on any given day, writers are seeking an alternate solution to stand out among the crowd.

The proven success of several editions of the following titles identifies the continuous demand for books on this subject matter:

- *Write the Perfect Book Proposal* by Jeff Herman & Deborah Levine Herman, second edition
- *How to Write a Book Proposal* by Michael Larsen, third edition
- *Nonfiction Book Proposals Anybody Can Write* by Elizabeth Lyon, third edition

To be sure, nonfiction titles abound: Approximately fifty thousand titles are published annually in North America alone, of which 85 percent are nonfiction. Approximately 75 percent come from first-time authors, translating into about thirty-two thousand published nonfiction books by first-time authors annually.

In regard to this large number, rejections still remain at an all-time high. Writers have been "misled" into thinking that there exists an easy standard when in fact the reality of the industry indicates just the opposite. For that reason, the time has come for a title that delves deeper into writing a successful proposal.

The highest demand for *10 Secret Steps* is from writers, both novice and professional, who desire inside knowledge or an increase in perspective on how to write a sensational book proposal. The need has never been greater and the competition never stronger.

As literary agent and principal of International Literary Arts, Ms. Brodowsky receives, on an annual basis, approximately sixteen thousand project queries. With over two hundred active literary agents in the United States, this number translates into approximately 2.4 million proposed project queries in search of a home each and every year. With the average 98 percent rejection rate, only

48,000 projects will secure either representation or publication. The balance of 2,352,000 will go unclaimed. Writers now, more then ever, are hungry for a better understanding of what it takes to succeed in this crowded marketplace.

There are six additional markets for this title in which sales potential is substantial. These include but are not limited to:

- **Book Clubs:** including Writer's Digest Book Club, Cincinnati, Ohio; Literary Guild Book Club, New York
- **Specialty Retailers:** including the Writers Store
- **Trade Organizations:** including The Authors Guild, The International Women's Writing Guild, Women's National Book Association, and the National Writers Union
- **Writers' Groups:** including annual conventions and conferences, book fairs and expos, workshops and seminars. *10 Secret Steps* is a workshop format. Ms. Brodowsky is a sought-after speaker and panelist at various conventions and conferences nationwide.
- **Internet:** Ms. Brodowsky and Mr. Neuhaus both possess their own Web sites that are easily accessed through major search engines. Ms. Brodowsky's professional Web site, InternationalLiteraryArts.com, is frequented by a high volume of new writers on a daily basis.
- **Speakers Bureaus:** The National Speakers Association has a membership of 3,500. Public speakers want to learn how to publish a book to enhance their professional careers.

EASY REFERENCE STATISTICS

Magazine Subscriptions: Circulation

Writer's Digest	200,000 +
Poets & Writers	70,000 +
The Writer	40,000 +
ByLine	3,000 +
Total	313,000

Total Average Titles Published Annually, North America 50,000
Nonfiction Categorized 42,500
Nonfiction by First-Time Authors 32,000
Book Club Membership: Writer's Digest Book Club 38,900 +

EXERCISE: List Five Statistics That Justify Your Book

It's time to start surfing the Web and making some phone calls. Locate five statistics from credible sources that show an audience for your book. You can also include trend statistics. Remember to keep track of your sources and clearly identify where you obtained the information. Be prepared for agents and editors to ask for verification.

Chapter 5
Analyzing the Competition

WHO YOUR COMPETITORS ARE AND WHY YOU'RE BETTER

The more competition the better!

It's true! If you're writing a joke book, it's good news that there are a lot of joke books. This tells you that people like joke books. If you're writing a book about the Civil War, it's good news that there are a lot of people who are interested in reading books about the Civil War. There's a Civil War niche. The presence on bookstore shelves of many competitive titles means there's a market for the general subject of your book. It means that publishers—and readers—have agreed there's a niche into which your book fits. Your task is to make sure, and then convince others, that there's room in that niche for your approach to the subject.

On the other hand, if you can't find books that are, in a general way, like the book you want to write, it may be a signal that your idea lacks marketability. The way an editor will determine whether he thinks your idea is marketable is by thinking of other titles like it that he knows have sold well. By presenting a sharp analysis of similar titles you are seizing the high ground on this debatable issue; you are staking out the market geography to the advantage of your idea.

We'll call the other books in your market niche the competition, because in some cases we expect that a buyer will compare several books and pick the one she believes will best fill a need. You'll be comparing your book to the other titles in its niche to make a case for the advantages your book will offer over the others. In order to do a comparative analysis of competitive titles, you'll first have to identify what other books are out there. Here's how:

- Google keywords on your topic and surf to www.Amazon.com, www.BarnesandNoble.com, book reviews, and other places where keywords will connect you to related titles.
- Visit the New York Public Library catalog (www.nypl.org) and search by keywords and titles for books in your niche.
- Go to the bookstore and look on the shelves.

Visiting a big bookstore, such as Barnes & Noble or Borders, is the best way to assess the competition. The books on the shelves are the books that are in stock. Chances are the older titles among them are the books that are automatically reordered. They are the books that are selling. Of course, it's possible that some titles won't be there at any particular time, but in the bookstore you'll be able to see most of the books that are successfully reaching your market. Try several bookstores, both brick and mortar and online.

If a book has been published within the past few months or the year, you won't know if it has been a success. If, on the other hand, a title is a few years old, and particularly if the copyright page indicates you're looking at a third or fourth or higher printing, that title is probably a successful seller. Determining the number of editions of any title can be done simply by turning to the copyright page located in the front of the book. For each separate edition the publisher will have listed a separate date. Focus your competitive analysis on successful titles. Comparative titles should not be more than five years old unless they are demonstrable perennials or classics. Very old books are too easily dismissed as being outdated and irrelevant.

Buy (or camp out at a table) and examine the books that seem like the best ones, the ones that have been reprinted the most times, the ones that represent several different approaches to your basic subject area. Take a close look at all these books. Analyze the structure, contents, style, tone, layout, and jacket or flap copy to see what the idea of each book is and how the publisher is pitching it.

Then start thinking in terms of comparisons. How is your book better than the competition? How is it more modern? How is it more comprehensive? How is it more interesting? Examine each competitive title carefully and compare it to your idea.

- **Look at the table of contents.** What are the topics addressed in the book? Are there topics missing, topics you cover that are not in this table of contents?

- **Look at several chapters.** Read them. What is the approach the author takes to the subject? Is it a good approach? Why is your approach better?
- **Check the notes or bibliography.** What are the sources for the book you're examining? Do you have different, better, or newer sources?

Remember, you want to write a book that is "the same but different." There's a core of information that "goes with the territory," and then there is a way of dealing with that information that's fresh and different from or better than what's been done before.

The competition is a beaten path to readers' doors. The path shows you what readers have purchased in the past. The path can also lead you to improvements in your idea to better serve the needs of your audience. Reading competitive titles will give you some ideas about ways you can refine and improve your own idea. Notice ways your competition might have been better and consider working those overlooked virtues into your book.

Editors are always looking for reasons to say no. It's your task to anticipate objections and provide positive responses in advance. Don't raise the troublesome issue; simply give the evidence in your favor.

If there are a lot of competitive books out there, the editor may say, "Oh, that market is too crowded," so you have to combat that idea. Use the crowded market as a springboard by showing how your title surpasses all the current titles. The key to this is to show how your book is strikingly different from the competition. You must demonstrate that your book will have a strong and unique appeal to the same audience that purchased the competitive books.

If there is little or nothing in the way of competitive titles, the editor may say, "I don't see the market for this title" or "I don't see how we could sell your book." What he means is, *Without comparative titles, I have no numbers—sales figures indicating good performance— to give the sales department to convince them they'll be able to sell your book.*

This is why finding competitive titles is important. They are the support you need to sell your idea. It's not good enough, if you've written a biography of Madame Curie, to point to a current best-selling biography of Abraham Lincoln. Biography as a genre is too broad for comparative analysis. It's not good publishing logic to argue, *I will write a biography; biographies have sold well in the past; therefore my book will sell.* You'll need to establish the market for your title by referring to a book on the same subject matter but then by explaining how yours will be different. The closer the content of the competitive title to the content of your idea, the more effective your comparative analysis.

A cardinal rule of comparative analysis: *Don't criticize the other books*. The publisher you're submitting to might have published them. Also, your point is not to demonstrate that the other books are bad, only that your book will be different, or has new information, or has a fresh point of view, or has more up-to-date illustrations. Your aim is to show that your book offers readers benefits that the competitive titles don't offer. You do this by being positive about your idea, not by being negative about the others. The skill with which you analyze the factors that are at work in the type of book you intend to write will enhance your credibility with editors.

For each competitive title:

- Write a clear statement of what that book intends to do.
- Make a general assessment of how well it achieves its aim.
- Differentiate your aim from the aim of the book in question.
- Pinpoint what your book will offer readers that will make your book more attractive, useful, interesting, etc.

Bullet-point summaries of the competition can be effective in pinpointing your book's competitive edge. This can also be done in the form of a chart. Across the top of the chart list various relevant features; down the side list the various competitive titles and your own. In each box indicate whether each book does or does not have the feature. For example, if your book is a guide to avoiding additives in foods, you might list down the side various assets: *Contains charts by additive showing presence in various foods, Contains charts by food types showing prevalence of various additives, Offers additive-free menus, Discusses latest studies on benefits and side effects of various additives*, etc. Naturally your title will feature most, if not all, of the important features!

Take a look at how we crafted the competitive analysis that sold this book.

COMPETITION

Our research on competitive books of this subject matter indicates the concept of crafting a winning proposal as an important topic. It also substantiates the claim that writers are seeking a clear perspective of the components that deem a proposal successful. However, there are no titles that address the topic from the three-point-of-view system: Agent, Author, and Publisher. This system allows readers to evaluate the maximum of inside information and go on to create a proposal that will stand out from the average.

Our research reveals four competing titles on the topic of nonfiction book proposals:

Write the Perfect Book Proposal: 10 That Sold and Why by Jeff Herman and Deborah Levine Herman, second edition, John Wiley & Sons, Inc., May 2001 (paperback list price $15.95)

> **Competing Factors:** Authored by industry professionals—title contains example proposals.

How to Write a Book Proposal by Michael Larsen, third edition, Writer's Digest Books, February 2004 (paperback list price $15.99)

> **Competing Factors:** Authored by industry professional—title contains example proposals.

Nonfiction Book Proposals Anybody Can Write: How to Get a Contract and Advance Before Writing Your Book by Elizabeth Lyon, third edition, Perigee, December 2002 (paperback list price $14.95)

> **Competing Factor:** Includes examples.

The Fast-Track Course on How to Write a Nonfiction Book Proposal by Stephen Blake Mettee, Quill Driver Books/Word Dancer Press, September 2001 (paperback list price $12.95)

> **Competing Factors:** Authored by an industry professional—contains an example proposal.

Competitive Title Analysis:

Jeff Herman and Deborah Levine Herman:
Write the Perfect Book Proposal is an accurate basic guide to writing proposals. Ten good examples are given in content along with comment. However, the authors make a point of the negatives of the example proposals rather than the positives. Readers don't want to know how an example proposal could be improved; they want examples of the best to guide them in the process of crafting their own. We also believe this title to be light on explanation of how to translate an idea into a standout

proposal. Instead, it offers a cookie-cutter approach to writing a "standard proposal."

Michael Larsen:
How to Write a Book Proposal provides the reader a wealth of explanation and detail on the requirements of writing a book proposal, but with only three examples to guide the reader, there is room to offer a book with more of what readers want..

> **Customer review quoted from Amazon.com on the two above-referenced titles:** David Cullen is a writer in Denver, Colorado, specializing in ethnographic and investigative reporting. More recently he has written for *The New York Times*.

> "I used this book (Jeff and Deborah Herman's) along with Larsen's *How to Write a Book Proposal* for my first book proposal and felt they made an excellent combination."

> "Larsen was great on explanation and details describing what each section required and why, but was light on examples."

> "This book (Jeff and Deborah Herman's) offered incredible examples, with great commentary, but was extremely light on guiding you through the process of creating your own proposal. Each chapter corresponding to each section runs a mere one to three pages. Examples are great, but direction is necessary as well..."

Elizabeth Lyon:
Nonfiction Book Proposals Anybody Can Write provides accurate, detailed information regarding the creation of the nonfiction book proposal. Her example proposals are broken into pieces and used throughout the text, taking away from the visual aspect needed. But, several of the examples used are derived from unsold material. Ultimately, we don't feel this falls under the term "successful examples."

Stephen Blake Mettee:
The Fast-Track Course on How to Write a Nonfiction Book Proposal provides insight into the creation of the book proposal in a short but concise 128 pages, pointing out often discarded but deadly mistakes made by many proposal authors. He provides only one example of a complete proposal.

---

10 Secret Steps—Immediately Distinguishable Values:

1) Three-Point-of-View System: Agent, Author, Editor
2) Twelve Successful Example Proposals With Positive Element Comment
3) Easy-to-Follow Ten-Step Program
4) Detailed Proposal Contents to Crafting the Above-Average—Not the Standard—Proposal
5) Easy Reference Tips
6) Evolution of This Proposal to Book Content

EXERCISE: Analyze Competitive Titles

Select five similar books and analyze why your book is better. Make a trip to the bookstore, the library, or buy them from Amazon.com or BarnesandNoble.com, but make sure to do your homework in this area. You will need to know what is already released, about to be released, and how your book is better, would complement, or surpass this competition. You will need to identify these points to both your agent and editor.

Chapter 6
Developing a Platform

PRESENTING A REALISTIC PLAN TO MAKE YOUR BOOK A SUCCESS

There's no denying it: The dream of every author is to get featured on *The Oprah Winfrey Show* or *Today*. In the world of books, that's like winning the lottery. National television publicity can create an instant best-seller. But now for a reality check. Unfortunately, the likelihood of appearing on one of the national television programs—unless you're a megacelebrity—is slim. So first and foremost, you need to be realistic in your proposal about your plans for promotion.

Too many authors think national television is the only means to publicity. In fact, you probably shouldn't even mention getting on *The Oprah Winfrey Show* in your proposal unless you personally know Oprah or one of her producers. Instead, you want to create a plan that's "outside the box." The publisher knows about all the traditional avenues of promotion; this is your opportunity to convince the publisher that you're going to be realistic yet creative and opportunistic. In other words, show the publisher that you're a relentless self-promoter (and we don't mean that in a bad way).

MARKETING IS NOT PUBLICITY

When you are putting together your publicity plan, it's important to take note of the difference between publicity and marketing. Have you ever noticed full-page ads for books in *The New York Times* or other major newspapers? Those ads can cost upwards of $100,000 and generally are paid for by the publishers. That's called *marketing* or *paid advertising*. Occasionally, a publisher will put up that kind of money, but don't count on it. Unless you're an established author, you don't even want to mention advertising in your proposal.

Just because you don't get a full-page advertisement in *The New York Times* doesn't mean you can't get noticed. What's going to propel your book to the best-seller list is what's called *publicity*. Essentially, publicity is free advertising—an interview in your local newspaper or a review in a magazine. Any time your book is mentioned in the media or people are "buzzing" about it, that's considered publicity.

The more publicity your book gets, the more likely people will know and want to buy your book. Since publishers are cautious about spending money, even on generating publicity that's free, in your proposal you're going to need to spell out the ways you're going to be a self-promoter and garner publicity yourself.

WHY DO YOU NEED TO PLAN YOUR OWN PUBLICITY?

The latest buzzword in publishing is "platform." It's a fancy way of saying that publishers don't want to spend money on promoting your book and that you need to pick up the slack. A platform is essentially the means you already have in place to promote your book. For instance, do you have a syndicated newspaper column? Do you have a Web site that receives X number of hits per month? Are you regularly quoted as an expert in newspapers, magazines, or on television? If you answered yes to any of these questions, you're off to a great start and have a platform that publishers will consider helpful in successfully launching a book. If not, you're going to need to make yourself more visible to the public.

First, let's consider what your publisher will do to promote your book. You don't need to specify these in your proposal because these are obvious to an editor reading your proposal.

Review Copies

You can count on your publisher sending out copies to the major trade magazines, such as *Publishers Weekly* and *Library Journal* as well as other major review publications through media mailings. This is relatively easy for the publicity department. They put together a target list of media outlets that might want to feature your book and then follow up with calls.

Press Release

The publicity department will write a release announcing the publication of your book, but make sure you read a draft. You know your book better than the publisher's publicist. You might want to include a sample press release in your proposal to show the publisher you know how to think in publicity terms. It will also indicate that you understand how the book will be positioned and marketed.

For Eric Neuhaus's proposal for *The World's Fittest You*, he included two sample press releases for the book. He simply added these press releases as appendices to the actual proposal. Not only did his agent love the idea, but in meetings with publishers, publicity, and marketing people they said they could immediately see how they could do their jobs and promote the book.

Here's the press release included in the proposal. In the exercise at the end of this chapter, you'll be writing a press release of your own.

SAMPLE PRESS RELEASES

For Immediate Release
Contact: Eric Neuhaus
Dateline: New York, NY
Headline: The World's Fittest Man Takes on America's Fitness Crisis in His Breakthrough New Book

APRIL, 200— There's no doubt about it— Americans are fat. And despite all the information out there about the dangers of obesity, the problem is just getting worse. The latest statistics show that 62 percent of Americans are either overweight or obese, compared with 48 percent in 1980!

Joe Decker used to be part of that problem—but now, with a revolutionary new book—*The World's Fittest You: The World's Fittest Man's Four-Week Total Fitness Program*—Joe is offering readers the solution!

Once, Joe was fat and out of shape. But through an amazing personal journey from fat to fit—a journey Joe will share with readers in his new book—Joe was able to transform himself from flabby farm boy to fitness hero. And Joe didn't just attain an average level of fitness—he's achieved fitness stardom—winning the coveted title of the *Guinness Book of World Records'* World's Fittest Man!

Joe will share with readers of *The World's Fittest You* not only the compelling saga of his personal transformation from fat to fit—he will also share his prescription for how the reader can become *The World's Fittest You*!

Joe's an ordinary guy who has achieved extraordinary things—he's a "regular guy," so he talks to his readers in a refreshingly straightforward manner.

No gimmicks, buzzwords, or complicated charts—just Joe's personal eating and fitness program—one that is proven to produce unbelievable results!

Readers will be motivated by Joe's inspiring life story in the first part of the book. Then in the second half of *The World's Fittest You*, readers will turn that motivation into action as they take on Joe's easy-to-follow program. With Joe's coaching and advice, they'll learn to gradually reduce fat from their diet—as Joe says, "Less Fat, Lose Fat"—and they'll learn how to *shock your system* with a breakthrough new fitness program based on up-to-the-minute research.

Now, with Joe Decker's *The World's Fittest You: The World's Fittest Man's Four-Week Total Fitness Program*, readers can stop being part of the American fitness crisis and start being part of the solution!

Piggyback Your Author Tour

These days, author tours are becoming rare. Not only are they expensive, but for publishers the payoff in sales can be minimal. A few readings at local bookstores aren't going to generate the kind of publicity to really pump up sales.

However, that doesn't mean you should ignore the author tour in your proposal. If you like the idea of going on tour—and most authors do—come up with a plan to "piggyback" your author tour with some other activities. For instance, you may want to time your tour with a family vacation or a scheduled trip to visit a friend. Small towns are particularly receptive to authors. Include a list of all the towns you plan to visit. For each town, list the types of venues (bookstores, churches, libraries, etc.) you'll reach out to as part of your tour.

Regular Speaking Engagements

The idea of publicity is to get your message about your book to the public. What better way than to speak at conventions or events? The bigger the better, and start doing it now. In your proposal you want to be able to say, "Next year I am booked to give X speeches in X cities."

If you're new to public speaking, your first step is to join one of the many public speaking groups such as the National Speakers Association (www. nsaspeaker.org). The NSA is a great networking and educational resource for building your public speaking opportunities.

Once you've become familiar with the basics of public speaking you're going to need to find some venues at which to speak. Start by brainstorming a list of local venues that might be interested in having you as a speaker. Conventions and conferences that tie in to your topic are always looking for credible speakers. But think outside the box, too. Local charities and fundraisers sometimes want to promote an event. What better way than to feature you as their speaker? Local independent stores often look for speakers to draw potential customers into the store. Libraries and rotary clubs also need speakers.

After you've identified your venues, come up with a few topics to speak about. You should try to tie your topic into your proposed book. Write a brief paragraph about each topic and make sure you give each topic an attention-grabbing title—just like you learned in chapter two of this book.

With your list of venues and potential topics, you're ready to do some cold calling and letter writing. Start by calling the heads of these groups and introducing yourself. Tell them about your topic and how your presentation can help them promote their businesses. If you're not comfortable making cold calls, write a pitch letter explaining your expertise and proposed speech. If you don't hear back with in a few weeks, follow up with a call.

How does public speaking relate to your book proposal? It's a great way to build your platform as an expert on this topic. Once your book is published, each time you give a speech or presentation you'll have the opportunity to sell your book to the audience members. This is called "back-of-the-room sales," and if you're speaking at a large event with, say, thousands of people, there is potential for selling a lot of books just at the event itself.

Getting Press

The easiest way to start getting press is by using the Web. Many Web sites are looking for good content. Start by writing a few articles or columns about topics related to your proposed book. These can be first-person stories or more traditional news articles. Whatever you write, make sure you sound credible and get your facts correct.

Once your articles are written, start surfing the Web. Make a list of the Web sites that might want to run the articles you've just written. You'll have the best success if you target Web sites run by individuals or small groups rather than big corporations like CNN or Fox News. Once you find at least ten Web sites that fit, e-mail the Web master or editor and see if they'll run your column. Web sites usually have a "contact us" link. Use this information to send them your material.

After you've achieved success placing your articles or columns on a few Web sites, you may want to try some local newspapers. Most local newspapers run columns or articles written by experts. Research which newspapers in your area publish this type of information. Next, call the newspaper and find out which editor handles these types of submissions and send some examples of your work. Getting your work into a newspaper is very tough and will take lots of persistence, but the payoff is great exposure.

Become a Media Resource

Even before your book is published you can become a valuable resource for the media. Believe it or not, the media needs experts like you. Whether on television, radio, or in newspapers or magazines, experts are quoted in just about every story. You want one of those experts to be you, but how do you get quoted?

As always, the first step is to start small. Read through your local newspaper and write down the names of the reporters that cover stories on the topics that relate to your expertise. If you're in a big city like New York or Los Angeles, target a smaller paper such as a free weekly. The reporters at these smaller papers are more likely to be receptive to your pitch. Once you have the names of a few reporters, call them up and introduce yourself. Tell them that you've read some of their articles on X and you are an expert in X. Tell them that you are available to be quoted if they are looking for a source for an upcoming article. Follow up by sending an e-mail with your résumé and directing them to your Web site if you have one (and you should).

With some persistence and follow-up with reporters you'll go from average Joe to expert Joe with media contacts. Keep the ultimate goal in mind: In your proposal, you will be able to demonstrate with specific examples how you were covered in the media. From a publisher's perspective this is great media exposure and evidence that you know how to publicize yourself—and ultimately your book.

Develop a Web Site or Blog

Whatever your subject matter, you must create a media presence online. Not only is a Web site easy and cheap to build, it helps you create "instant" credibility. The most important aspects of your Web site are that it's professional and easy to navigate. Also, you want to choose a domain name that says something about you and your expertise. Most authors find it convenient to use their full name as the name of the site. That's fine, but you also can try something more creative like the name of your business or service you offer if it has a catchy or memorable name. Remember, your Web site name is a reflection of who you are and what you do.

Ideally, you may want to hire an expert Web designer to help you organize and design your Web site. Ask your friends and colleagues for referrals to a good Web designer. Before you choose a designer, make sure you see examples of his previous work and find out how much it will cost. When you meet with a designer, come prepared with Web site formats you would like to model. Make a list of these Web sites and show them to the designer.

If you don't have the resources to hire a designer and you don't know the first thing about Web design, don't despair. There are actually quite a few companies that offer "do-it-yourself" Web design. GoDaddy.com (www.godaddy.com) offers a service called WebSite Tonight®. This service gives you the tools and resources to create your own Web site without having to rely on a designer or Web programmer. Register.com (www.register.com) offers a similar service that you might find useful.

A blog is even easier to set up than a Web site since blogs are mostly just text. Blogger (www.blogger.com) is a great resource for helping you set up a simple blog. You can also use Typepad (www.typepad.com). If you're keeping a blog, remember to update it as often as possible. Blog readers (which include agents and editors) like to read updated information. If they see that the last entry is a few months old, they might assume that the blog is no longer active.

Whether you decide to create a Web site or a blog or both, make sure your bio and contact information are readily accessible. The main complaint we hear from editors and agents is that they don't want to spend a lot of time navigating your Web site for basic information. To make things easy for Web visitors, create tabs or links at the top of your page so your credentials are easy to find. You may also want to include a photo of yourself as well as links to your media clips and appearances. Editors and agents particularly like to see that you've had some media exposure. Fancy bells and whistles like music and graphics might look nice, but make sure they're not too distracting. Editors and agents are busy, and if it takes too long to get the right information, you've lost your window of opportunity.

Some Web sites and blogs like the ones listed below have become perfect vehicles for launching books:

- *Julie and Julia: 365 Days, 524 Recipes, 1 Tiny Apartment Kitchen,* by Julie Powell, grew from blog (http://juliepowell.blogspot.com) to book when Powell's online journal about her attempt to cook every recipe in a Julia Child cookbook became a hit on the Internet. Powell then took her blog, expanded upon it, and the book was born.

- *The Darwin Awards: Evolution in Action*, by Wendy Northcutt, started out as an e-mail, then became a Web site (www.darwinawards.com) and eventually became a book about people who "remove themselves from the gene pool in a sublimely idiotic fashion."
- *The True Stella Awards: Honoring Real Cases of Greedy Opportunists, Frivolous Lawsuits, and the Law Run Amok*, by Randy Cassingham, also originated as a Web site (www.stellaawards.com).
- *Bitter Is the New Black: Confessions of a Condescending, Egomaniacal Self-Centered Smartass, or Why You Should Never Carry a Prada Bag to the Unemployment Office*, by Jen Lancaster, grew out of the author's blog, www.jennsylvania.com, which chronicled Lancaster's downward spiral after losing her high-paying job.
- *The Weblog Handbook* by Rebecca Blood. Blood took notice of the trend toward blogging and established her own blog (www.rebeccablood.net/handbook) to chronicle the history of blogging and how it impacts society. By positing herself as an expert of the world of blogs, Blood was contracted to write *The Weblog Handbook*.
- *An Army of Davids: How Markets and Technology Empower Ordinary People to Beat Big Media, Big Government and Other Goliaths*, was authored by Glenn Reynolds, the founder of the popular political blog Instapundit.com (www.instapundit.com).
- *Straight Up and Dirty: A Memoir* by Stephanie Klein. Klein's blogging of the details of her life as a single woman in the city on her site, Greek Tragedy: Stories of My Life (http://stephanieklein.blogs.com), led to comparisons to *Sex and the City*'s Carrie Bradshaw and eventually to book and TV/film deals.

Promotional Tie-ins

Believe or not, there's a holiday just about every day of the year. See how your book fits into one of these "holidays" and plan a creative way to tie your book to the event. It's an easy hook when you're pitching to the media.

This is also a great way to show the publisher that you're thinking outside the box about other ways to generate publicity. Remember, the publicity department at a major publishing house is swamped with work. Each publicist may be trying to publicize ten books or more at a time. Any ideas that can generate additional publicity without utilizing the publisher's resources can definitely score extra points in your proposal.

E-mail Newsletters

If you have a Web site with an active e-mail database of readers, tell the publisher you're going to send out an e-mail to all of your readers (hopefully in the thousands) about the publication of your book. This is your core audience. You can take this idea a step further and ask your core audience to forward the announcement to five friends who might be interested in buying your book. And so on. This is a cheap, effective way to promote your book. Publishers love it because it's low cost and effective. Don't forget the Internet—blogs are a great way to generate buzz, too. Create a list of the top bloggers who might want to read and review your book. Include a list of these bloggers in your proposal.

HOW DO YOU RESEARCH AND WRITE A PUBLICITY PLAN?

In your publicity plan you're going to need to identify the elements of your platform and the ways you're going to help your publisher promote the book. Again, don't be generic and state the obvious. Don't tell the publisher about sending out your book for a review in *Publishers Weekly*. They know that. Instead, offer a specific action plan of what you will do.

So how should your publicity plan be organized? First, organize your publicity action plan into a list of specific ways you are going to generate publicity for your book. For each item on the list such as "Web site," "author tour," and "speaking engagements," describe the steps you would take through that vehicle and what type of publicity results you intend to get for each.

PUBLICITY BOTTOM LINE

Ask any publicity professional and she'll tell you that the best type of publicity is word of mouth or buzz. Publishers are now paying top dollar to generate buzz through agencies that specialize in what's now called *buzz* or *viral marketing*.

The New York Times describes viral marketing as "an ancient form of communication that many marketers have updated by using new technology like blogs, podcasting, and online message boards." (*The New York Times*, Julie Bosman, 1/23/06) Basically, viral marketing means good word of mouth, and it can have a huge impact on book sales.

Good buzz can be more powerful and effective than traditional advertising. Companies that specialize in buzz marketing can get your book into the hands of bloggers, writers, and other networks of key individuals who then spread the word to their friends, families, and other associates. The publisher of the book *Freakonomics*, for example, employed the Boston-based marketing agency BzzAgent as part of its publicity campaign, and that book became a best-seller (*The Boston Globe*, Scott Kirsner, 11/14/05).

Here's how we crafted the publicity section of the proposal that sold this book:

PUBLICITY AND PROMOTION

Both Ms. Brodowsky and Mr. Neuhaus understand the importance of self-promotion in marketing a book of this type. They are both skilled writers and entrepreneurs with previously published books. In short, they know what it takes to publicize, promote, and sell books.

We will publicize the book by targeting four areas: magazine articles, direct mail campaigns, trade shows, and public speaking engagements/workshops.

- **Magazine Articles:** Ms. Brodowsky and Mr. Neuhaus will write articles in writing and other trade publications about the process of writing a book proposal.
- **Direct Mail and E-mail:** We will purchase mailing lists targeting writers.
- **Trade Shows:** Ms. Brodowsky and Mr. Neuhaus will attend trade shows for major book expositions as well as specialized fields where experts might want to learn about book writing.
- **Speaking Engagements/Workshops:** As panelists or featured speakers on the topic of proposal writing or any part of the publishing process, we will sell copies of the book directly through the trade market. We will also be targeting workshop leaders in regard to using *10 Secret Steps* as course material.

Mr. Neuhaus specializes in writing about health/fitness/self-help/cooking. Therefore, he will target his experience in this field toward organizations whose members might also be potential writers. As a television news producer and adjunct professor of broadcasting at New York University, Mr. Neuhaus will also promote his book through affiliations in television, journalism, film, and radio. Some of the groups include:

- Fitness trainers and professionals (American College of Sports Medicine, IDEA Health & Fitness Association, American Council on Exercise, National Strength and Conditioning Association)

- Registered dieticians (American Dietetic Association)
- Chefs and cooks (The French Culinary Institute, The Culinary Institute of America)
- Doctors (American Medical Association, American College of Sports Medicine)
- New York University
- Television producers and journalists (Producers Guild of America, American Society of Journalists and Authors)

As a literary agent, Ms. Brodowsky will target her promotion toward the many writing and author groups mentioned in the target audience section. In conjunction with the publisher's efforts and that of Mr. Neuhaus, Ms. Brodowsky has the following to contribute:

Public Speaking:

Ms. Brodowsky is a sought-after speaker and lecturer throughout the trade industry. She averages between twelve and twenty-four events on an annual basis. She is requested by various sponsors and organizations including:

- Writer's Digest Books
- Women's National Book Association
- The International Women's Writing Guild
- Romantic Times Booklovers Convention
- Pennwriters, Inc.

Ms. Brodowsky will actively utilize these and other trade speaking opportunities to promote and publicize *10 Secret Steps*, increasing book sales.

Ms. Brodowsky is willing to travel for book-related promotion and in-store appearances. As an added benefit to bookstores signings, Ms. Brodowsky will provide a half-hour question-and-answer forum for bookstore writers' groups.

Web Related:

Ms. Brodowsky will utilize her professional Web site, InternationalLiteraryArts.com, in the promotion of *10 Secret Steps*. This Web site, visited daily by a high volume of new and previously published writers, is a natural source of promotion for this book. She will also utilize her listings on other industry sites such as WritersNet and Publishers Marketplace.

Trade Organizations:

Ms. Brodowsky will utilize her contacts throughout various trade organizations such as:

- The Authors Guild
- American Society of Journalists and Authors
- The National Writers Union

Workshops:

Ms. Brodowsky and Mr. Neuhaus will contact various writers' groups in regard to using *10 Secret Steps* as course material. They will offer a discount for group sales as a benefit. Ms. Brodowsky and Mr. Neuhaus will also conduct a predetermined number of workshops together annually; the program contained in *10 Secret Steps* lends itself to this format. At the request of various writers' groups, Ms. Brodowsky will be teaching workshops based on her first book, *Secrets of Successful Query Letters,* in 2004.

EXERCISE: Brainstorm!

Brainstorm a list of the ways you can use the media to get publicity for your book. Be as realistic as possible and start acting on some of these to begin building your publicity platform even before you finish your book proposal.

Chapter 7
Selling Yourself

DELIVERING THE IRRESISTIBLE AUTHOR BIO

Why is the author bio important?

The biography in your proposal is more than just a rough draft for the bio that will appear on the jacket flap when your book is published. It's a presentation of who you are, and it's one aspect of the proposal that will be more extensive than what appears in the book itself.

Your idea is important, your approach is important, and the content of your book is important. Equally or more important is who you are. Your credentials are important in several ways:

- They establish your credibility as a source of the ideas or facts you will be presenting in your book. They answer the question, "Why should the reader trust this author?" The bio should confirm that you are an expert on what you're writing about.
- They predict how significant your name, or your public persona, might be in selling your book. For a work of fiction, the name Stephen King is enough to sell a million copies, no matter what the title of the book is. A nonfiction book by Dr. Phil McGraw gets a head start because his name is well known. Your name may not be known to a mass audience, but if it's known in your niche, the publisher can project a certain number of sales based on that fact. Here the question is, "Does the author's name itself add potential sales?"
- They establish how effective you will be at selling your book. The contacts you have, the networks you can access, the ongoing publicity levers you can manipulate—all these mechanisms mean you can market your book. The publisher will not have to go it alone; you have muscle of your own.

- They answer the question, "How can the author help the publisher sell the book?" The bio should confirm your ability to sell your book.

COMPOSING A SELLING BIO

Your bio will sell you if it's accurate and impressive. It will be accurate and impressive if you are, in fact, well qualified and knowledgeable and if you do, in fact, have strong credentials. If you don't, no amount of hype can put it over. In other words, tell the truth and rely upon it. Your bio should tell who you really are, and it should honestly list your personal and professional qualifications as the author of your book. If you don't have the right qualifications, perhaps you should be writing a different book.

Your bio should be accurate and carefully written. It should be straightforward and should, by all means, place your qualifications in the most favorable light possible.

How should you handle negatives in your résumé? The point of the bio is to sell you as the author of the book. Aspects of your personal biography that are not relevant to your book need not be included. However, you should address any aspect of your personal history that bears directly on your credentials as an author and your ability to represent your book through publicity later. If you've written a book about beating the stock market and you did time for illegal stock transactions, this fact may detract from your credibility. On the other hand, it may add to it. In any case, you must include the fact in your biography, arguing presumably that your experience adds to your credibility. Under no circumstances should you suppress information that would alter the publisher's assessment of the marketability of your book.

The bio should include whatever is relevant to demonstrating that you're an expert in what you're writing about. It should establish that you are a credible person. It should establish that you know your subject. It should establish that you have a network that coincides with or connects to the book's natural audience.

The most important facts in your bio are those that relate directly to your authority and credibility as to the content of your book and those that relate directly to your ability to move copies of your book—to get them sold. If you've previously published any related articles on your subject matter, include this information in your bio. This will lend you instant credibility. It is also a good rule of thumb to present your agent/editor with copies of the related published clips. If you are like many new writers and have no previously published articles, you may want to try contacting some local newspapers or journals. More often than not, you will find they may have an interest in an article based on your book project. And if at first you don't succeed … try again.

The less important facts are those that have more to do with you as a person, such as where you live, where you went to college, your spouse's name, and how many children you have. Unrelated professional accomplishments are also less important—other books you've written on different subjects do serve, however, to establish that you are a published writer, and you have previously managed to put a book or books together. It's always good to list all of your published books for your agent/editor. This will come in handy when the agent/editor is pitching you as a prospective author and again when an agent/editor is in search of an author for a project that requires your area of expertise.

A bio is not a résumé; a lot of information that might appear in a résumé will not appear in the bio section of a proposal. The purpose of the bio is not to sell you as an employee by describing the fullness of your accomplishments as a person. Its purpose is to focus more sharply than a résumé does on a very specific part of your personal history—that part that has prepared you to write this book and made you the perfect person to do so. The subtext of the bio is always *why this person is perfectly qualified to write this book brilliantly.*

You're not selling just yourself; you're selling your expertise and your platform.

What is your personal platform? It includes:

- **Your network or organization.** If you can sell books directly to this group, it's important to tell the publisher how many. If your organization is well known, make clear the relevant details.
- **Your lectures, performances, appearances, or gigs.** Any frequent contacts you have with institutions, groups, or networks to whom books can be sold directly, or who function as multipliers and intensifiers of advertising or publicity dollars.
- **Your celebrity.** You don't have to be world-famous! If you're locally famous, describe the extent of your fame. Publishers often start out publicizing books to mini-markets; they can build on good results to expand sales into larger areas. Your local fame can be a foot in the door.
- **Your energy and any previous efforts that demonstrate it.** Did you promote a previous book by loading your car and selling copies door to door? Did you sell copies of a self-published version of your current book to chain or local bookstore? Did you do a series of lectures on your topic? Publishers have limited promotion budgets, so they are always inclined to take on an author who is energetic about "flogging" her own book.

Here are the bios we used to help sell this proposal:

AUTHOR BIOS

Pamela K. Brodowsky is an experienced literary agent, co-author of *Staying Sane*, the series (Da Capo Press, November 2005), and founder of International Literary Arts, a full-service literary property agency covering the creative spectrum. She is a popular speaker at various writers conferences, including BookExpo America and The International Women's Writing Guild. Brodowsky has been a guest speaker in various broadcast programs, teleseminars, and conventions nationwide and is highly sought after in her field. Prior to opening her agency, Ms. Brodowsky spent over seventeen years in various sales and marketing positions, including corporate financial sales. She resides in Moscow, Pennsylvania, along with her husband and two children.

Eric Neuhaus is a writer, journalist, and award-winning television producer. He is the co-author of *The World's Fittest You* (Dutton, January 2004), which sold at auction for a six-figure advance. He has written for numerous magazines, including *Smart Health, Physical, Experience Life,* and *Menz*. He is also an adjunct professor at New York University in the division of Film, Video, and Broadcasting, where he teaches newswriting. He started his career as a story editor and producer at ABC News' *20/20*. There, he developed and produced over ninety television magazine segments. His reporting earned him national recognition, winning an Emmy Award, Emmy nomination, and numerous other achievements. Mr. Neuhaus is a graduate of Wesleyan University, holding a B.A. degree in sociology. He earned his M.A. degree in American studies at New York University. He is a member of the National Writers Union, The Authors Guild, and Producers Guild of America. He lives in New York City.

EXERCISE: List Your Qualifications

Make a list of all your qualifications to write this book. Your agent and editor need to believe fully that you are the right person to write this book. By listing your credentials to back up your proposal for both credibility and sales reasons, you are providing the agent/editor with author ammo that is needed throughout the presentation phase. List only what pertains to the project at hand.

Chapter 8
Creating Chapter Outlines

ORGANIZING YOUR BOOK INTO CHAPTERS AND TOPICS

Now it's time to get to the nitty-gritty of your proposal. You've got the concept, the market, and even some promotional plans for publicizing your book. What about the content? How will all that information be organized? What will be the format of your book? Do you plan to include photographs and artwork? All of these questions should be answered in your proposal. You want to present a complete package to the publisher with as much detail as possible.

Planning the format of your book now will ultimately help you write the book after you've made the sale. Think of the outline as the roadmap to your book. When it's time to write, all you'll need to do is connect the dots.

WHAT IS THE CHAPTER OUTLINE?

Pick up any nonfiction book and the first thing you'll see is a table of contents. This is essentially your chapter outline. Most books contain between seven and ten chapters. Each chapter should represent a major idea or topic in your book. If your book has more than ten chapters, you might want to consider breaking down your structure even further. You can try grouping the chapters into "Parts" so that "Part 1" contains a few chapters, and so on.

With books that are programmatic—for instance, a program for learning a new skill, getting fit, staying healthy—your table of contents should flow logically so each chapter builds on the knowledge of the previous chapter. In this book, you can see how each chapter represents a step in the proposal writing process. Following the steps teaches you a new skill. This is the formula for most how-to books. If your book fits this format, by all means follow this template. Don't think you need to be creative with the structure. Rather, highlight your creativity in the chapter titles and content.

For biographies and anthologies you can have more leeway with the structure. The most obvious structure for this type of book is chronological. But don't feel locked into this format. There are lots of other ways you can organize the material, such as thematically or alphabetically.

Whatever type of book you are writing, choose the titles of your chapters wisely. Here's your chance to be clever and creative, if it's appropriate to your topic and tone. The titles don't have to be long, but make sure they have a punch. If your book revolves around a catchy concept or phrase, don't be afraid of using those words in the chapter titles and subheading. In Neuhaus' book *The World's Fittest You,* the overall concept was "fittest." Using an attention-grabbing word like "fittest," he made sure to use that word in some of the chapter titles such as "Becoming the World's Fittest You" and "Fit, Fitter, Fittest." Within the chapters Neuhaus continued to use the "fittest" concept. Here's how he did it:

THE WORLD'S FITTEST YOU

Introduction From Fat to Fittest: Becoming the World's Fittest Man
Chapter 1 My Promise
Chapter 2 Getting Started: Becoming the World's Fittest You
Chapter 3 The FIT Equation
Chapter 4 The Power of Positive Eating
Chapter 5 Shock Basics
Chapter 6 Feeling the Shock
Chapter 7 Intensifying the Shock
Chapter 8 Enjoying the Shock
Chapter 9 Fit, Fitter, Fittest
Chapter 10 Challenge Yourself!

Keep in mind, though, that in some books being clever works; in others it's best to be straightforward with the material and ideas so it's clear to the reader what will be included in the book.

WHY IS THE CHAPTER OUTLINE IMPORTANT?

Remember, clarity and logic are key to a good chapter outline. The editor reading your proposal needs to see that you have covered all of the information and packaged it into a form that is accessible to readers. Since publishers are buying a proposal and not a complete manuscript, they want to be assured that you have enough material for the book. The last comment you want from an editor is that your proposal feels more like a magazine article than a book. A strong, fleshed-out chapter outline with chapter summaries that clearly describe the content will convince editors that your topic is worthy of a book and that you have all the information to write it. Here are five ways to organize the material in your book:

1. Time
2. Importance
3. Classification and Division
4. Step by Step
5. Argument

HOW DO YOU WRITE A CLEAR AND ORGANIZED DETAILED OUTLINE?

Once you've nailed down the chapter outline you're going to need to take your outlining to the next level. Start by listing subheadings for each chapter. Save these subheadings because you might want to use them later. In the meantime, use the subheading to write a detailed narrative about what information you'll include in the chapter. Be specific but don't write more than a paragraph.

The format of these chapter summaries should be complete sentences and questions that engage the editor. Write your sentences in the active voice with active verbs, such as *describes*, *compares*, *details*, and *reveals*. Try to avoid starting each sentence with "This chapter will ..." You want to engage the editor in lively prose, not put him to sleep.

WHAT'S YOUR BOOK FORMAT?

In addition to the chapter outline, indicate in your proposal some basic physical elements related to the size and format of the book. Remember, these elements will change once your book is sold, but be prepared to offer a snapshot of your vision of the ultimate product. You should include:

- **Length of book:** Give a word count of the total number of words in your book. A good average to follow is that each page is about 300–400 words depending on the size of the book and the size of the font used.

- **Format:** Give an overview of how you envision the format of the book. Will there be sidebars with additional information? Will you be including graphs and charts? Will you be including photographs and illustrations? Keep in mind that if you're including photographs and illustrations, you should specify how you will obtain these graphic elements. Will the photographs and illustrations be created specifically for your book or will you be acquiring existing material? The answer to this question will have an impact on the cost of production, so be prepared to state the estimated cost of producing original photos and illustrations.
- **Front matter:** Include any information about a foreword, testimonials, and endorsements. A foreword is a great opportunity for you to find a celebrity or other notable person to introduce your book. If you have any endorsements from other experts or authors, note those, too.

Here's how we described the format and topic outline in the proposal that sold this book. Keep in mind that the organization of your book, including chapter titles and headings, will likely change once your proposal is accepted and your editor has the opportunity to give you feedback. We haven't included the entire outline or the chapter summaries here but you will find more examples of outlines and chapter summaries in Part Two of the book.

BOOK FORMAT

The book will be 250 pages. The first half of the book will be the instructional guide on how to write a proposal. Each chapter is one of the ten steps in the proposal-writing process. The format for each of the "step" chapters will be consistent and easy to follow, showing the reader exactly what the step is, why it's important, and how to get started. At the end of each chapter a "getting started exercise" is included to help the reader apply the instructional material of the chapter and get underway.

The second half of the book will feature twelve successful proposals. Here we will show why each proposal was successful from our three-point perspective system. The analysis will appear at the end of each proposal. The appendix will list valuable resources for writers.

TOPIC OUTLINE

Acknowledgments

Introduction
A Note to Our Readers

PART ONE

Chapter One: Defining Your Idea
Great Ideas Take Shape
Topics: What is a "good idea" or hook?
Why is it important to hook your audience?
How do you formulate and find a good idea?
Exercise: Clearly identify your idea in 25 words or less.

Chapter Two: Standing Out From the Crowd
Creating the "Tell & Sell" Title
Topics: What makes a good book title?
Why do titles matter?
How do you create a title with power words and puns?
Exercise: Generate three titles and do an informal market test with friends and family.

Chapter Three: Crafting the Opener
Creating the Powerful and Persuasive High-Point Summary
Topics: What's the opener or concept statement?
Why is it important?
How do you write the opener?
Exercise: Draft a high-point summary.

Chapter Four: Defining Your Market
Analyzing Who and How Many Will Buy Your Book
Topics: Who is your audience?
Why do you need to know the marketplace?
How do you research your market?
Exercise: List five statistics that show a market for you book.

EXERCISE: Organize Your Notes

Organization is the key to writing a good table of contents. Read through all of your notes and material, and write a simple table of contents. Remember to look at some of the examples in this book and visit your local bookstore for more ideas about outlining.

Chapter 9
Writing Sample Chapters

WRITING KNOCKOUT SAMPLE CHAPTERS

Good sample chapters are absolutely critical. The editor is looking for a smart idea she can sell to an established target audience, but by training and inclination she wants to be sure that what's actually on the pages—the book itself—is going to be strong. This is why your proposal must offer well-written samples of the actual text. The brilliance of your idea, the claims you make in your summary, and the credentials in your bio are all for nothing if the chapters you write for your proposal are weak.

THE FLAVOR AND A TASTE OF WHAT'S TO COME

The length of your proposal will vary and so will the extent of the sample you submit. Submit between thirty-five and seventy-five pages of sample text. It doesn't matter much whether this comprises one, two, or three chapters; the important thing is to display what the book will be like—and how good it will be.

The sample must demonstrate how you write, what the tone of your book is, how it reads, what kinds of connections you make, how you reason, or whether (if it's supposed to be funny) it's funny. Most editors have at some time been burned by manuscripts that don't measure up to the promise of glib, well-put-together proposals. They read the chapters very carefully, because they know that sometimes a writer is more skilled at writing the proposal than at writing the book. From your point of view, writing good sample chapters is essential to writing a slam-dunk proposal.

It's also a start on writing the book itself.

It's best to submit the first few chapters. In almost all cases, chapters in a book are in a certain order for a reason, and it doesn't make sense to read them out of order. There's a tendency for authors to want to give a selection or a smattering, but you shouldn't ask an editor to respond positively to haphazardly ordered chapters. The purpose of the chapters is to approximate what reading the book will be like. When the book is finished you will have put the chapters in just the right order, the order in which you want them read to best make your points. So it's counterproductive to offer chapters that someone will have to read in a less than optimal order.

So include the opening chapters in your proposal. It's fine if the first chapter is an introduction or a prologue. The editor will read your sample—more or less like a normal person—and if he likes it, he will, like any other normal reader, want to read more.

Make sure your sample chapters are carefully edited. It is not professional, nor will it sell your book, if there are typos, dropped words, or weak phrases. It's important for your sample chapter or chapters to be complete and convincing. If an early chapter is not complete, it's a good idea to add some connecting paragraphs designed to finish the argument, if not in full then at least enough to satisfy the editor. The sample chapters are not meant to be a tease, offering partial information to suck a publisher into paying you an advance in order to find out what's going to happen! Of course, your summary will have given the editor the complete picture of your concept and content, so she will know your argument, the range of information, your special areas of concentration, your opinion, your analysis of controversy, your view of historical subjects, etc. You want the sample chapter to represent, in brief, what reading your book will be like, giving the reader what he came for—information, advice, help, amusement, or whatever.

The sample chapters should be comprehensible as a package. They don't have to make the entire argument or cover the entire subject matter of the book—the overview will present a good summary of the total project—but they must present a coherent piece of the content. If you're writing about weapons that made a difference in great wars of history, present a strong chapter that gives your complete presentation of the catapult so the editor can see how you make your case that this weapon was crucial. If you're writing a biography, make sure your chapter gives a complete episode in, say, the early years of the subject—an episode that delivers a complete narrative. If you're popularizing a scientific subject, your first chapter should present the context and simple form of your general ideas, which in later chapters you will analyze in detail with many examples. A second sample chapter would be an example of how you are making your presentation so the editor can tell just how well you succeed in making complex ideas understandable.

It's usually a good idea in any chapter, just as it is in any book, to state your case and then wrap it up. There should be a strong lead paragraph or several, then a middle in which you follow through on what you've postulated at the start, and finally a conclusion in which you nail down how your discussion has in fact demonstrated what you set out to demonstrate.

The editor will be reading for the richness of your content and the clarity of your structure. She will also be acutely aware of your tone. Is the book pitched properly to its audience, neither over their heads nor beneath their intelligence? Is it pleasant and readable? Is it personal and lively rather than dry and stuffy?

Finally, remember that the editor reads a lot of proposals, so he's looking for shortcuts to rejection. He's looking for easy tip-offs that the project isn't worth the risk he's taking every time he advocates spending the company's money to give a writer an advance. Strive to avoid giving him any such tip-offs. A crucial tip-off is any flaw in formatting, any grammatical error, any typo. You are expected to eradicate these things from your proposal; otherwise the editor suspects they will be present in your book as well, and he doesn't want that.

READ IT, HAVE IT READ, AND READ IT AGAIN

Find the best possible readers for your chapters—and for your entire proposal—before you submit it. Husbands, wives, other relatives, and friends can function as "average readers," and their feedback can be valuable. Sometimes, however rigorous we might want them to be, these readers can be more inclined to give praise than useful criticism. So it's worth trying to get other professionals to read your chapters. In particular, have someone proofread the final version, just to make sure there are no tell-tale misspellings, typos, or dropped words.

It may also make sense to have your proposal professionally edited. A professional editor will give you objective feedback about your structure, about how clear your writing is, and about the effectiveness of your entire presentation, offering suggestions for strengthening whatever might be weak in your proposal. Some cautionary advice, though: Research any editors thoroughly before committing to work with them to avoid any costly mistakes in the end. Ask them for a list of book projects that they have worked on and the contact information of the authors. When you have good reason to anticipate success in selling your book, the services of an editor can be a relatively inexpensive insurance policy against the kinds of mistakes that can scuttle a large advance.

EXERCISE: Write the Lead Paragraphs for Your First Three Chapters

In writing the lead paragraphs for the first three chapters your project will begin to evolve naturally. Here is where you will begin to find your voice, the tone you will use throughout your book, which will need to remain consistent.

Chapter 10
Packaging Your Proposal

Putting It All Together

You've made it to the final step of the process! Now that your proposal is written, you'll need to get it into the hands of a publisher—someone who has the ability to buy your concept for a book. In most major publishing houses, there are "acquisition editors." These are editors who are always on the hunt for new projects and are anxious to read (and buy) new material. Generally, each division of each publishing company has its own editor who acquires books for that division.

The question now: How do you get your blockbuster proposal into their hands and get them to read it? If want to shoot big—in other words, the major New York publishing houses—you'll need a literary agent to get your proposal into their hands. As a rule, the major houses rarely read unsolicited or un-agented material. You might have heard that it's impossible to get a literary agent, so why even bother? That's completely wrong. Surprisingly, many writers simply approach literary agents the wrong way. So how do you effectively approach agents so they want to represent—and sell—your work?

WHAT IS THE QUERY LETTER AND WHO DO YOU SEND IT TO?

The industry standard for approaching and contacting a literary agent with a project is to write a query letter. A query letter, at its most basic level, is a sales pitch. You are writing to an agent to sell your project idea. Remember, most agents receive hundreds of query letters each week so you really need to make this letter count. Read it over a few times then have a friend or colleague read it. This is the first and sometimes the only impression you can make. Avoid common mistakes like grammatical errors or misspellings.

That's an immediate red flag to an agent that you're a careless writer. The bottom line—a query letter is an opportunity to put your best foot forward.

The next question: With hundreds of agents out there, how do you know who to send it to? The best place to start is at your local bookstore or library. Go back to the books you've listed in your competitive title section and carefully read the acknowledgments section. Invariably, the author credits the agent who "discovered" the project and made the sale. Another place to look is the Web site Publishers Marketplace (www.publishermarketplace. com). There you can search for agents within particular categories such as "health" and "lifestyle." You can also sign up for a free Publishers Marketplace e-newsletter each week that lists books sold and the agent who made the sale. Finally, you'll want to consult the *Guide to Literary Agents* or *Writer's Market*, both published by Writer's Digest Books and updated yearly. These contain contact information and submissions guidelines for reputable agents.

A few notes of caution about agents. When choosing an agent, make sure you investigate his credentials and experience. Reputable agents don't charge "reading" fees but rather make their money based on commission of the sale of your book. If an agent asks for a fee up front to read your proposal, don't bother. One great way to investigate an agent's credentials is through The Association of Authors' Representatives (www.aar-online.org). This organization is an important resource because only vetted agents can become members of this organization. Members of the AAR are not allowed to charge fees and should be able to be trusted. Ultimately, you want to choose an agent who is reputable and has a good track record of sales over time. Using the AAR Web site, you can check the sales history of agents, too.

HOW DO YOU WRITE AN EFFECTIVE QUERY LETTER?

If you've completed your proposal, all the information for your query letter is right at your fingertips. There's no need to reinvent the wheel. The purpose of the proposal is to sell your idea, so all you need to do is simply boil down the material in your proposal into a one- or two-page letter. Here's the basic format you should follow:

Your Lead

An agent likes to know you've done your homework. In your lead, mention a book she has represented or if you've read about her in one of the trade magazines. At the very least, mention where you found her name (perhaps *Writer's Market*) and that you know she specializes in the subject area of your proposal. Your next sentence should hook the agent into reading more. The easiest thing to do is lift this from the "concept statement" or "overview" section of the proposal. You may need to rework the sentences slightly in order to really grab the agent's attention.

Your Body

Once you've gotten the agent's attention you can tell more about your proposal in a paragraph or two. Again, the information here should come right from your proposal and include:

- the size of the market (see chapter four)
- your promotional platform (see chapter six)
- the need for your book (see chapter five)
- why you're the best person to write it (see chapter seven)

These sentences should be very tight, concise, and to the point.

Your Conclusion

Wrap things up quickly. Thank the agent for considering the project and offer to send the proposal as soon as possible. You also can direct the agent to your Web site or blog (if you have one) to get more information about you. Agents will do this, so always make sure your Web site is nicely designed and includes only relevant information to your professional work. In other words, remove your family photos and other distracting information from the site that may detract from your credibility as a writer.

Now the hardest part: You wait. You may be tempted to call the agent to follow up the next week and make sure he received the letter. Don't do this. You've sent an unsolicited query, so you need to give the agent time to review your query. If an agent likes your idea he will contact you and ask you to send your proposal. Generally, if they are interested, agents respond quickly. They assume you've sent the same letter to many agents. If the agent thinks he can sell your project, he won't waste any time getting in touch with you. A delay on his part could cost him the sale.

Here's an example of a query letter for *The World's Fittest You*. Always address the agent and agency by name and include your contact information. We've removed that information from the letter below as an example. When

Eric sent out the letter below to over twenty agents, each one was addressed individually and a majority of the agents responded quickly to the letter. In fact, some agents called the same day they received the letter. Ultimately, Eric chose to work with Joelle Delbourgo of Joelle Delbourgo Associates, Inc. She helped to shape the proposal and then sent it to over fifteen publishers and set up meetings. The proposal sold at auction to Dutton for six figures, a number that makes authors—and agents—very happy.

Date
Agent Name (include full name)
Agent Address (include full address)

Dear Agent (include full name),

I am writing to you to see if you would be interested in representing Joe Decker and me for a book we're writing tentatively titled *The World's Fittest Man's Guide to Getting Fit.*

I came across your name as an agent who specializes in nonfiction health and how-to books. With your expertise in this genre, I thought you would be a good person to help to shape and sell our proposal to publishers.

Joe Decker was dubbed "The World's Fittest Man" after he broke the *Guinness Book of World Records'* twenty-four-hour Physical Fitness Challenge. He is also a certified personal trainer with his own fitness company. Joe made national headlines last spring when he broke the world's fitness record. He appeared on the national network morning news shows (*Today* and *The Early Show*); on the front page of *The Washington Post* Health Section; in countless major national newspapers; on the daily entertainment television magazine shows; and in major magazines including *People, Men's Health, Men's Fitness,* and an upcoming issue of *GQ.*

Not only is Joe extremely marketable in terms of getting featured in national media outlets, but he has important information about fitness that he'd like to get out there in the form of a book. The book itself has two purposes. First, to help motivate and inspire obese people to lose weight. For this reason, Joe's personal weight-loss story of going from fat to fit will be featured in the first part of the book. Second, to help people at all fitness levels train better for specific sports activities. This part of the book will begin with Joe's personal account of training for and competing in the Fittest Man Competition. Following this, the rest of the book will be devoted to specific fitness and nutrition advice that Joe used to train for the competition. Each chapter will be devoted to one of the thirteen events from the competition. For example, Chapter One, "Cycling," will explain how Joe trained for this event and include stretching exercises, weight-training activities, and nutrition information.

Obviously, the title of World's Fittest Man gives Joe a credential that would hook customers into buying the book. However, we see the book as part of a larger marketing plan. The book will be launched with a Fat City Book Tour. The title of the tour will be Fat City, USA: The World's Fittest Man vs. The Fattest Cities. Joe will begin the launch in Houston, the fattest city in America (according to *Men's Fitness*) and continue through twenty cities. During that time, we'll be attracting local media and securing bookings on the national morning news programs. Finally, we are also in the process of developing a reality-based television show featuring Joe, similarly titled *Fat City, USA: The Fittest Man vs. The Fattest Cities*. The show will follow four obese people from the fattest cities as they transform themselves from fat to fit. What's more, the show gives Joe more national media exposure and generates more interest in the book.

As for my background, I am a journalist and former television development producer for ABC News' *20/20, Primetime,* and *Downtown*. Like Joe, I am also a fitness buff, although I'm not planning on breaking any world records soon.

If you're interested, I would be happy to send you more detailed information about Joe and our proposed book. In the meantime, you can reach me at 212-555-1212. I look forward to hearing from you.

Sincerely,

Eric Neuhaus
Address
Phone number
E-mail address

Here's another example of a query letter that helped to secure an agent and ultimately a sale. Eric helped Steve Greenberg put this letter together, which was sent out to about twenty agents. Again, always address the agent by name. Agents were excited about the project and many responded to our query. We decided to go with Andrew Stuart of The Stuart Agency because of his expertise in selling humor books. He had recently sold *The True Stella*

Awards and previously sold the best-selling *The Darwin Awards*. After some reworking of the proposal, we had an offer from Sterling Publishing:

Date
Agent Name (include full name)
Agent Address (include full address)

Dear Agent (include full name),

I found your listing on Publishers Marketplace and thought you might be interested in this project.

Have you ever heard of bird diapers?

Interested in a talking toilet paper dispenser?

What about meat-flavored water? Yum!

Surprisingly, these are not David Letterman gags but actual products available for sale on the market. Steve Greenberg, dubbed the Innovation Insider, is the media go-to guy for goofy and wacky gadgets. Now, for the first time, Steve is bringing together the goofiest gadgets of them all in a proposed book, *Gadget Nation: A Journey Through the Underbelly of American Invention*. I am writing to see if you would be willing to represent Steve and me for this great new project.

Steve's book will uncover the one hundred goofiest gadgets of all time. Each unique product will include a hilarious picture of the product, its sometimes outrageous packaging, and an interview with the inventor revealing the story behind how each way-out invention came to market.

To date, there's only one other competing book. That book is focused on patents and does not deal with actual products that are sold on the market. At the same time, America's appetite for gadgets and inventions appears insatiable. The popularity of specialty catalogs like *The Sharper Image*, *SkyMall*, *Clever Gear*, and *Hammacher Schlemmer* makes this abundantly clear. What's more, who hasn't asked the age-old question, "Why didn't I think of that?" Each year more than sixty thousand patents are filed by private citizens who hope to strike gold with their product ideas. This book will appeal to those would-be inventors, but some of the products will have readers saying, "I'm *glad* I didn't think of that!" Essentially, this book is a must-have fun gift for the inventor—and consumer—in all of us.

Steve, a regular commentator and expert on all things gadgets, has the ideal platform to launch this book. His offbeat and wacky on-air personality has made him the television media darling for demonstrating new products. He's appeared routinely on national talk shows such as *The Daily Buzz, The Caroline Rhea Show, FOX & Friends*, Lifetime's *Our Home*, and others. Steve also does satellite media tours for several newscasts across the country. For three years, Steve appeared nationally every weeknight demonstrating innovative products on the Discovery Channel's *Your New House*. For six years, Steve was on HGTV's very popular *Dream Builders*. For *Dream Builders*, Steve has traveled the country showcasing the latest in home design, construction, and trends. For five years, HGTV also used Steve's reporting skills for coverage of the hottest new home improvement products at NAHB's International Builders Show.

Steve also writes for several magazines and Web sites. His "Innovation Insider" features appear in each edition of *Smart HomeOwner* magazine. Steve also writes for *Backyard Living, Log Home Living, Ocean Drive, Manhattan Style,* and *DailyExaminer.com*.

I will be Steve's writer and have previously ghostwritten two books: *The World's Fittest You* (Dutton, 2004) and *Iron Yoga* (Rodale, 2005). As a former producer with ABC News' *20/20*, I have many current media contacts and will use those to help promote this book.

For more background on Steve and me you may visit our respective Web sites:

www.stevegreenbergtv.com

www.ericneuhaus.com

We are completing a full book proposal now and would be happy to send you a copy for review. We look forward to hearing from you.

Sincerely,

Eric Neuhaus
Address
Phone number
E-mail address

SENDING THE PROPOSAL

When you receive the go-ahead to send the proposal, do so quickly. Print the proposal on 8½-by-11-inch white paper. Make sure to use a standard font type such as Courier or Times New Roman. Don't use strange fonts or colors—let the quality of the proposal speak for itself. Many agents are turned off by packaging bells and whistles. Staple or clip your proposal neatly together.

In addition to the proposal, you may want to include media clips of your work. Agents and editors like to see that your work has been validated in the press. If you've appeared on television you can include a DVD of your appearances. Television experience is a great selling point for your proposal and can greatly increase your chances of getting your proposal noticed.

GOING "AGENTLESS"

Many smaller publishing houses readily accept proposals that are not represented by agents. In fact, a few of the sample proposals included in this book did not have agents. If you decide to go this route, send your query letter directly to the editor at the publishing house and then follow the same procedure for sending your proposal. You'll find a great listing of small publishers in *Writer's Market* or on WritersMarket.com.

Keep in mind that working without an agent has advantages and disadvantages. The biggest advantage is that you won't be paying a 15 percent commission. All the sales of your book go directly into your pocket. On the downside, you're going to have to be prepared to do your own negotiating (a task the agent manages). Once you get past the elation that someone wants to buy and publish your book, you'll need to agree on a price. Don't be shy about going back to the publisher and asking for a larger advance. In most cases, publishers are prepared for this type of negotiation. For instance, if you get an offer of five thousand dollars, go back and ask for eight thousand. Chances are, the publisher will split the difference and you'll end up at sixty-five hundred. Not bad for speaking up. However, don't go back with an unreasonable figure. If you get five thousand dollars, don't go back with twenty thousand. The publisher will probably see this as totally out of range and it may put you out of the negotiation process completely.

EXERCISE: Create a Persuasive Query Letter

Read through your proposal. Using the cut-and-paste feature on your word processor, cut the sentences that distill the major selling points of your proposal and paste them into a new document. Name that document "query letter." Now link the sentences to create a persuasive letter. Next, identify three agents who specialize in the type of work you are writing. These will be the first three people you will submit your query to.

Part II
The Sample Proposals

Now that you've followed the steps and exercises to help you craft your superior proposal, we've added a real bonus to help you even more. In this part of the book, we've gathered together twelve outstanding proposals to give some real life examples of what agents and editors are looking for when they read a book proposal. You'll also hear from the writers themselves about the process they used to get started and ultimately get the results they wanted—a published book. Yes indeed, these are all proposals that have sold and are successfully published. One final note, in the interests of space we've removed some of the cover pages, sample chapter outlines (noted with an asterisk), and sample chapters from the proposals. If you are interested in reading a sample chapter from one of these proposals, we encourage you to buy a copy of the proposed book and support the authors who have generously offered their proposals as models to help you on your quest for publication. Gook luck!

Proposal 1
PR on a Budget

Published in fall 2006 by Dearborn Trade Kaplan Publishing

LEONARD SAFFIR Author

I was always thinking of a book on public relations on a budget when my agent called me and asked if I would write such a book. We came up with the title PR on a Budget and the publisher came up with their subtitle. This is my third book. I used the Internet, mainly Google, plus a long list of people I know in PR and PR publications to help me get the information I needed. It took about one month to write. Since my agent had a publisher in mind, the whole process went smoothly.

PAM BRODOWSKY Agent

Leonard was referred to me by a business acquaintance. I was in search of a major PR man for a specific project. His credentials impressed me greatly. He has worked for some of the biggest and the best firms in the world. He had two previous PR books already published and is well known in the media. In short, Leonard is a great package.

MICHAEL CUNNINGHAM Editor

Our sales and marketing list was still fairly young at the time I saw this proposal, and this looked like a good project to pursue since we didn't have anything PR-related at the time.

At Kaplan we work very closely with our authors to form a partnership on the sales and marketing front, so we are looking for an author who can support the book upon publication. The original proposal did not include a marketing support plan from the author, and this is one of the most critical pieces that we review when considering a project. Given Leonard's background as a PR professional, I was confident that he had much to offer. I asked Leonard and his agent to put together a plan that would take advantage of all his contacts as well as the activities of his consulting business. Oftentimes, an author is conducting many great programs on his end that could go a long way to support the book, and the author's marketing plan in the book proposal is the perfect opportunity to toot his own horn and really sell himself to the publisher.

Leonard has had an amazing career in the field of public relations where he served as the executive vice president with one of the biggest and best known PR firms in the world. His work with blue-chip clients provides an interesting perspective into some of the most successful campaigns, but his later experience as a consultant who advised start-ups and other smaller enterprises provided the unique balance we were looking for in this type of book.

PR on A BUDGET
How to Get Maximum Exposure for Your Minimum Dollar

Book Proposal
By Leonard Saffir

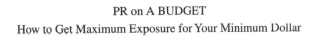
International Literary Arts, LLC
RR 5 Box 5391 A
Moscow, PA 18444
(570) 689-2692

This is a great title with a clever subtitle that says it all. "PR on a Budget" says clearly what this book is about in four powerful words. "How to Get Maximum Exposure for Your Minimum Dollar" states what this book will do for its reader. The key to a great title is making it short, sweet, and to the point. Use as few words as possible. A great title will attract attention and tell its reader what he can expect to gain from reading the book.

Table of Contents

Providing a proposal table of contents allows agents and editors to easily navigate through your proposal without having to sift through the text to locate answers to their questions. This is especially important when submitting a lengthy proposal. Although the table of contents for a proposal can vary due to the organization of your sections, a good rule of thumb is to put them in descending order from strongest to weakest. For example, if you are a previously published author, with a great sales record, you wouldn't want to leave your author bio for last, but rather place it up-front after your overview. You are trying to grab the attention of potential buyers so put your best foot forward. (Note: The page numbers do not match this re-creation of the proposal.)

Overview

Tenika Morrison of Puyallup, Washington, found herself with a groovy new online vintage clothing store but no money to get the word out.

That would have turned off most entrepreneurs but not the 25-year-old Morrison. Over several weeks she devoured everything she could read about public relations on the Internet. Her efforts paid off. With her new knowledge, she wrote a short, fun, and detailed press release that brought her excellent results.

When Kathleen Ragland wanted to get some media notice for her Boca Raton, Florida, art gallery, she turned to a new kind of public relations service company. She purchased a package that included a telephone consultation with an experienced PR professional, a press release written in proper journalistic style, and distribution to all relevant media in Florida. Her cost was about $500. On the success meter she scored a 10 because it was quick, easy, and relatively inexpensive and she "got ink," as coverage in a newspaper is called.

With the influx of so many new entrepreneurs into the business world—women starting their own businesses and all of the new high tech and dot com companies—there's an unparalleled need to help them get the word out about their companies, products, services, and people.

The Market

The market has never been better than it is today for a book offering public relations savvy on a budget.

Your overview section will be your first impression on prospective agents and editors. This section needs to be one of your strongest. You need to set the tone for what is to come in a powerful, short narrative. This is not the place to include all the details of your project but rather to sum them up in a to-the-point opener.

With two sample situations, the author reinforces the fact that his idea is a worthy one. Using real-life examples of situations where your proposed book may have been helpful to someone is a clever way of showcasing the need for your book. It says there is an audience ready and waiting.

- Over 23 million small business owners in America.
- Millions of medium-sized companies looking to get the most out of their PR dollars.
- Large corporations looking to drive more attention to them without having to spend millions.
- Management and account staff at small- and medium-sized public relations firms looking for new ways to serve their clients inexpensively.

Why This Book and Why Now?
While PR firms are sprouting up over the countryside like weeds, and blooming along the way, so are their fees. Many of today's entrepreneurs are forced to pass on PR.

Start-ups, as well as small and medium-sized businesses, charities, and non-profit organizations have more important things to spend their money on than costly PR agencies.

For those who think their "widget" is the coolest around and are going it alone with PR, getting publicity is often a confusing, hit-or-miss process. Reporters and editors are inundated with poorly prepared or inappropriately targeted press releases. More than half the press releases received by a chain of community newspapers in Palm Beach County, Florida, are addressed to editors who have long been replaced or deceased.

Incorporating public relations in business plans, may be the difference today between success and failure. PR's importance is

---

Researching your market to its fullest extent is of the utmost importance. Use statistics, demographics, and organization memberships to detail your markets. Show who, how many, and why your book will help them. A bulleted list with numbers supporting the book's audience makes an easy reference for the agent/editor.

Emphasize the need your book is fulfilling. For this proposal the need is PR, but PR is expensive and small companies don't have the revenue needed to get the word out. This author is providing an affordable alternative to the need. Show how your book is going to solve a problem or provide a solution to those in need.

undeniable. Recognizing the power of public relations is one thing, harnessing it is another.

Public relations is not rocket science. It is possible to handle a business' or organization's public relations in a manageable and logical fashion, providing a little time is spent learning your way around.

That's what this book is for … a trip through the bizarre bazaar of public relations. Yes, help is on the way. *PR on a Budget* is the answer for the financially-strapped start-ups, those struggling companies who have had to drop their PR firms and the timid who are afraid to start a new business because of the high cost of getting the word out.

Scope & Focus

The book offers advice on working with the media and building a successful public relations program. Written in a light, breezy style, it includes an abundance of tips on how to get noticed. For those with PR experience who have seen their budgets decline, this book will show you how to keep churning.

Costs for services covered in this book range from free to a few thousand dollars a month on a project basis.

Oftentimes, the only difference between a big agency charging $10,000 a month and a smaller one charging $2,000 is $8,000.

Then there's a firm that guarantees at least five published articles every month in approved publications or there's no charge. There are plenty of small PR firms who charge a few thousand dollars a month for a retainer, and the book explains how to pick a good one.

The final paragraph of "Why This Book and Why Now?" defines the entire premise of the book. The author states very clearly what this book intends to cover and who it is for. Always be direct when telling editors and agents the most important part of your proposal: the essential idea.

As this author does, give specific numbers and figures. Doing so shows that you are an expert in your field and understand the material. Editors and agents like to see specificity whether it's the amount a PR agency charges or another type of figure.

PR on a Budget is written by a PR professional who once helped run one of the world's top public relations firms and also toiled in the vineyards of entrepreneurship with no money to hire a PR agency.

Leonard Saffir's former Fortune 100 clients paid his agency millions of dollars for his knowledge—much of what is in this book. Saffir reveals numerous examples of his personal experiences, interesting and at times humorous. He not only draws from his big agency experience for this book, but, as a former award-winning newspaperman, Saffir also uses his journalistic skills with interview material from top PR industry leaders. The book includes ideas and tips from renowned PR practitioners such as Bob Dilenschneider, Richard Weiner, Bob Seltzer, and Bill Novelli, current or past CEOs of top global agencies. They also believe that one can obtain good results on a low budget or no budget.

With his long award-winning background in public relations, Saffir brings extra promotional support to a publisher. For his most recent book, he was successful in getting national publicity, arranging a number of interviews, and setting up a book signing at one of the nation's leading independent bookstores.

Saffir will work with the publisher's marketing department to help create and implement a marketing and public relations campaign strategy and the tactics to make PR on a Budget among the leading all time best-selling PR books.

Early in your proposal, tell your agent or editor why you are the best person to write your book. State what you've done. Showcase your best talent, qualifications, education, and training, or real-life experience. If you have had success in the category of the project you are proposing, show it. Writing about yourself in the third person is an effective way to do this without sounding pretentious. Establish your expertise by providing background information. State where your information will come from.

Editors want to know that you'll be involved in the process of marketing and publicizing your book, and that you're not going to sit back and wait for something to happen.

<u>**Competitive Titles:**</u>

Today's leading books on PR include:

- *Effective Public Relations* by Scott Cutlip—Prentice Hall; 8th edition (1999), Hardcover, 608 pages, List Price $126.00, Amazon Sales Rank—24,440
- *Full Frontal PR* by Richard Laermer—Bloomberg Press (2003), Hardcover, 256 pages, List Price $31.94, Amazon Sales Rank—154,447
- *Public Relations Writing* by Thomas Bivins NTC/Contemporary Publishing; 4th edition (1998), Paperback, 385 pages, List Price $ 29.52, Amazon Sales Rank—33,724
- *The Public Relations Writer's Handbook by* Merry Aronson—Jossey-Bass (1998), Hardcover, 224 pages, List Price $ 32.95, Amazon Sales Rank—183,544
- *Public Relations for Dummies* by Eric Yaverbaum—For Dummies (2000), Paperback, 384 pages, List Price $29.99, Amazon Sales Rank—28,244

While *all* of the above titles are written on the subject matter of Public Relations and all provide good practical advice, *none* of them come from the unique standpoint of *PR on a Budget: How to Get Maximum Exposure for Your Minimum Dollar. PR on a Budget* is about how to get great PR exposure while not having to put out an exorbitant amount of money. The timing has never been better.

Amazon rankings are a great way to indicate that a book is selling well, but make sure you use books with good rankings. Otherwise, editors and agents may see this as a sign that your book might not sell. These rankings are good, considering that many of the titles are a bit old.

This shows that there are a number of existing books on PR, but none with this intended approach. This says that the author's book is going to be "unique" in its category.

Stating your proposed title throughout your proposal tends to make it grow on the reader, particularly if it's well crafted. It helps agents and editors begin to conceptualize your book.

PR on a Budget: How to Get Maximum Exposure
for Your Minimum Dollar

Table of Contents
Chapter One: What Is Public Relations?
Chapter Two: Everyone Needs PR
Chapter Three: Big Agency vs. Small Agency
Chapter Four: Strategy & Tactics
Chapter Five: Brainstorming
Chapter Six: Spin or Win
Chapter Seven: On Target
Chapter Eight: Getting the Word Out
Chapter Nine: There's More Out There Than *The New York Times*
Chapter Ten: Successful Paupers
Chapter Eleven: Internet Public Relations
Chapter Twelve: How to Stage Manage the Interview
Chapter Thirteen: Turn Newsletters Into Gold
Chapter Fourteen: Dos and Don'ts
Chapter Fifteen: Media Pointers
Chapter Sixteen: Read, Read, Read
Chapter Seventeen: Surveys, Surveys, Surveys
Chapter Eighteen: Down But Not Out

Just as this author did, start the table of contents on its own page so it is easier to read and separate from the other informational text.

The titles to your chapters are very important. Editors and agents often scan the proposal table of contents to get quick a sense of your book. At a glance your agent and editor should be able to distinguish all that your book is about from your table of contents, as well as what it will cover and how it is organized. These chapter titles are clear and to the point and tell the editor and agent that the author has a firm grasp on the overall content of each chapter.

Here's how ***PR on a Budget*** unfolds:

Chapter Outline

Chapter One answers the question: *What is Public Relations?* The chapter explains the differences between public relations, advertising and publicity. Advertising you pay. PR you pray. The advantage of media coverage of a company is the credibility of a third party endorsement that it gives the company for use with its target audiences. PR is the engineering of perception, according to Leonard Saffir's definition as described in his two previous books.

Chapter Two, *Everyone Needs PR,* discusses the importance of PR in a business model backed up by numerous examples of how public relations made the difference. Quotes from PR leaders are included here (and elsewhere).

Chapter Three, *Big Agency vs. Small Agency.* Leonard Saffir has helped to run one of the biggest PR agencies in the world and one of the smallest agencies in the world, his own one-man shop, and every size in-between. Big is not always better. He describes the differences and suggests that the right small agency may work even better for the wannabe success.*

Chapter Seventeen, *Surveys, Surveys, Surveys* tells how you can be a player without possessing a stack of big chips. Saffir tells about a one-question survey of Fortune 500 CEOs, conducted by an administrative assistant, that landed his agency's client on the front page of the *Wall Street Journal.*

Your chapter outline is a detail-oriented description as to what will be covered in each chapter. This section should provide an in-depth understanding of what your book will include and how you will present it. Use an easy-to-read format as this author did. Bold chapter numbers, italicized titles, and regular font and point size for the text.

In your chapter summaries, write as if you are speaking to the reader. "You" is used frequently, as well as direct, imperative statements. This helps draw in the agent or editor.

Though we've omitted some here, the author included summaries for all chapters as required..

Chapter Eighteen, *Down But Not Out*. Public relations literacy is spreading. Those who realize the critical nature of PR will have to seek PR literacy on their own. This book is Leonard Saffir's contribution to those who can't afford big agencies.

Yes, it's lonely at the top and you have gone this far and now you have a question. No one to turn to? Wrong. Go directly on-line to Leonard Saffir, the author of this book. In his lifetime Saffir has probably faced every conceivable PR problem. He boasts he knows all the answers or where to find them. Simply e-mail the author. He'll get back to you with an answer, for free of course. lenpr@bellsouth.net

Your chapter summaries are a great opportunity to showcase your writing ability. Be direct, but write in a style that will reflect how the actual book will be written. This author is to the point, but conversational. His summaries show that his book won't take the topic too seriously, but it will convey all the material in a straightforward manner.

There is no need to sum up this section. Just as this author has done, simply end with the last chapter. It should have its own natural conclusion. This one is especially nice because the author shows that he isn't afraid to make himself available to readers, something that will help to promote the book and increase sales.

About The Author

Leonard Saffir is the author of two books. His first, *Power Public Relations: How to Get PR to Work For You,* was published in hardcover in 1992 and soft cover in 1994 by NTC Contemporary Books (now part of McGraw Hill). The same publishing company published his second book, *Power Public Relations: How to Master the New PR*, in 2001.

Communications departments in numerous colleges and universities have used both books as required reading.

Saffir has spent a lifetime affecting the ways we view our corporations, our politicians, our heroes, and the host of products and services we buy and use every day.

He served as executive vice president of Porter Novelli, one of the largest PR firms in the world. For long-time client Philip Morris USA, Saffir developed and worked on numerous major projects in corporate image, sports, entertainment, music, and the arts. He was a creator of the highly successful Marlboro Country Music program and led Marlboro into Indy Car auto racing. He worked on numerous integrated marketing programs for Philip Morris and image building programs for Philip Morris Corporation. He created the first crisis communications plan for Porsche USA and developed a technology-driven pressroom for the giant Detroit Auto Show for Michelin. Other former clients include MasterCard, Pepsi Cola, Bristol Myers, Mattel, General Foods, Kraft, the Cigar Association of America, the National Enquirer, Amtrak, Johnson & Johnson and Gillette, whose Sensor

---

Use your most powerful credentials first. If you have had success with previous books you've written on your subject matter, state that immediately—just as this author has shown he has written two previous PR books and follows that with detailed information demonstrating his expertise.

If your previous books have been used as textbooks or for university courses, be sure to include that information for your agent and editor. It shows that your writing has been showcased in areas other than the normal trade.

razor blade launch has been listed as one of the top 10 greatest PR programs of all times.

He is the recipient of the Public Relations Society of America's prestigious Silver Anvil and Big Apple awards and several PRSA Certificates of Commendation.

Saffir has contributed to *The New York Times, The Washington Post, The Miami Herald, South Florida Sun-Sentinel*, and *Good Housekeeping* magazine.

He worked for Hearst's International News Service in its New York, Dallas, and Tokyo bureaus.

He started four newspapers, three dailies and one weekly.

Saffir has won numerous journalism awards and is a past president of the Overseas Press Club of America. He served as chief of staff and press secretary to U.S. Senator James L. Buckley, 1970-76.

As an entrepreneur, as well as a consultant to many start-up companies, Saffir has considerable experience in getting the word out with little money.

If you have been employed by nationally recognized organizations, be sure to include them. This author lists the various highly visible clients for which he has worked. Tell your agent and editor about all of your related connections. Mention the best of the best in descending order. Include your accomplishments, your media experience, and your previously published works. If you have experience working in media, make that clear. Why? Because working in media shows you have crucial connections that ultimately can get your book more exposure. And we all know, the more exposure your book gets, the better sales will be.

Proposal 2
The Killer Book of True Crime Trivia

Will be published in spring 2007 by Sourcebooks

TOM PHILBIN & MICHAEL PHILBIN Authors

True Crime has always been a subject my brother Mike and I have long been enamored with. I was focusing only on murder trivia, but when I expanded the concept it all fell into place. I had a number of titles; the current title was the publisher's idea, which I'm not in love with because I think it's ambiguous. It's not my first book, I've had thirty-nine nonfiction books published plus fifteen novels—all about crime.

The concept, like so many book ideas, gestated in me for years. My approach to the agent is this: I try with all my heart and soul to please the agent because I know if I please her, I have a better shot at selling the book. The proposal is key to selling books. Don't forget: After it leaves your hands, the agent has to sell it, and you want to give her as much ammunition as possible. And listen to the agent: They usually know a lot more—as they should—about the market than you do. The book took me and my co-author three months to write.

Over the years I tried to sell it a few times, but never really had a broad enough concept, which turned out to be all kinds of true crime trivia, not just murder. I think it's a great idea to look at your book through the eyes of potential publishers. The biggest obstacle to selling this one was that publishers didn't know where to put it. It finally ended up in true crime, where it belongs. Always try to imagine where your publisher will place the book on the shelf.

PAM BRODOWSKY Agent

Tom came to me as a referral from a mutual friend. I found him to be very knowledgeable in both the True Crime category and various other subjects. He has more than sixty books to his credit and is a top notch writer. I have always been fascinated by true crime, so this was a direct hit for me.

PETER LYNCH Editor

The first thing that grabbed my attention was the topic of the book. We had been interested for a while in publishing in the true crime category but needed the right project with which to begin. As a new publisher in the category, we would need to bring something new or different to the reader. The authors' approach was different because instead of another look at a particular case, they proposed to give the true crime fan an ultimate resource of facts and trivia. We know that this approach works in other areas, such as bathroom readers, so the concept seemed an ideal way to offer a new type of book for true crime fans.

Because story is so important in true crime, we felt that this book would need to have more and longer stories than originally included in the proposal. Therefore we asked the authors if they would agree to adding these to their book, and if so, to provide samples of stories they would write. The authors agreed and provided excellent samples, allowing us to agree on making an offer for publication.

The authors were very knowledgeable about true crime readers and what types of trivia would appeal to them. By fully understanding their audience, they were able to create a book that would have high potential for quality and sales.

THE KILLER BOOK
OF
TRUE CRIME TRIVIA
By Mike and Tom Philbin

International Literary Arts, LLC
RR 5 Box 5391A
Moscow, PA 18444
(570) 689-2692

The impact from a powerful title can mean sales for your book. This title is sharp. It immediately says something about the book, and the word "killer" is often used as slang to mean "the best." So, in short, this title is working for the book in two ways: It says what it is about and that it is the best available.

Proposal Contents

1. Introduction/Overview
2. Audience/Market
3. Format
4. Competitive/Comparative Titles Analysis
5. Authors Bios
6. Chapter Lineup With Sample Entries

Your proposal should always include a proposal table of contents. Treating each section of the proposal as its own will allow you to focus more directly on the content. Providing numbered sections in order of placement is one way to create this proposal table. This is an acceptable method if your proposal is short, like this one. But if you are planning to submit a lengthy proposal, it is best to identify your sections and to provide page numbers so each section can be located quickly.

Introduction/Overview

This book is for people who like to read about true crime. One of its attributes is that it's very easy to read; the information comes in bite-size portions. In a sense, it is like a big bowl of hot popcorn fresh from the popper, kernels that crime aficionados will find interesting, surprising, informative and/or shocking—and, of course, delicious.

Every chapter will have the crime facts served up in various forms. There are lists—we all love lists—Q&As, anecdotes, a feature called "Who Am I," which gives a series of clues on someone's identity and then invites reader to guess who the person is—or was—as well as crime jargon, games, interesting quotes ("Notable Quotables") and much more. The idea is to enhance the appeal of already fascinating information.

We think that Tom and Mike Philbin, who are brothers, are in a good position to evaluate what to include in the book because they are typical, they believe, of the kind of people who will be reading it. Both have had long-standing interest in true crime; or to put that another way, were born with a ghoul gene. They view the book as entertainment, and will keep that in mind constantly as they collect and prepare material for it.

There should be a light, airy, open look to the book, and illustrations would help.

Depending on budgetary situations, the more the merrier. In addition to photos of people, the authors plan to include simple black-and-white artwork and sections from autopsy reports, death

---

This great opening paragraph highlights the distinctive selling point of the proposal—"bite-size crime facts" that crime aficionados will love. Using descriptive words and metaphors makes for lively and engaging prose. The "popcorn" comparison is unique and fun. You're really going to have to hook your reader, so anything in the first paragraph to get your message to "pop" helps.

In the overview, give a taste of how your work will be presented and what you plan to include. Clearly convey the picture in your mind to your prospective reader. If you plan to use illustrations, specify how many, but don't go overboard. Illustrations can be costly, and you don't want the production cost to outweigh the book's worth.

certificates, and other memorable trivia of the famous and infamous such as Tupac Shakur, Phil Hartman, and JFK.

The book will include at least fourteen chapters that cut across, as it were, all kinds of criminal activity, from cons to capital murder.

Astonishingly, a crime book of trivia in the same vein as this one has never been published! There are crime encyclopedias but not any containing short, punchy, bite-size facts—from a single line to a paragraph or two—that cover such a broad area of crime like this one does.

There is ample evidence, as detailed below in the Market/Audience section, that this book should attract a large readership. Crime is big in our culture now, and this book should be more delicious entertainment that people will gobble up.

Audience/Market

People love crime, and this is reflected today in the popularity of both books and TV. *The New York Times* current nonfiction paperback best-seller list has three crime books in the top seven: At number two is *Worth More Dead* by Ann Rule. (Pocket Books); at number three is *The Devil in White City* by Erik Larson (Vintage); and at number nine is *In Cold Blood* by Truman Capote. In TV, as reflected in the Nielsen numbers, an astonishing six of the top ten shows are crime shows. *CSI* (CBS) is number one with 28,728,000 viewers; *Without A Trace* (CBS) is number three with 20,440,000 viewers; *NCIS* (CBS) is number five with 18,126,000; *Cold Case* (CBS) is number eight

Here the authors show they are filling a gap. Now make note: It is *not* that a true crime book has never been published but that one presented with this approach has yet to be published. This project is clearly unique to its market.

Stating that *The New York Times* best-seller lists has three crime books in the top seven is a great way to prove the market as these authors have. Agents and editors love best-selling comparables. Be sure to be right on target with your claims. Stating that your book would be comparable to another that it is clearly not is not advisable. Saying that your book may appeal to that same audience may be a better approach.

with 16,624,000 people watching; *CSI: NY* is tied at number eight with *Cold Case* and number ten—only on the air five or six weeks—is *Criminal Minds* (CBS) with 16,218,000 viewers. Plus there are numerous true crime shows such as *FBI Files*, A&E's nonfiction *Cold Case* and *Court TV*, which spawns numerous crime specials, as well as covering criminal cases itself all day. And just recently the publishers of *People Magazine* demonstrated what they thought about the viability of the subject by publishing a quality 144-page "one shot" entitled *TRUE CRIME Stories ... Cases That Shocked America.*

Format

Hardcover, or sturdy trade paper, 450 pages with 30 to 40 black and white illustrations.

Competitive/Comparative Titles Analysis

There is not, as mentioned, a single book like this one. There are plenty of books on crime, but the vast majority of these are on individual topics, such as the recounting of a tale or murder, or crime collections or encyclopedias, which are expensive. For example, Facts on File sells crime encyclopedias for $75 a volume. *The Encyclopedia of Crime and Punishment* sells for a whopping $570.00. *The Killer Book of True Crime Trivia* is in a different league. A paperback *Macabre Miscellany* (Virgin Publishing 2005) is similar in form—short and punchy—but it covers a lot of areas other than crime, and the focus is on gory and gruesome, such as the horrible ways people die (like being swallowed headfirst by a loft python and the like.).

Back all your claims with numbers. This is a great way to prove your audience. Here the authors refer to crime shows and list the number of viewers. These statistics help define the audience.

When you describe your format, you want to include any additional photographs or illustrations that will be in the book. The more information you can give, the better.

Stressing the point that there is not a single book on the market with this unique approach reminds the agent and editor that this book is something new and needed for the category. Do this throughout your proposal, but be careful not to be redundant.

There are, as mentioned, encyclopedias of crime but nothing on trivia. One paperback that covers a lot of True Crime ground at a reasonable price ($13.95) is *The Mammoth Book of True Crime* (Carroll & Graf) by Colin Wilson. This book has done quite well. It contains analytic essays by the author on various true crimes, but it differs vastly from *The Killer Book of True Crime*. The material in *Killer* is short and sweet, and even the longer anecdotes that it contains could not be described as essays.

Author Bios

Tom Philbin and his younger brother Mike have been close to crime (and its consequences) for many years. They come from a New York cop family. Their grandfather walked a beat in Manhattan for thirty-six years, their uncle Jimmy Williams was a much-decorated detective in the old "Fort Apache" precinct, Jimmy's son Blake was a plainclothes cop in the Bronx, and their father was an investigator with the Immigration & Naturalization Service who lectured for years at the NYPD on criminal immigration matters. Tom is a long-time freelance writer and has written nine cop novels under the Fawcett Crest banner in the Precinct Siberia series, one Fawcett Crest Mystery, *The Yearbook Killer*, two novelizations of cop movies *Blink* and *The Rookie,* and in 1997, he won the grand prize, the "Badge and Quill" award for "Excellence in Writing" from the International Union of Police Chiefs for his book *Copspeak: The Lingo of Law Enforcement and Crime*. Mike Philbin is a musician by trade, but he knows how to run a Remington and, as mentioned earlier, is a long time crime buff.

Be specific in your analysis of what the other competitive books do and don't include. You can do this by focusing on form as well as content.

Demonstrate your abilities to write your proposed project. The authors do this by detailing their prior publishing credits and the ways they have been involved in the crime category.

Also included in this proposal package (not shown here) were several crime fact examples in their intended formats. A sample chapter and examples of your writing can sometimes make the difference between a sale and no sale.

Proposal 3
Now What Do I Do? The Woman's Guide to a New Career

Published in May 2005 by Capital Books

JAN CANNON, PH.D. Author

The idea for this first book came from my experience working as a career counselor for over ten years. I received calls from people looking for career help, but unable to afford working with me for an extended period of time. Unfortunately, many people see the price of career advising as a cost rather than an investment. I thought that it was time to make my "system" available to a wider audience at a reasonable price. I also decided I could use it as a text for the many workshops I lead, currently in Boston, Providence, and Denver (and looking to expand). From evaluations, I've learned that often the participants have wanted more time spent on the topic of job searching, and this book would be a way to offer that. I decided to focus it on career searches for women because 1) women buy more books, 2) my workshops are for women, and 3) I learned from all my research that targeting an audience is the best approach. As for the title, that was the publisher's idea. Mine was much more pedantic: *Job Search at Mid-Life: A Woman's Guide to Finding Satisfying Work.*

The proposal evolved over a period of months. I started with an annotated table of contents and added the various parts to that. My research consisted of going to my local Barnes & Noble, collecting about eight books on how to write a book proposal, and then sifting through them for their salient points while I drank several cups of coffee at the café. I took lots of notes. I took special notice of those areas that all books referenced: research the competition, create a marketing plan, target the audience, etc. I also took a three-hour workshop on writing proposals through an adult education program. It was targeted to magazine editors, but I picked up some additional valuable information about writing the cover letter to go with the proposal. All in all I think the proposal evolved over about ten weeks. The hardest/longest part was the market research on the competition—it was a moving target.

I decided I wanted a small press because I felt I could get the book to market faster that way. I chose not to seek an agent for the same reason, although I ultimately would have sought an agent if I couldn't sell my book myself. As it turned out, one of the small press editors passed the proposal on to a friend who is a New York book agent. She called just days after I got the offer from Capital Books.

Once I decided on a small press publisher, I took *Writer's Market* from the library and identified ten publishers I thought sounded like the right ones for my kind of book. I sent them cover letters and the proposal, which included a marketing plan, annotated table of contents, three sample chapters, a bibliography/resources section, and my résumé. All of them responded with typed letters saying they were not the right publisher but that someone out there was. I was encouraged because I didn't get any form letters; so I identified ten more publishers, also from *Writer's Market*, and repeated the process. This time I got an offer from Capital Books in Virginia (and the call from the agent). Almost one year later, just as the book was ready for publication, another publisher called and wanted to make an offer. Guess I finally made it to the top of the slush pile.

I don't feel like I faced any problems. The contract was a challenge, but I had good advice from a friend who's a media lawyer, so it really wasn't too difficult to navigate.

KATHLEEN HUGHES Editor

Jan Cannon's book proposal fit into our publishing program as defined on our Web site. She had obviously done her homework about what we were looking for. Then, as I read on, I could see that she is also an author with good realistic marketing ideas and a business with a direct link into the career market.

Jan included exactly what we ask for in our submission guidelines: a cover letter, an annotated table of contents, two sample chapters, and marketing ideas. I did follow up by sending her our Author Questionnaire, which she filled out right away.

The author's credentials and realistic vision of where her book could be sold and how she could help to sell it sold me on the proposal.

WHAT'S THIS BOOK ABOUT?

Job Search at Mid-Life: A Woman's Guide to Finding a Satisfying New Career is designed to help older women face the challenge of finding new jobs. An entire career can be started, developed, and completed in the active years before Social Security or retirement benefits begin. *Job Search at Mid-Life* provides a new way of looking at the self, jobs, and opportunities.

Many women are in jobs they don't like. Most never really explored their dreams. Or maybe they don't know how their abilities relate to specific job possibilities. This book encourages women to learn about themselves and to value their years of paid and unpaid experience. While the book includes the "nuts and bolts" of career research, résumé writing, and interviewing, the emphasis is on developing a clear sense of one's strengths, talents, interests, and mid-life goals, and then finding the right job. The workbook-like format is easy to use and includes self-assessments and exercises.

Job Search at Mid-Life concludes with extensive resource lists.

WHO'D BUY IT AND WHY?

Baby boomers resist thinking of themselves as old. Thus, a book for women that emphasizes mid-life opportunities is likely to appeal to this market, aged 40 to 64, predicted to be the largest age demographic by 2010.

Job Search at Mid-Life is written for women who would likely turn to books for information. It's for women over 40 who want or need to

---

The first three sentences of this overview describe the book's unique angle and its target audience: older women. The book provides a "new" way of looking at the self, jobs, and opportunities.

This second paragraph really lays out the specific idea and need for the book. It also includes a brief sentence about the content of the book, which will be in workbook format (another distinguishing benefit).

State your target market clearly. In this proposal, the target market is the growing population of female baby boomers between the ages of 40 to 64. (A growing market is a very good thing.)

make career changes. This book is also for women who are re-entering the job market or who have never worked for pay. Of course, the current employment insecurity in most fields increases the market for career change literature, but this book is relevant in any economy.

Career counselors and therapists who work with women at mid-life could turn to this book as a useful resource.

While the clerk at one mid-size bookstore looked up relevant keywords on her computer version of *Books in Print*, I told her about this project. She replied, "What a great idea! My mother could sure use a copy."

WHAT ELSE IS ON THE SHELVES?

Internet searches of www.amazon.com and www.bowker.com resulted in several recent titles that seem similar or for the same market. Here is a brief analysis of their contents and how *Job Search at Mid-Life* is different.

- *I Don't Know What I Want, but I Know It's Not This,* Julie Jansen (Penguin, 2003): Very good with assessments as a first step, but not much help with the job search process. *Job Search at Mid-Life* covers both.

- *What Color is Your Parachute?* Richard Bolles (Ten Speed, annual): A perennial best-seller. Most clients I've seen say they've started but never finished this book because it's too long. *Job Search at Mid-Life* is less complicated and less dense.

Extra value is added to the target market by pinpointing a "hidden" market that publishers might not even know existed. Many how-to books have the potential to be a great resource for professionals as well as the everyday bookstore consumer.

The upbeat, positive writing style conveys the message that one is never too old to move in a new direction, which shows that the author knows how to address her audience appropriately.

If appropriate, include some anecdotes and first-hand reasons why your book is better than the competition. What better evidence of filling a gap in the marketplace than readers themselves.

- *To Find a Job ... Start a New Career*, Marvin Rafal (Andrews Mc-Meel, 2003): This book looks at the employee from an employer's point of view and then offers ways to find a more fulfilling job based on past work experiences and personality type. *Job Search at Mid-Life* focuses on the job seeker, either working for an employer or herself, whether or not she's worked before.

- *The Seasons of Your Career*, Kathy Sanborn, Wayne Ricci (Mc-Graw-Hill Trade, 2003): Focuses on the employee in the workplace. *Job Search on Mid-Life* focuses on career change.

- *Work It!*, Allison Hemming (Fireside, 2003): A guide to surviving a layoff with information about networking, résumés, and interviews for finding a new job. *Job Search at Mid-Life* cover these topics and adds assessments and information about self-employment.

- *Reinvent Your Career*, Susan Solovic (Career Press, 2003): Approximately half of this book is devoted to losing a job/surviving on the job. *Job Search at Mid-Life* focuses on exercises to move through assessments and the job search.

- *What to Do with the Rest of Your Life*, Robin Ryan (Fireside, 2002): Of the 200 pages in this book, 30 were devoted to job hunting strategies, 15 to negotiating salary, 32 to how to get promoted, 12 to asking for a raise, and 35 to taking the business to the next level. *Job Search at Mid-Life* is focused on deciding what job to seek and then how to get it.

You will need to provide an analysis of the competitive titles that clearly shows a gap in the marketplace, as this author has done for a mid-life job search book. Go in-depth and tell why your book is different, how it will complement the others, and why it will stand out on the shelves among them. Don't be critical of other books, though. Give specific reasons why your book is going to be different in a positive, not negative, way.

- *Women for Hire,* Tory Johnson, Robyn Spizman, Lindsey Pollak (Women for Hire, 2002): Excellent first-job advice. *Job Search at Mid-Life* is designed for the woman with more experience as well as one seeking her first job.

- *Dancing on the Glass Ceiling,* Candy Deemer, Nancy Fredericks (McGraw-Hill Trade, 2002): Advice only for working women, not job seekers.

- *What Should I Do with the Rest of My Life?* Po Bronson (Random House, 2002): Profiles of career changers. *Job Search at Mid-Life* helps to answer that question, and then offers the means to find it.

MY PLANS TO PROMOTE THIS BOOK

Book reviews and/or author interviews:

- professional journals for career and psychotherapy
- alumni magazines (I am a member of three college and university alumni associations)
- newsletters: American Association of University Women, AARP, career-related organizations
- Internet newsletters on career change: www.job-hunt.org (circ. 15,000 opt-in subscribers) and others
- Boston and Cleveland (my hometowns) newspapers; radio and television programs

When writing your competitive section, be sure to list the most current competitive books versus older books that may no longer be in print, and list only those that are direct competition.

List all organizations and resources that you will use to publicize your book. The title of this section shows that the author is going to take an active role in publicity.

Start your publicity push in your hometown. If you you live in a large city or in two or three places, that's an even bigger advantage. You can call all of those cities home. Local media love to do stories on successful members of their city.

Internet advertising:

- as a columnist for an online career site for the Boston Herald (www.print.jobfind.com), I have a banner ad that can feature this book
- career-related or women's issues-related Web sites
- viral marketing through my career tips subscribers
- www.cannoncareercenter.com

Through my professional networks:

- International Association of Career Management Professionals, Career Counselors' Consortium, International Coach Federation, National Speakers Association

Presenting workshops and seminars:

- I teach and speak to various organizations on issues for women throughout Massachusetts. I have proposals out to organizations in Providence, Los Angeles, Cleveland, Chicago, New Orleans, and Denver for similar all-day workshops.
- Back-of-the-room sales are always available. I've made bookstore presentations on other authors' titles related to careers and would welcome the opportunity again.

A LITTLE BIT ABOUT ME

I'm the president of Cannon Career Development, Inc., where I've been counseling individuals and groups in my own practice

---

Set up a Web site for your project prior to submitting your proposal. It's easy and will draw attention from your target market and increase your visibility in the marketplace. This author also says she'll use viral marketing—a cheap way to generate buzz. This is one of the most effective ways to get the word out.

This author teaches seminars, which shows she is in front the public spreading her message. An author can sell a lot of books based on back-of-the-room sales. If you teach seminars or workshops and you have a schedule with an average number of attendees, include that information in your proposal. Agents and editors will love to hear how many books you can sell through these events.

since 1995. I work with clients of all abilities and ages, having run several successful six-week 50+ Job Seekers groups this past year. I've presented many public seminars on job search topics, most recently "Career Discovery Workshop for Women," "Working the Room with Confidence" and "How to Find a Job That's Not in the Want Ads." My job experience as a dental office manager, English teacher, small business owner (manufacturing children's wear under the Sandbox Sportswear label), college administrator, and single mother of two young adults (I've been widowed for over fifteen years) have given me life preparation, as well as the academic credentials I've earned along the way, to author such a book. At mid-life, I wonder what my next career will be.

WHEN YOU CAN EXPECT THE WHOLE BOOK IF YOU LIKE THIS SAMPLE

The approximate length of *Job Search at Mid-Life* will be 200 pages (typed, double-spaced). Nine of the twelve chapters are completed and the entire manuscript can be available in three months from contract.

Show that you're active in putting yourself in front of the public as an expert. Agents and editors like to see that you're busy promoting yourself and your work.

Showing your platform throughout several sections in your proposal reinforces the "what you can do for your book" hook. It says you're not just going to sit back and wait for something to happen but that you are going to make it happen.

Contents

CHAPTER 1. Is It Time for a Change?

- What's the right job?
- The importance of YOU in your work
- The trap of a quick decision

Mid-life is a time for exploration and self-expression, not resignation.

CHAPTER 2: Who Am I?

- Getting in touch with the self-needs, desires
- Decision-making style
- Dare I try something new?

Personal assessment may seem like a luxury and unrelated to finding satisfying work, but it's crucial. Without it, the ultimate result may be an unsatisfying or inappropriate job based on inadequate knowledge of your strengths and interests. And then, before long, you may need another search.

CHAPTER 3: How Am I doing?

- Life circumstances
- Level of energy
- Financial status

What do I really want to do with my life? What haven't I done yet? What do I want to leave behind as my legacy? What's going on for women at mid-life? Changes in health, relationship, and or

---

The first few chapters in this proposal are titled with provocative questions. If it fits with your topic, this is a good way to hook the reader. The three simple bullet points and short paragraph clearly show how the question will be answered. This organization tells everything about your hook in a short and effective format.

Remember, your goal is to make this section of the proposal as clear as possible to the reader. Too much text can be exhausting. This proposal condenses ideas into powerful, to-the-point summaries. The use of bullet points throughout this outline is a clear-cut way of showing the agent or editor at a glance what each chapter will cover.

finances can affect or cause change. No matter what a woman's status, this is a time for some personal reexamination.*

CHAPTER 10: **Getting Sidetracked**
- "Real" issues about age
- Staying "up" in the process of career change
- Techniques for getting "unstuck"

Constraints to a successful career search can appear in many guises. Family needs, poor health, finances, and beliefs about which jobs are appropriate all can be seen as obstacles to obtaining a good job. Techniques are provided for addressing these limitations and staying focused on the job search.

CHAPTER 11: **Creating a Support Group for Change**

Many women find a small group format helpful as they wrestle with career change issues. The advice, sharing of experiences, and support from other women on a similar quest can be extremely useful. This chapter focuses on helpful hints for finding or starting such a group.

CHAPTER 12: **You Can Do It!**

Women at mid-life have many options open to them. While it's imperative to plan for retirement and to acknowledge that you're not likely to work forever, it's also possible to see mid-life as the gateway to another twenty or more years of satisfying work. A positive, proactive attitude is crucial. Women who integrate the realities

---

If all of the chapters in your book don't fit in the same summary format, don't force them. This author changes format by eliminating the bulleted lists to better meet the needs of her content.

If you are writing a how-to book, make sure to keep the tone of your chapter titles upbeat and powerful. Remember, you're the cheerleader for your audience. This is particularly important with topics in which motivation is an essential feature of the book.

The author included summaries of all the chapters in the book, but some were eliminated here for space.

of their lives with their own personal goals, wishes, and talents are most likely to make the right career choices. This chapter will give you ideas about how to use the skills learned in seeking a new career for making change in other aspects of your life, too.

APPENDIX A
  • Resource lists

APPENDIX B
  • Organizations

APPENDIX C
  • Bibliography

A great way to add value to your book—and agents and editors love this—is to include an appendix with helpful resources for readers. Your resource list can take many different forms, but you'll probably want to include some Web sites since many readers are looking for ways of getting information online.

Proposal 4
Gadget Nation: A Journey Through the Underbelly of American Invention

Will be published in 2007 by Sterling

STEVE GREENBERG Author

Over the years I had the opportunity to interview many "garage inventors." The one characteristic they all had in common was the unwavering passion for their product. Many were ridiculed by family and friends, yet they still forged ahead. Often these inventors would spend their life savings trying to make their product a success. I was so intrigued by these men and women that I pitched the idea as a TV program to several of the networks. I had interest, but it never actually happened.

I had never written a book before, but when I was approached about coming up with a book idea, my thoughts jumped back to my failed TV show idea. As a TV program or as a book, I really believed that "garage inventors" are truly a slice of Americana. There's nothing more American than our entrepreneurial spirit, and nothing captures that spirit more than "garage inventors."

The original concept of the book was humor. So I thought I would focus on silly inventions, or goofy gadgets. Here were some of the initial possible titles:

"I'm Glad I Didn't Think of That"
"Greenberg's Guide to Goofy Gadgets"
"The World's Weirdest Widgets"
"The World's Worst Widgets"
"The World's Goofiest Gadgets"
"Not So Smart Stuff"
"Gadget Disasters"
"Goofy Gadgets: The Book"

"Gosh Awful Gadgets"

"What Were They Thinking?"

"Lame Gadgets"

"Loser Gadgets"

"Gadget Graveyard"

"Gadget Oops"

"Mis-Gadgets"

"Greenberg's Guide to Bad Gift Ideas"

"Strange But True Gadgets"

"Gadget Failure"

"Garage Inventors" was cut early on and I think I went forward with "Goofy Gadgets." Honestly it didn't feel right, but that was the title. When we finally found a literary agent to represent the book, he had a few title ideas, including "Gadget Nation." The moment I heard that title, I knew it was perfect.

In the first few stages of the book, I had a partner who did the research, and it took us about a month to write the proposal. We sent it out to about twenty agents. Several were interested almost immediately. E-mails were exchanged. One agent really stood out from the pack. Andrew Stuart totally got the concept right from the get-go. We met for lunch, and I could tell he was the right guy for the job.

ANDREW STUART Agent

What grabbed me most about this proposal were the good writing, good sense of humor, and good command of the market. Also, the author had an original idea and a great platform to back it up. This idea really tapped into the market for quirky nonfiction. Steve's excellent platform—award-winning, extensive experience in the field—ultimately helped to sell this proposal.

STEPHAN KIDD Editor

The title got my attention right away. I knew immediately what the book was about, or at least what I wanted the book to be about through the title. Luckily, it was featured prominently on a title page to give it significant resonance. The initial proposal was very complete and thorough. In fact, I abridged the proposal for the acquisitions board. When that whetted their interest, I sent the proposal in full. Steve's background as the "Innovation Insider" was so extensive, I couldn't imagine anyone else writing the book. Plus, I was dazzled by his twelve Emmy awards.

OVERVIEW

Have you ever heard of bird diapers?

Interested in a talking toilet paper dispenser?

What about meat flavored water? Yum!

Surprisingly, these are not David Letterman gags, but actual products available for sale on the market. Steve Greenberg, dubbed the "Innovation Insider," is the country's leading expert on strange and wacky gadgets. Steve routinely offers his innovation insights on such national talk shows as *The Daily Buzz, Fox & Friends*, Lifetime's *Our Home*, and numerous others. Steve also does satellite media tours for several newscasts across the country. Now, for the first time, Steve is bringing together the craziest gadgets of them all in a proposed book called *Gadget Nation: A Journey Through the Underbelly of American Invention.*

This book will uncover the 100 most bizarre gadgets of all time. The discussion of each unique product will include an amusing picture of the product and its often outrageous packaging, and an accompanying text that highlights the unique story behind it. The text for each product will be around 400–600 words, and the writing style will be fun, informative, and very tongue-in-cheek. Each chapter will be based on interviews with the inventor, revealing the genesis of the invention and how it came to market, as well as information on how the product has fared in the marketplace. The narratives will reflect humorously on the use-value of the gadgets as they try to answer the ultimate question: "Did the world need this invention?"

With the use of questions, the author immediately hooks the reader with a humorous, off-beat tone that makes him read on.

Providing your credentials and expertise at the top of the proposal is a great way to show you have a strong platform. The author emphasizes his media exposure, which is a strong selling point.

This last paragraph is a great tell-all paragraph. It covers what the book is about, how it will be organized, and how the author plans to get his material. By providing an agent and editor with this crucial information, you are helping to assure them that you can write an effective book.

INTRODUCTION

We live in a world where medical miracles and high tech marvels are almost commonplace. New cure-all prescription drugs fill our pharmacies on a daily basis, and last year's electronic products become this year's dinosaurs as smaller, stronger, and smarter versions are launched each week. Most of us look at these innovations as something we could never invent. We're lucky if we even can figure out how to use them.

Every year, however, there is a group of inventions that shows up in the marketplace that makes us say, "Why didn't I think of that?" Products like the Thigh Master™, Post-It Notes™, Hairagami™, and Liquid Paper ™ are examples of money making ideas that most of us believe are within our creative capabilities. I'm sure any one of us could have invented the paper clip. We just didn't do it.

Now before I go any further, I want you to know that I'm a big fan of all inventors. As the "Innovation Insider," I travel around the country showcasing some of America's smartest new products. In my mind there's nothing more American than that entrepreneurial spirit that all inventor's share. Inventors have made this country great. Thomas Edison, Henry Ford, Alexander Graham Bell, Steve Jobs, William Hewlett, and David Packard have all changed our lives forever. In this country, if you hit the right idea, your life and the lives of your children, grandchildren, and even great grandchildren will never be the same.

Approximately 60,000 patents are filed each year by private citizens. That's a lot of people grabbing at that brass ring. When I talk to garage inventors, I'm always impressed with their passion.

The narrative for this introductory section is well written and easy to read. The tone is fun and upbeat. This shows agents and editors that the author has strong writing skills and can deliver on the promise of a humorous book on inventions.

The author's anecdote about his own expertise in this area personalizes the proposal. This is a great way to grab your reader's attention and show your connection to the material.

Backing up your book idea with a statistic or demographic gives strong evidence for the book's market. You will want to do this for each market segment you identify in your proposal.

They truly believe they have the next must-have product. Friends and family may tell them that they are nuts, but they push forward. Just picture this: you tell your family that you want to sink part of your savings into your latest invention, bird diapers. You really have to believe in those diapers to ignore the disbelief and possible ridicule from your loved ones. Almost all of them have said they want their products to be a success not only because of the money, but also because they genuinely want to change the world. There's an indescribable joy in seeing your invention sitting on a store shelf. It's like having a bit of consumer immortality. Inventors believe their problem-solving products will make the world a better place.

That said, not all new products make the world a better place. Some inventions are just plain ... bizarre. And that's what this book is all about. It's a collection of some of the strangest products out there. And when I say "out there," I mean "out there." From meat-flavored water to a talking toilet paper dispenser, from haircut umbrellas to campfire butt warmers, I've rounded up some of America's goofiest gadgets and talked to the inventors behind them. You'll meet the men and women who had an idea and turned it into something we can all buy. Readers will learn why these inventors have put their passion, their energy, and often their own money into these peculiar products.

Getting people to understand and support the inventors and their goofy gadgets is oftentimes a real uphill battle. Friends and family can't recognize the genius behind the inventions. The inventors were often told that they are just plain crazy and need to find

Using funny anecdotes and phrases like "just picture this" help to enliven your proposal and engage an agent or editor. Make sure your ideas jump off the page.

Give some context and meaning to your proposal. Yes, the idea of goofy gadgets is funny, but this author takes the extra step and explains how he can develop that into a book. He makes it clear that this is more than just an encyclopedia of gadgets: It's something richer and deeper. The interviews with the inventors make this project stand out from the competition.

a hobby. But despite the abuse, these garage inventors never gave up and in some cases have done surprisingly well. The bird diaper inventors sell about 1,200 bird diapers each month. Go figure.

I think it's safe to say, however, that many of these gadgets are examples of innovation gone terribly wrong. Cases of good people, bad gadgets. After you look at most, you should find yourself breathing a sigh of relief and saying, "Boy, am I glad I didn't think of that!"

Occasionally sublime, though usually bathetic, these products, and the stories behind their creation, offer ample illustration of the indomitable passion that feeds the spirit of invention. At the same time, they provide a funhouse mirror of some uniquely American attributes: the obsession with convenience, the fascination with gimmickry, and the eternal dream of getting rich quickly. Whether or not the Chia Pet or the FlowBee Vacuum Haircut System have made the world a better place is your call.

AUTHOR BIO

Whether he's doing it on camera or in print, **Steve Greenberg**, the Innovation Insider, makes the world of new products a little more user-friendly.

Steve routinely offers his innovation insights on such national talk shows as *The Daily Buzz, The Caroline Rhea Show, Fox & Friends*, Lifetime's *Our Home*, and numerous others. Steve also does satellite media tours for several newscasts across the country. A producer for Al Roker Productions, National Geographic, and the

By linking the topic of the book to larger issues of American culture, the author also shows that the book is going to appeal to a larger audience than other humor books would. Defining your market into sections you may find that your book is a cross-over title, meaning that it may appeal to more then just one market. Make sure to stay true to your claim when doing so, and back all of this information up with numbers.

Tell your agent and editor what you have done, when and where, and what you are doing now. This is no time to hold back. State what you are capable of. If you have had national hits, include them in your list.

Hallmark Channel, Steve has cultivated extensive contacts through-out the media world, particularly with national talk shows.

For three years, Steve could be seen nationally every weeknight demonstrating innovative products on the Discovery Channel's *Your New House*. For six years Steve was on HGTV's very popular *Dream Builders*, for which he traveled the country showcasing the latest in home design and construction trends. For five years, HGTV also used Steve's reporting skills for coverage of the hottest new home improvement products at NAHB's International Builders Show.

Steve writes for several magazines and Web sites. His "Innova-tion Insider" features appear in *Smart Homeowner* magazine. Steve also writes for *Backyard Living, Log Home Living, Ocean Drive, Manhattan Style,* and *DailyExaminer.com*.

Before he made innovation his beat, Steve was a full-time tele-vision news reporter. While working at the CBS-owned station in Miami, Steve traveled to Cuba five times, has covered Hurricane Andrew, followed Hurricane Emily to the Carolinas, and has re-ported stories in Mexico, Honduras, Bahamas, and around the U.S. Steve's reports have been seen on *CBS: This Morning* and routinely on CBS's national news feed service. Steve has been honored with twelve Emmy Awards for his television news work and for his spe-cial broadcasts, including his own educational children's program *Doc Steve's Amazing Science Seekers*. He has received the highest broadcast national award from the American Heart Association, and he has received special recognition from the Florida Medical As-

---

Writing for magazines, Web sites, journals, and such is a great way to gain publicity. Using your byline for a means of advertising your new book will help to get the word out.

Don't be shy in your bio. You always want to include any awards and special distinctions you've received. Agents and editors can see this as a great selling point for the book. For instance, if you've won a number of highly regarded awards for your work, you can refer to yourself as "an award-winning" writer or whatever type of expert you are. Awards give you credibility in the marketplace. This author's vast experience proves him to be credible and professional.

sociation for his coverage of the HIV Haitians detained at Cuba's Guantanamo Bay Naval Base. Steve also took first place in the Sunshine State Awards for feature reporting.

MARKET

As one of the country's leading experts on the gadget market, Steve Greenberg is intimately familiar with America's insatiable appetite for gadgets and invention. It is nothing less than a national obsession. The popularity of specialty catalogues like the *Sharper Image*, *Sky Mall*, *Clever Gear*, and *Hammacher Schlemmer* makes this abundantly clear. What's more, who hasn't asked the age-old question, "Why didn't I think of that?" Each year more than 60,000 patents are filed by private citizens who hope to strike gold with their product ideas. This book will appeal to those would-be inventors, but some of the products will also have readers saying: "I'm *glad* I didn't think of that!" This book will be a must-have fun gift for the inventor—and consumer—in all of us.

Gadget Nation is not just for those interested in the excesses of inventiveness. From the hugely successful *The Darwin Awards* to the *Weird U.S.* titles to *Candy Freak*, there's an enormous audience for books offering an idiosyncratic perspective on contemporary life.

PUBLICITY

Steve, a regular commentator and expert on all things gadget, has the ideal platform to launch this book. He's already "branded" himself as the "Innovation Insider," a title that he's protectively trademarked.

Rather then using specific statistics, the author effectively shows a strong market for his book through references to popular culture, such has magazines and catalogs.

The author shows demand for his book by connecting it to the success of other books. If you do this, make sure the books you are comparing to yours have indeed sold a significant number of copies. You want to convey to your agent and editor the simple message that your book will also sell.

As a relentless self-promoter, his offbeat and wacky on-air personality has made him a television media darling for demonstrating new products. His connections in the media world are extensive. His professional relationships include Al Roker and producers at *The Oprah Winfrey Show, The Ellen DeGeneres Show, The Tony Danza Show, Extra, E!,* WNBC-TV, NYC's *WB Morning News,* ABC *World News Now,* CBS's *The Early Show,* DIY, HGTV, and various individual stations across the country. Steve routinely demonstrates gadgets on national television shows such as *The Daily Buzz* and *Fox & Friends,* and also does satellite media tours for 25–30 newscasts across the country every 4–6 weeks. For the past few years, Steve has worked with HWH-PR. Lois Whitman is the president of HWH-PR and a close friend of Steve's. She has offered the use of her PR machine to help generate buzz about *Gadget Nation.*

Go to www.stevegreenbergtv.com to see some video clips of just a few of Steve's television appearances. Each clip will prove how telegenic and media savvy he is, and that he makes a desirable booking for any local or national talk or news program (www.stevegreenbergtv.com click on I2 on the spinning wheel). The most obvious story that should be an easy pitch for television would have Steve doing a "show and tell" of goofy gadgets from the book. While some of the products in the book have been already featured on TV (which demonstrates the media interest in this subject), most will be new to the media.

While the "goofy gadgets" story can be pitched anytime throughout the year, there are obvious tie-ins to gift-giving holidays.

Establishing yourself as an expert in your field is very important in nonfiction books. Show your agent and editor that you are the *one* to write this book. For publicity purposes, you need to include what you have done, what you can do, and who you have access to. Here, the author has great media connections and makes a point of stating how these contacts can ultimately help in publicity efforts.

Web sites are a great way to show you have a strong platform. The author has video clips on his Web site, which will help show agents and editors his dynamic personality.

Christmas is clearly the biggest gadget tie-in period, but Steve can also do "goofy gadgets" for Valentine's Day, Mother's Day, Father's Day, and yes, even Halloween.

Steve's humorous take on gadgets makes him a natural for humor-based talk shows ranging from *The Ellen DeGeneres Show, Late Night with David Letterman,* and *The Tonight Show* to *The Tony Danza Show* and *The View*.

Steve is also willing to launch a Web site with a national challenge of finding the country's craziest gadget. The challenge and Web site would fuel the book's publicity campaign.

Steve's contacts and drive will get this country talking about *Gadget Nation*.

COMPETITION

Although there are titles that examine weird inventions, there are no other books that take the approach of *Gadget Nation*. Ted Vancleave's *Totally Absurd Inventions: America's Goofiest Patents* (Andrews McMeel, 2001) focuses on patents, but does not deal with actual products that are available on the market. There's also a series of books by Kenji Kawakami on Chindogu, the art of inventing useless products (*Big Bento Box Of Unuseless Japanese Inventions*, Norton, 2005; *101 Unuseless Japanese Inventions: The Art of Chindogu*, 1995, Norton). However, these products are very specific to Japanese culture. And again, these books don't focus on actual products on the market. These "unuseless" inventions are just prototypes. Indeed, the popularity of these books indicates the potential market for a book on outrageous inventions.

By giving specific ways of publicizing his books this author shows that he is thinking about publicity and will be helpful once the book is published. Don't give false promise; List only your true possibilities.

List your book's possible spin-offs. If you think your book would warrant a television show, say so. Contests, if appropriate, are also a great way of generating buzz and attracting people to your Web site.

The popularity of invention books is a strong indicator that there is market for this book. Show that other books on your subject matter are selling well to defend why your book should exist.

TABLE OF CONTENTS

The following is just a sample of some of the goofy products the book will include. See Appendix A for photos of selected products.

Introduction
When Gadgets Go Terribly Wrong/Good People, Bad Gadgets

Chapter 1: Home

—**Hair Cut Umbrella**—You wear this umbrella around your neck so that it catches the clippings when you cut your own hair. You look like an idiot, but the floor stays clean. (see Appendix A for photo)

—**My Pet Fat**—It's not a pet that requires you to change its litter or needs to be walked; in fact, it's not much of a pet at all. It's a big ugly, yellow, plastic lump of fat. Its inventor thinks his Pet Fat will help you visualize 10 lbs. of excess fat. It's not enough that you have to carry around your own excess fat, now you can purchase a real-sized plastic model of this fat. (see sample chapter)*

Chapter 2: Car

—**Groovy Tool**—If you have a pick-up truck, you need a Groovy Tool. It's designed to clean out those nasty grooves in the back of a pick-up truck. And let's face it, dirty grooves have haunted pick-up truck owners for decades.

—**Executive Laptop Steering Wheel Mount**—Mount your laptop or notebook to your car's steering wheel and catch up on all your

If you have additional information that you're not quite sure how to include in the main section of your proposal, then create an appendix for that information. It's a great place to include photos or additional information that backs up your research and supplements your ideas.

The author includes some hilarious examples to get the attention of readers. (More examples were included with the actual proposal, but were cut here for space considerations.) These examples show that the topic of the proposal is viable and sellable.

work in your car. Of course, you probably should use this gadget only when your car is parked. (see Appendix A for photo)

Chapter 3: Food/Kitchen

—**Travel Hot Dog Cooker**—Plugs into the cigarette lighter and will cook six hot dogs and warm the buns, too. (see Appendix A for photo)

—**Octodog**—This device slices a hot dog into an octopus shape. (see sample chapter)

—**Food Suit**—Pockets are what separate man from beast. Most clothing is not only designed to protect us from the elements, but it creates storage spaces so we can carry our keys, wallets, etc. But what about lunch? Wouldn't it be great if you could carry a few meals in your clothing? That's the problem this product attempts to solve. The Food Suit is designed to store food. With the Food Suit you won't reach for your wallet, instead you'll reach directly for that turkey sandwich you've been carrying around all morning. (see Appendix A for photo)*

Chapter 4: Pets

—**Meat Flavored Water**—This is bottled water that tastes like meat. No, it's not for people on a low-carb diet; instead, it's for your meat-loving pooch.

—**Soft Claws Colored Nail Caps for Cats**   Many feel that removing a cat's claws is wrong. Many others think that claw marks up and down your new furniture is also wrong. That's

In the final proposal, the author included photos and pictures of the gadgets. This really added to the presentation value of the proposal. If you have photos or illustrations that are integral to the proposal, you can cut and paste them into your final proposal. Ultimately, if you use the photos or illustrations in your book, you'll have to get the proper permissions, but using them for illustrative purposes in your proposal without permission is fine.

The tone and style of these chapter summaries are fun and humorous. These summaries give the agent and editor a sense of how the book will read.

why Nail Caps were invented. They slip on your kitty's claws and protect your furniture, while making your kitty's claws look very glamorous. (see Appendix A for photo)
—**Bubble Buddy Bacon Flavored Dog Bubbles**—It's a battery-powered gun that shoots out bacon-flavored bubbles. Your dog will spend hours chasing the bubbles and later dreaming about the Denny's Grand Slam breakfast special. (see Appendix A for photo)*

Chapter 5: Sports/Toys
—**Electronic Bug Zapping Racket**—Looks like a tennis racquet but can zap bugs. It makes killing bugs more like a sport. (see Appendix A for photo)
—**Presidential Action Figures**—12-inch-tall presidents speak many different phrases in their own voices. The sound bites are taken from campaigns, inaugurations, and other speeches. Best of all, you can put them in some very compromising positions. (see Appendix A for photo)
—**Love Triangle Turkey Deco Set**—Turkeys that simulate sex positions. (see Appendix A for photo)*

Make sure you have a logical breakdown of information in your chapters. Here, the author used types of products—kitchen, sports, etc.—to break down the gadgets into groupings, which shows agents and editors that he has a grasp of the material.

Make sure your chapters have a natural flow to them, titling all of them with headings that match. For instance, you don't want to have some that are extremely lengthy while the rest are short and to the point.

The chapter summaries continued in this fashion but are not included here.

Published in June 2005 by Avery

SHERI COLBERG, PH.D. Author

The idea for this book came from a realization that the recent epidemic of kids developing type 2 (formerly known as "adult onset") diabetes is completely avoidable—and possibly reversible with early intervention. As an exercise physiologist, my perspective is always that most health problems can be prevented or mitigated with adequate amounts of physical activity. As a person with type 1 diabetes since childhood, I also realized that the same strategies (i.e., nutritional and exercise-related) that I use to control my blood sugars can be employed to prevent type 2 diabetes in children.

The working title I had for the book was *No More (Type 2) Diabetic Kids!* At some point in the editing process, the editor at Avery felt that a shorter title would work better, and we agreed upon its published title, *Diabetes-Free Kids*.

This book is actually my second. My first published work of nonfiction, *The Diabetic Athlete*, was published by Human Kinetics in 2001. It is a book aimed more at effective diabetes management during any type of physical activity in anyone with diabetes, but particularly insulin users.

I researched the concept in a number of ways. To start with, I searched Amazon.com and other bookstores for titles related to diabetes and children, but I found almost entirely books related to type 1 (formerly "juvenile-onset,") diabetes, which has comprised the majority of cases of diabetes in children until recently. I also searched the scientific literature pertaining to the topic (e.g., what has been published about type 2 diabetes and children by the

American Diabetes Association) to try to ascertain how much of a problem this disease has become in the past decade. Finally, I also "googled" the topic to find any relevant and current articles, such as when the cover of *Time* magazine had a cover story on type 2 diabetes in adolescents back in 2003. Once I have my ideas in my head, I actually write very quickly. I researched how to write an effective proposal on the Internet and then put my proposal together in less than a week. For me, the whole process from start to finish—i.e., from initial idea to mailed proposals—took about three weeks for my first proposal.

I went to the public library and searched through several books listing literary agents, focusing on ones that stated an interest in nonfiction books on health and fitness topics. I also located the names of several agents by looking in the acknowledgments sections of published health-related books. I initially narrowed my list of possible agents down to twenty and mailed out copies of my proposal, along with my curriculum vitae to establish my platform in diabetes and exercise, to those agents. I made certain to include an SASE with the correct postage to receive my proposal back with each agent's comments. Once my agent had contacted me (she called me as soon as she read my proposal) and agreed to represent my slightly revised proposal, she sent copies of it to numerous publishing houses on my behalf, along with some articles that I had written and other supporting materials.

The main problem that I faced during the process of selling my proposal resulted from the fact that my book focuses on the prevention of diabetes along with the treatment of type 2 diabetes in children and adolescents. It appeared that many publishers were somewhat reluctant to take on a book without a guaranteed audience, and the actual number of children with type 2 diabetes still has not been adequately determined (not that surprising given that even a third of adults with the disease are undiagnosed). The other problem was that, even though I teach classes in sports nutrition and have for many years, the editor wanted me to add a co-author who had an official degree in nutrition—a registered dietitian, or R.D.—that they felt was necessary to sell the book more effectively. Consequently, I had to find someone to work with me on my book.

LINDA KONNER Agent

It's rare for someone who is an expert in one field to also be a good writer, but Sheri is. Her proposal, while full of solid and occasionally technical information for parents of diabetic kids, was nevertheless clear, easy-to-read, and well organized. After having worked with Sheri now on three books (one we're currently in the process of selling), I am convinced that she could write an excellent proposal on any topic, whether within her area of expertise or not. Her information is fresh (or at least is presented in a fresh way), and her own credentials in the field complement the material perfectly. She's also a mother—another plus for this particular book.

Sheri is not only an expert in her field, complete with Ph.D. (which editors love to see because it helps to boost a book's credibility), but also she thinks and writes clearly and well, a rarity among academics. She writes conversationally and, therefore, immediately engages the reader in the material. Further, she knows how to Make a Book, i.e., she can take her information and organize it solidly into a plan or program people can actually follow and benefit from. Many would-be authors, even those with exceptional information to work with, don't know how to make it reader friendly and useful, which is key to almost all the books I represent.

DARA STEWART Editor

What grabbed me most about the proposal was its timeliness. Obesity among children is a major health issue right now, and this proposal sought to address that issue. The surge in occurrence of type 2 diabetes in children is happening in epidemic proportions.

After receiving the proposal, I needed a bit more information about the author's platform and ultimately requested that an expert on nutrition in children was added to the project. What impressed me most about the proposal was Sheri's enthusiasm for the subject matter.

Contents

If your proposal is long, be sure to include page numbers in the ever-important table of contents to help an agent or editor navigate through each part. These page numbers are not accurate for the proposal as it is depicted here, but match with the 8½ x 11 proposal the author originally submitted.

Summary

As recently as two decades ago, the onset of type 2 (formerly called "adult onset") diabetes in the younger set was almost unheard of. Currently, however, one in three people newly diagnosed with the life-long, potentially debilitating condition is a teenager—or younger. This explosion of type 2 diabetes in our youth is understandably frightening to parents.

No More (Type 2) Diabetic Kids! is the only book on the market that explains this growing phenomenon and gives parents and other involved adults the information and advice that they need to help prevent the onset of type 2 diabetes in their children and to most effectively control the condition in those who already have it. Written by a college professor and researcher with a Ph.D. in exercise physiology, this book contains a mixture of explanatory and practical information about type 2 diabetes, nutrition, blood sugar balance, physical activity, and more that will give parents, health care professionals, and other adults the knowledge they need to prevent type 2 diabetes or greatly reduce its severity once it has been diagnosed.

Knowledge is power with regard to prevention and control of type 2 diabetes. *No More (Type 2) Diabetic Kids!* covers the basics of exercise physiology, metabolism, and nutrition as they relate to the prevention and control of type 2 diabetes in youth and others.

Some of the topics covered are as follows:

The author makes good use of statistics in the opening paragraph to show a real need for the book and hook the reader. Use any dramatic statistics you can find to indicate your book is needed to begin your proposal. Then, you can expand upon them in the market section.

- Prevention and control of diabetes and its complications
- Causes and diagnosis of type 2 diabetes in youth
- Nutritional strategies to reduce risk and lower blood sugars and insulin resistance
- Blood sugar responses to physical activity and the importance of regular exercise
- Strategies to increase daily physical activity
- Oral medications and insulin for the treatment of type 2 diabetes in youth

No other book currently on the market specifically focuses on the prevention of type 2 diabetes in youth and gives specific recommendations that will help type 2 diabetic and pre-diabetic children alike. The result of Dr. Colberg's years of professional and personal involvement with diabetes, physical activity, and nutritional issues, *No More (Type 2) Diabetic Kids!* is an invaluable resource that will appeal to any parent or adult interacting with inactive and obese children who are at highest risk for developing type 2 diabetes.

Author

    Sheri R. Colberg is an exercise physiologist and associate professor of exercise science in the Exercise Science, Sport, Physical Education and Recreation Department at Old Dominion University in Norfolk, Virginia. Having earned a Ph.D. from the University of California, Berkeley, she specializes in research in diabetes and exercise. She continues to conduct extensive clinical research specifically in type

Using concise paragraphs, powerful diction, and handy bullet points, the author provides a clear and compelling overview of the book.

Alternately driving home the timeliness and urgency of the subject and boldly presenting the first-time nature of the proposed work opens the proposal with a tight, virtually impenetrable argument.

2 diabetes and exercise with funding from the American Diabetes Association, and she has authored close to forty research and educational articles on exercise and diabetes, as well as one book, *The Diabetic Athlete* (Human Kinetics, 2001), currently in its second printing.

In addition to her many credentials that enabled her to write her previous book and *No More (Type 2) Diabetic Kids!*, including working as an exercise specialist in a diabetes treatment center, Dr. Colberg has thirty-five years of practical experience as a (type 1) diabetic exerciser. A frequent lecturer on diabetes and exercise across the nation to both professional and lay audiences, she is also a reviewer for many diabetes- and exercise-related scientific journals, grants, and books, a member of two diabetes publications advisory boards, a fellow of the American College of Sports Medicine, and a professional member of the American Diabetes Association.

Dr. Colberg currently resides in Virginia Beach, Virginia, with her husband and their three boys, who have given her ten years worth of practical experience as a parent as well. An avid recreational exerciser, she enjoys swimming, biking, walking, tennis, weight training, hiking, and yard work, as well as playing with her three (usually) active sons.

Audience

Of the 17 million people with diabetes in the United States alone, about 95 percent have type 2, a condition considered to result primarily from a state of insulin resistance in the body. More than 150,000

By stating her great credentials and experitse in relation to the topic, the author gives the publisher tools for promoting her. Showing agents and editors that she is professionably marketable instills confidence in them that she is the best author for the book project.

Writing your about the author section in third person may make it easier for you to state your credentials in an objective way. It also will seem more natural when an agent later submits your proposal to an editor.

American youth currently have some form of diabetes, and at least 13,000 more kids are diagnosed each year. Although type 1 (formerly "juvenile-onset") diabetes has predominated among the younger set, type 2 (formerly "adult-onset") diabetes is reportedly becoming an epidemic among adolescents, closely paralleling the rise in overweight and obese teenagers. In fact, it has been estimated that as many as 45 percent of all newly diagnosed cases of childhood diabetes are now type 2 rather than type 1, and many experts believe an even greater explosion of type 2 youngsters is looming on the horizon in the near future. The rise in type 2 diabetic youth is not limited to the United States either: In Japan, the incidence of type 2 diabetes in those under eighteen has reportedly reached three to four times that of the cases of type 1.

Furthermore, the development of type 2 diabetes in youth is almost entirely preventable, especially in "at-risk" kids, including overweight youngsters who are between ten and nineteen years of age, have a family history of type 2 diabetes, and are members of certain racial or ethnic groups (African American, Hispanic, and Native American). *This book, therefore, will be invaluable to parents everywhere, but also to grandparents, concerned relatives, health care professionals, educators, and other adults involved with high-risk youth.* Unlike a fad diet book, this book will be important for years to come as a guide to both control and prevention of type 2 diabetes in youth. This book, unlike other available ones, will both educate the reader and provide him or her with useable, practical advice about type 2 diabetes and children.

The author gives great statistics to show the need for this book. Not only does she show how many people suffer from the disease, but also that the spread of the disease is widening, pointing to a growing potential market. Use numbers to show your market exists and, whether it's a growing market such as this one. You can also do this by providing reference to current coverage of the topic in newspapers and on television.

The author explains how the book will be a resource over time. Publishers are always looking for books to fill their backlist—books that will sell for many years to come rather than just during the latest fad.

Competition

To my knowledge, there are only three books currently on the market that specifically address the topic of type 2 diabetes in youth. The first, *The Doctor's Guide to Diabetes and Your Child: New Therapies for Type 1 and Type 2* (Allan Sosin and Sheila Sobell, Kensington Pub Corp, Nov. 2000) differs from the proposed book in that it focuses more on the treatment of type 1 diabetes than the prevention or control of type 2. Furthermore, it only sketchily addresses the importance of physical activity (in only part of one chapter), choosing to focus more on nutrition, supplements, and medications in the treatment of the condition.

The second competitive book, *Managing Type 2 Diabetes in Children and Adolescents* (Arian Rosenbloom, Janet Silverstein, and Elizabeth Baldwin, McGraw-Hill/Contemporary Books, May 2003), is written more as a textbook-style reference book for healthcare professionals than as a practical guide for a wider, lay public audience. Furthermore, it is only 128 pages, but its list price is $34.95, making it less affordable for the public at large. The proposed book would be a much more user-friendly guide, offering practical advice along with educating the reader about possible solutions to the current type 2 explosion in youth.

Finally, a third book, *Type 2 Diabetes in Teens: Secrets for Success* (Jean Betschart Roemer, John Wiley & Sons, June 2002), is written directly for the teenager living with type 2 diabetes, addressing such issues as "dating with diabetes." However, unlike the

Be sure to back up any claims you make about other competitive books. One of the first things and agent or editor will do if she wants to find out about the competition is conduct a quick online search; you should do the same. Make sure no books pop up that are competitive if you state in your proposal there aren't any. Here the author clearly backs up her claims.

Describing your book as "user-friendly" is a great selling point and important way to distinguish it from the competition. Also discussing the price points of other books and how yours can be less expensive shows that your book can appeal to a wider audience.

proposed book, it stresses neither the importance of physical activity in lessening the severity or symptoms of diabetes nor its role in the reversal or prevention of type 2 diabetes in adolescents.

Special Marketing and Promotional Opportunities

A college professor teaching exercise physiology and sports nutrition, Dr. Colberg is also a highly visible educator and researcher in the topic the proposed book addresses. Not only has she already written a book in this particular field (*The Diabetic Athlete*), but she has also published numerous educational and research articles in prestigious journals in her area of expertise: exercise and diabetes. These articles have recently appeared nationally and internationally in publications such as *Diabetes Care* (the American Diabetes Association's clinical research journal), *The Physician and Sportsmedicine, ACSM's Health & Fitness Journal, Journal of Diabetes and Its Complications, The Diabetes Educator, Diabetes Self-Management, Voice of the Diabetic, SportEX Health* (a UK journal), and *Bodybuilding.CZ* (translated to Czech).

Considered an expert in her field, Dr. Colberg has recently been interviewed and quoted in many national publications including the following: *Diabetes Interview, Men's Health, Men's Fitness, Today's Health and Wellness, Countdown* (ADA lay publication), and *Joe Weider's Muscle & Fitness*. She is currently on the editorial board of *Diabetes Interview*, a monthly publication for the diabetes community for which she serves as an exercise advisor and frequent

Highlighting your publishing experience is an important way to stress your proven expertise in a given area. You can do this by simply listing the articles and other published materials you've written on this topic.

Listing her media interviews, the author demonstrates that she has a proven media platform and is an expert that journalists will turn to when they are seeking to write stories about this topic.

article contributor. She also serves as a contributing editor for a new diabetes publication, *Diabetes Focus*, which is published quarterly and available in drugstores nationwide.

Her prior book, *The Diabetic Athlete* (Human Kinetics, 2001), is currently being marketed worldwide and has recently been translated into Japanese, Portuguese, and Spanish to target additional foreign markets. Written with the same combination of educational and practical advice proposed for her new book, it has been rated highly by many reviewers (e.g., four stars in a professional review by Doody Publishing). Her book is available on more than twenty diabetes-related Web sites, including the ADA's bookstore. A tribute to her book's success in reaching its target audience, Dr. Colberg routinely receives e-mail from around the globe asking her questions and thanking her for writing her informational "bible" for the diabetic exerciser.

As for public appearances and lectures, Dr. Colberg travels nationwide to present on the topic of diabetes (both types 1 and 2) and exercise, most recently lecturing at ACSM's Health & Fitness Summit in Reno, the American College of Sports Medicine annual meeting in San Francisco, and the USAF Fitness Summit in San Antonio in 2003. She is also scheduled to address the Diabetes Exercise & Sports Association (DESA) members at their annual meeting in Chicago this December (expected audience of 275–300 people). The Diabetes Partnership of the Virginia Peninsula is also sponsoring her to address their Third Annual Diabetes Symposium on the control and prevention of diabetes with exercise in November of

The author shows that she has a great track record in writing books that sell. As evidence, she cites the international appeal of her prior book. If you have written a prior book that has done well in the marketplace be sure to point this out in your proposal. Even if the project you are proposing now is of a different vein, this matter is still of great importance because it shows that you know how publishing works and you are fully capable of writing and promoting a book.

With a list of speaking engagements, the author gives further evidence that she has a strong platform to launch this book. If you are lucky enough to have a speaking schedule lined up prior to submitting your book proposal, be sure to include a copy of that schedule for your agent and editor.

2003 (expected professional audience of 150–200 healthcare providers). Additionally, she will be presenting the results of her recently completed research study on resistance training and skin blood flow in type 2 diabetes at the national annual meeting of the American Diabetes Association in Orlando in June of next year (2004).

Working as a consultant for Animas Corporation in 2001, she was seen on television across the nation in a taped video news release promoting physical activity for diabetic users of insulin pumps. Her other television appearances include taped and live interviews for the D'Feet Diabetes Gala Telethon aired locally in Hampton Roads (VA), an interview for a local station's (Channel 13) newscast called Women's Health Beat, and a "Smart Tip" segment on diabetes and exercise that aired during local newscasts in San Diego, Denver, Bakersfield (CA), Indianapolis, and Johnstown (PA). Furthermore, she has appeared online on DiabetesStation.com as an invited "speaker" on occasion as well as "Diabetes Forecast—Live!" as an expert on diabetes and exercise along with Gary Hall, Jr. (2000 Olympic gold medalist in 50-meter freestyle swimming who has type 1 diabetes) and his physician, Dr. Anne Peters. Dr. Colberg has also made radio appearances on "Hagen's Health and Fitness Show" and KMPH News Radio (Fresno, CA).

Once published, the proposed book is likely to be offered through professional organizations such as the American Diabetes Association and the American Association of Diabetes Educators as well as through the regular trade book market. Its wide appeal

The author of this proposal is clearly considered an expert in her field. She mentions several experiences with different types of media. Television and radio spots and online exposure are great for publicity. If you have any opportunities to become an expert in your field, be sure to take advantage of them and then mention them in your proposal.

Giving other avenues for sales of your book is a great way to show that you are thinking beyond the traditional bookstore. The author gives specific groups that will help to sell her book. List all that apply to your book.

is likely to make it required reading for all parents, physical educators, pediatric professionals, and other adults working with children throughout the world, as the type 2 diabetes epidemic in youth is not limited to the United States.

Manuscript Specifications

The length of the proposed book will be in the range of 175 to 200 pages. It will contain "inspirational" photos throughout (at least 1–2 per chapter), including pictures of physically active kids, healthy food choices, and other positive reinforcers along with illustrations to demonstrate some physical activities such as proper stretches.

The completed manuscript can easily be finished in 2–3 months following the signing of the contract.

As this author does, directly tell your agent and editor exactly what they can expect from your book. Include information about length, format, and special features. Prove that you have really given this some thought and be realistic.

Outline
Table of Contents:

Part I: Prevention of Type 2 Diabetes in Kids
Chapter 1. Who's Likely to Get Diabetes?
Chapter 2. The Environment and the Obesity Epidemic
Chapter 3. What To Eat or Not To Eat
Chapter 4. Good Nutrition for the Whole Family
Chapter 5. Exercise: A "Cure" for Diabetes?
Chapter 6. Daily Physical Activities for Everyone

Part II: Control of Type 2 Diabetes in Kids
Chapter 7. Controlling Blood Sugars is Key
Chapter 8. A Nutritional Plan for Health
Chapter 9. Exercise is the Best Medicine
Chapter 10. Other Diabetic Medications
Chapter 11. Obstacles to Good Control
Chapter 12. Make It Simple, Stupid

Appendix A Food Shopping Guide
Appendix B Sports and Nutrition Web Sites of Interest

Selected References by Chapter

Annotated Table of Contents:
Part I: Prevention of Type 2 Diabetes in Kids

Make sure the table of contents (TOC) for your book is clear and comprehensive. This TOC uses simple chapter titles that lay people will understand. Each chapter title also makes it clear what you will learn from the chapter. Agents and editors want books that have take-away value for readers; the appendices contain a food shopping guide and Web sites of interest, which are perfect for that.

Structuring your book into different parts is a great way to divide information into digestible sections. The author separates the book into two main parts that make logical sense. By visually breaking up the information, parts also help readers get a clearer idea of what they can expect from the book.

Chapter 1. Who's Likely to Get Diabetes?
- How important is good health to you and your family?
- The real cause of obesity and type 2 diabetes in kids
- Who is at risk for diabetes?

The purpose of this chapter is to introduce the reader to the underlying causes of diabetes in youth and to assess who is at risk for developing it and why. The chapter begins discussing whether parents need to be concerned about the possibility of type 2 diabetes developing in their children. It goes on to prompt the reader to assess his or her family's health attitudes and habits with regard to sugar consumption, physical activity, and immediate gratification It then proceeds to discuss specific populations at highest risk for manifestation of type 2 diabetes among the younger set.

Chapter 2. The Environment and the Obesity Epidemic
- What constitutes obesity and overweightness?
- Does obesity by itself cause type 2 diabetes?
- Environmental factors affecting obesity and the current epidemic
- Do fat kids invariably become fat adults?

This chapter addresses the role that obesity plays in the development of insulin resistance, a pre-diabetic state. The importance of other environmental factors in obesity and insulin resistance—poor dietary habits and physical inactivity, in particular—are discussed with regard to the current research in those areas. The extent of the obesity problem in children and the population as a whole in the United States and abroad is

The chapter outline is logical, clear, and well organized. The author does a good job of bullet pointing the main topics of the chapter and then giving a brief, informative paragraph explaining how those bullet point items will be answered and addressed. This is a quick and effective way to cover a lot of information in a little space.

also discussed in further detail, along with the importance of prevention of overweightness and obesity in children and into adulthood.

Chapter 3. What To Eat or Not To Eat
- Just how bad are soft drinks for you anyway?
- How to tell the good foods from the bad ones
- Glycemic index and load
- Why dietary fiber is your friend

This chapter discusses why some drinks and foods contribute to insulin resistance, obesity, and type 2 diabetes, why others do not, and what to look for. It also goes into detail about the importance of glycemic index and glycemic load in determining the effect on insulin responsiveness and resistance. Finally, the chapter addresses the importance of avoiding highly refined carbohydrates and certain fats and the health benefits of consuming greater quantities of high-fiber, low glycemic index foods in terms of satiety, obesity prevention, and blood sugar control.*

Chapter 12. Make It Simple, Stupid
- Remember the basics: anti-"chip" activities
- One day at a time … for the rest of your life
- The importance of good habits

The final chapter reiterates the key points to remember for effective prevention and control of type 2 diabetes in youth. It also the stresses the importance of making permanent health changes and forming optimal nutritional and exercise habits for lifelong good health.

Chapter titles are an effective way to engage your reader. Keep them clear and to the point. You can even inject a little humor into your titles even when the topic is serious in nature.

Remember, the last chapter of your book should feel like an ending or a logical conclusion. Here the author uses the content of the last chapter to demonstrate how the information presented in the rest of the book can be used over a lifetime.

The author included summaries for all of her chapters, but chapters four through eleven were not included here due to space constraints.

Published in September 2006 by Dearborn Trade Kaplan Publishing

WILLIAM G. RAMROTH, JR. Author

The idea for this book is not my own. An acquisition editor from Dearborn Publishing contacted my agent and asked if she had contact with any authors who were architects and could write a book about project management geared toward design professionals. Fortunately, she did: me. I wrote a proposal with a working title of *Project Management Handbook for Design Professionals*. Dearborn shortened it to *Project Management for Design Professionals*. This was my second book.

It is a big help to know something about what you are writing about. Since I have been managing design projects for about thirty years, very little research was needed in order to write the proposal. I reread some of the books I had, thought about what I have been doing most of my working life and searched the Internet a bit. It took about three weeks to write the proposal.

Selling this proposal was easy from my end. I e-mailed the proposal to my agent and she e-mailed it to Dearborn. Within a couple of days the acquisition editor was interested. She asked for and I provided information about a promotional plan. I knew next to nothing about how to write one, but again, my agent was a big help and told me how to do it.

PAM BRODOWSKY Agent

Bill has been a long standing client of mine who originally came to me via a query letter like so many other potential authors. It took me very little time to spot his potential. He is a very talented writer who exhibits his extensive knowledge throughout his writing. He comes with the credentials for the projects he chooses to write, which helps greatly when it comes to the sales aspect. In short, he makes life easy for an agent.

VICTORIA SMITH Editor

First and foremost, the book is in my specialty and fell in line exactly with my initiatives and strategic goals for my list of books. Sending proposals/manuscripts to the appropriate editor with the right specialty is very important. It's a big waste of time for both the author and the editor to send out unsolicited proposals/manuscripts to an editor without respect for her specialty. Fellow editors don't always pass along proposals to their colleagues. If you don't know the appropriate person to send it to, a quick call to the receptionist, department's assistant, or even the editor is worthwhile.

Also, Bill's proposals are all very well thought out, easy to navigate, and thorough, without including *too* much information. Thumbing through a thirty- to forty-plus page proposal can be very cumbersome.

I was interested in the project based on the proposal provided. However, I believe I did have additional questions, which is actually a good thing. For every project that I've presented, I always go back to the author with more questions for clarification. First, there's *no way* an author can possibly anticipate every question an editor or team may have. If an editor is asking questions or requiring more information, it's generally because she is interested in the topic and the author's platform. Another thing to keep in mind is that most editors don't make a decision to publish a book on their own. Generally, either a publisher or committee are involved in the decision as well. Creating a dialogue with the editor prior to making a decision or presentation will help the editor get a better feel not only for the project, but also for the author and his dedication to the project.

Bill is a terrific writer. In a technical field like architecture, many authors are dry and make the writing very impersonal. In Bill's proposal, he provided enough sample manuscript that I was able to get a feel for his writing, his message, and his passion for the topic, without an unwieldy or lengthy proposal. He's also very timely, open to suggestion, and easy to work with.

Book Proposal

PROJECT MANAGEMENT
FOR DESIGN PROFESSIONALS
by
William G. Ramroth, Jr. AIA

International Literary Arts, LLC
RR 5 Box 5391 A
Moscow, PA 18444
(570) 689-2692

It is very important to follow the industry standard for the title page of your proposal. You will need a one-of-a-kind title that describes your book, who it is for, or what it will do. You will need to identify that it indeed is a book proposal and include your byline as you wish it to be credited on the proposed project. When submitting to agents, your contact information is included in the spot where the agent's information is here.

OVERVIEW

Construction of the Cathedral Santa Maria del Fiore in Florence, Italy, began in 1296. Its first architect, the sculptor Arnolfo di Cambio, never had a plan for finishing it. He had no idea how to dome-over the enormously wide crossing, the area of the church where the nave and transepts intersect to form the Christian cross typical of all medieval churches. Nevertheless, he began building. Maybe he figured he'd think of something as he went along. But he didn't. None of his successors for the next 125 years solved the problem either. Nobody knew how to finish the project. It took a Renaissance genius to complete it. In 1420, Filippo Brunelleschi designed and began construction of the magnificent octagonal-shaped dome that covers the 130-foot wide crossing. He completed the dome in 1436. It took 140 years to complete the project!

Today, no building project should start without a plan for completion and it better not take 140 years to finish either! The world has sped up. Today's performance expectations have accelerated and are very high. Clients and principals of design firms expect every project to succeed. No client or design firm principal wants a project to take a day longer than necessary. Literally, time is money. Both the client and principal are anxious to complete the project and, with the Project Manager, share in the accolades that come with a successful project. But, should the project fail and the finger be pointed, the Project Manager is likely to stand alone. Managing projects for success has never been more important. The task of doing so falls squarely on the shoulders of the Project Manager.

Prior to this page, in the original proposal, the author included the standard proposal table of contents. It was eliminated here for space and because you have already seen several examples of tables of contents.

The author begins with an engaging and interesting story that hooks the reader immediately. Then, he transports us in time from the Renaissance to the current day and describes why this book is needed "now" more than ever. He does an excellent job of explaining his material in a creative and captivating way.

This book will give Project Managers working within the design professions the information and guidance needed to succeed. The book will serve as a toolbox, with instructions explaining how to use all the management wrenches, pliers, hammers, and screwdrivers needed to properly manage multi-disciplinary design projects.

The book will explain how to plan and monitor projects towards meaningful milestones. It will discuss how to make timely decisions. It will include methods for establishing and managing the project team, the design budget, and the project schedule. It will discuss the importance of project quality control, which requires planning and diligent monitoring throughout the project. This book will suggest ways to bring out the best work out of the various design team members. It will discuss client management, for the successful Project Manager has to manage the client, too! The book will discuss the characteristics of the good Project Manager, ways to lead the team, and how to avoid pitfalls. It will discuss common project management challenges and problems and address how to resolve them by using specific examples and work charts.

Finally, the book will include a comprehensive project manager checklist and rules of thumb, general principles that can assist and guide the Project Manager. The checklist will be developed from the principles, examples, and information presented throughout the book.

Not many students of architecture, engineering, or design started out their schooling saying to themselves, "I want to be a Project Manager." Students typically want to be architects, engineers, designers,

Here the author details what his book will do for its reader and how the reader will benefit from reading such a book. Showing how your book will benefit someone else is a great selling point. Books with strong benefits are what publishers are looking for.

This is a very well crafted, thorough overview that takes the reader from the beginning of the book to the end. It covers the entire scope of the project without being excessive. It's your job to describe your book project in a way that allows the agent or editor to envision it from your summary.

and planners. Once graduated, they begin working within their chosen professions. As they work and gain experience and competency, they slowly move up the professional ladder and are given more responsibility. Eventually they are given their own project to run. Unfortunately, little, if any, of their education prepared them for managing projects.

Project management needs to be learned, just like designing a building or engineering a post-tensioned concrete slab. The best way to learn project management is through a combination of good advice from others and actually managing projects. This book offers practical advice that can be applied directly to managing design projects. It is based on the author's twenty-five years of experience managing multi-disciplinary design projects, ranging in size from small remodeling projects to large, complex building programs with budgets over $100 million.

This book will include examples of project management techniques that work well, plus lessons from the school of hard knocks about things that did not go so well. In project management, it is just as important to know what *not* to do as it is to know what *to* do. Chapter 10, "Common Project Management Problems," will discuss various workplace challenges, give specific examples, and suggest ways of avoiding or resolving them (see Chapter 10 summary). Chapter 11, "Project Management Checklist," will summarize the project management information and challenges presented throughout the book in a checklist format for easy reference (see Chapter 11 summary).

At the top of this page, the author points out that there is a gap that needs to be filled—engineers, architects, designers all will run their own projects, but they have never received the proper information to know how. Then he shows how his book contains the advice they need to complement the experiences that will enable them to become effective project managers. He makes a great argument for why his book is needed.

Project Management Handbook for Design Professionals will be approximately 80,000 words in length. It will include approximately twenty-five diagrams and drawings to demonstrate some of the project management principles that will be discussed.

MARKET ANALYSIS

Project Management for Design Professionals will appeal to all members of the various design professions. This includes architects, landscape architects, interior designers, city planners, and the many disciplines within engineering including civil, structural, mechanical, electrical, geotechnical, and many other types of engineers. In addition, it will appeal to managers and project managers within the related construction industry. It will prove useful to project managers of government agencies and corporations that regularly are involved with building projects of various types. It will also attract project managers and readers from other industries with a curiosity about or interest in project management.

The content of the book will be presented in a style and use language that is understandable to a general lay reader. Technical terms will be kept to a minimum and when used they will be fully explained.

There are approximately 100,000 licensed architects in the United States based on a recent survey by the National Council of Architectural Registration Boards (NCARB). The U.S. Bureau of Labor Statistics puts the number of licensed architects at 113,000. According to the Council of Engineering and Scientific Specialty

The author clearly establishes his audience by detailing the various professions that would benefit from the prospective title. This allows the agent and editor to consider all the categories in which the book will be salable.

Here the author shows that he will present the book in a practical manner that the project will be easy to read and understand. This in turn tells the agent or editor that the book will be widely accepted and not a technical book that will require an in-depth understanding of the subject matter. Always strive to make your projects as reader friendly as possible.

Boards (CESB) there are over 2 million practicing engineers in the United States, while the U.S. Bureau of Labor Statistics states there are 1.47 million engineers. According to the U.S. Bureau of Labor Statistics there are over 1.2 million non-licensed practitioners within the architectural and engineering professions, which include drafters, engineering technicians, designers, apprentice architects and engineers-in-training. The Bureau of Labor Statistics states there are 32,000 urban planners. The American Society of Interior Designers states there are over 33,000 interior designers based on a 1997 U.S. economic census. The American Society of Landscape Architects (ASLA) has over 18,000 members. Combined then, there are over 80,000 interior designers, urban planners and landscape architects. In addition, there are tens of thousands of university students studying architecture and engineering, aspiring to become architects or engineers.

There is a mature, rich, and fertile market for books about the practice of architecture, engineering, and related professions. The market is far from saturated. Books about architecture and engineering are published every year. A subject search of www.Amazon.com yields over 68,000 books discussing architecture and over 170 million discussing engineering. Amazon lists over 3,000 books that discuss project management. However, if the subject search is limited to "project management for architects" the number of books drops to 2. Only 12 hits occur with a subject search of "project management for engineers" and 3 for "project management for design professionals."

When targeting a very specific niche market you want to make sure that you give as much concrete information that supports the claim that there's a market for your book as possible. In addition to citing government data, the author has included membership in some of the leading trade organizations. He also points out an additional market of university students—a great niche market that many proposal writers fail to address in their market analaysis.

It is always beneficial for an author to provide demographics when available. It helps the agent or editor to see the possibilities for your title. These numbers can easily be found on the Internet.

A word search on www.Google.com brings a total of over 20 million hits for the words "practice of architecture," over 30 million hits for "practice of engineering" and over 150 million hits for "project management."

The author is aware of the following recently published books about project management:

- *Project Management for Dummies*, Stanley E. Portny, 2000, For Dummies Publisher. Paperback, list price $21.95, Amazon rating #7,267. This book gives a general overview of project management. It is not specific to any particular discipline or profession.
- *A Guide to the Project Management Body of Knowledge*, Project Management Institute, 2004, Paperback, list price $49.95. Amazon rating #318. This book is the third edition of the Project Management Institute's guide to project management. It is a general project management guide for companies, nonprofit organizations, and government agencies.
- *Project Management: A Systems Approach to Planning,* Scheduling and Controlling, Harold Kerzner, 2003, Wiley. Hardcover, list price $80.00, Amazon rating #7,271. This is the eighth edition of this book which is geared towards business and engineering undergraduate and graduated students, functional managers, and upper-level executives.
- *Earned Value Project Management, 2nd Edition,* Quentin W. Fleming and Joel M. Koppelman, 2000, Project Management Institute, Paperback list price $23.00, Amazon rating #11,850.

Using the Amazon sales ranking is a way to identify how your competing titles are selling, the lower the number, the better the sales.

Showing comparables that have several editions helps to say these books sell.

Explaining a little bit about the content of each book is important. It shows you did your research and have a good grasp of what else is on the market. Using recent competitive titles is also essential to demonstrate that you have kept up with market trends.

PROMOTIONAL PLAN

Most design professionals are members of one or more professional societies or organizations, such as the American Institute of Architects (AIA) and the American Society of Civil Engineers (ASCE). In addition, most Design Professionals subscribe to or regularly read one or more magazines or professional journals tailored to their specific discipline's interests and needs.

To promote *Project Management for Design Professionals* the author will write and send out promotional material to the editorial staff of the most commonly read magazines and periodicals that cater to design professionals. The author will do the same for the major professional organizations. The author will review the promotional material with the publisher, accept, and incorporate any suggestions, and coordinate this effort with the publication date of the book, so that the timing of the promotional material has the greatest effect and relevance. Below is a list of major periodicals that cater to and are commonly read by design professionals.

- *Architectural Record* (received by approximately 40,000 members of the American Institute of Architects, AIA)
- *Civil Engineering* (received by approximately 100,000 members of the American Society of Civil Engineers, ASCE)
- *Spectrum* (received by 360,000 worldwide members of the Institute of Electrical and Electronic Engineers, IEEE)
- *ASME Journal* (received by all members of the American Society of Mechanical Engineers, ASME)

Here the author details what he can and will do for the promotion of his book and how he can assist the publisher with its efforts. This is a section you want to pay particular attention to. Describe all your contacts, affiliations, memberships, and previous media experience.

Don't assume that your agent or editor knows acronyms for organizations. Many agents and editors say that authors sometimes list acronyms without naming the organization. This author includes the full organization name and acronym just in case he wants to refer to the group later in the proposal.

- *The Construction Specifier* (circulation 26,000, received by all members of the Construction Specifications Institute, CSI)
- *Landscape Architecture* magazine (LAM) (official magazine of the American Society of Landscape Architects, ASLA, circulation of 19,000)
- *Planning* (received by 13,000 members of the American Institute of Certified Planners, AICP)
- *Engineering News Record* (commonly called ENR has 78,000 subscribers and a pass-along readership of 257,000)
- *Professional Engineering* (circulation of 80,000)
- *Architectural Digest* (circulation 30,000)
- *Design Cost & Data* (circulation 13,000)
- *Inland Architect* (quarterly magazine. Author does not know circulation numbers)
- *Harvard Design Magazine* (circulation 12,000)
- *New Civil Engineer Plus* (NCE+) (circulation 60,000)
- *Facilities Design and Management* (circulation 6,500)
- *Texas Architecture* (received by all architects registered in Texas. Author receives this magazine but does not know circulation numbers.)
- *Metropolis* (circulation 54,000)
- *Building Operating Management* magazine (circulation 70,000)

Below is a list of the most common professional societies and organizations to which the author will send the book promotional mate-

When you're including readership statistics, don't forget to figure in pass-along readership. This figure refers to the number of readers who read the magazine after it's passed along to them by a friend or colleague. Specialized publications, like the ones mentioned in this proposal, can sometimes be more than double in the initial subscriber base. Point out these larger figures when they're available, but don't guess. If the data doesn't exist, then just stick with the actual circulation. Don't be afraid to point out information you don't know.

rial. The author is currently a member of three of these organizations, the AIA, NCARB (certified to practice architecture in all fifty states and U.S. territories), and USGBC (LEED certified which means Leadership in Energy and Environmental Design).

- AIA, American Institute of Architects
- ASID, American Society of Interior Designers
- ASCE, American Society of Civil Engineers
- ASME, American Society of Mechanical Engineers
- IEEE, Institute of Electrical and Electronic Engineers
- IES, Illumination Engineers Society
- ISA, Instrumentation Society of America
- NCARB, National Council of Architectural Registration Boards
- USGBC, U.S. Green Building Council
- ASLA, American Society of Landscape Architects
- AICP, American Institute of Certified Planners
- CSI, Construction Specifications Institute

There are a number of bookstores throughout the United States that cater to the design and construction industries. In general, these stores are located in large metropolitan areas. Many of them have an active online mail-order business. It is the author's experience that these stores have a "new books section," which is promoted in their bannerhead. Also they send out e-mails to their customers when they receive new books of interest. The author proposes to send these bookstores promotional material regarding the book. Currently, the

If you want to be a successful nonfiction author, it's important to join organizations that can help you gain credibility before you write your book and that can help you promote your book upon its completion. This author is a member of twelve organizations. You may not be able to join that many groups, but you should at least consider being a member of one or two.

Here the author tells what he is going to do and how he can help with getting the word out—he's going to send out promotional material to bookstores. Anything you can do to promote your book that doesn't require time or money from a publisher is great.

author is aware of the following design and construction industry bookstores. Since the author is from the San Francisco bay area, he is most familiar with bookstores in the bay area; however, he will research and locate others in other metropolitan areas.

- The Architect Store.com (online bookstore)
- Construction Book Express (online bookstore)
- William Stout Books (San Francisco bookstore specializing in architecture, engineering, and construction industry books and reference materials. Also an online bookstore.)
- Builders Book Source (San Francisco bookstore)
- Stacey's Bookstore (San Francisco bookstore with an emphasis on technical books for all professions.)

ABOUT THE AUTHOR

William G. Ramroth, Jr., is the author of *Pragmatism and the Method of Modern Architecture,* McFarland Press, scheduled for publication in the first quarter of 2006. The book is about the development of pragmatism and modern architecture in the nineteenth century with a discussion about the various elements of pragmatism in the design method of modern architecture.

Mr. Ramroth is a practicing architect with over thirty years of experience in architectural design and project management. He has served as the project manager for numerous building design projects ranging in size from small remodeling projects to multidisciplinary design programs of over $100 million dollars in construction costs.

It's always a plus to provide a list of specialty stores in addition to the regular trade channels where your book may be well received. You can research this easily on the Internet. Do your homework. The more sales avenues you can locate, the better.

State your most relevant credentials first. This author has published a book on this topic before, which adds immediate credibility to the project. It shows that he knows what he is undertaking in the proposed project and that he is capable of getting the job done. He also mentions that he has served as the project manager for design programs of over $100 million dollars, which demonstrates he is trusted in his area of expertise.

He has bachelor's and master's of architecture degrees from the University of Oregon. He is a member of the American Institute of Architects (AIA) and is certified by the National Council of Architectural Registration Board (NCARB). He is LEED certified by the U.S. Green Building Council (USGBC) as a leader in the design of energy-efficient and environmentally sensitive "green" buildings. He is a member of MENSA.

He has been a guest lecturer at the University of Oregon, where he lectured and participated in seminars regarding methods of synthesizing the aesthetic, structural, financial, and technology parameters that affect the design of buildings. He has been an in-house lecturer and trainer for a large engineering and architectural firm in the subjects of project management and the development of effective communication skills.

Additional publications include:

- *Upgrading the Great Hall Ceiling, APT Bulletin*, Vol. XIX No. 3 1987, The Association for Preservation Technology, Washington DC.
- *Energy and Building: A Study of the Energy Consumption of Structural Systems*, Thesis presented to the Graduate School of the University of Oregon, August 1974.

List all of your pertinent background information along with your memberships and affiliations. If you're not a member of trade organizations in your area of expertise, consider joining some. They provide great networking resources once your book is published.

If you have been requested to speak on your topic, say so. If you think that there is a good chance that an organization would invite you back upon the publication of your book, state that as well.

For all previously published works, list the name of the publisher and the original date of publication.

PROJECT MANAGEMENT FOR
DESIGN PROFESSIONALS

TABLE OF CONTENTS

This is an outstanding table of contents. It is well organized and has a natural flow from chapter to chapter. The title of each chapter is simple and it is easy to understand what the content of each chapter will be.

You can indicate in your chapter outline if your book is going to have chapter notes and a bibliography. Many popular and mainstream books don't usually include this type of information. But when you're writing a specialized academic book like this one, including this information in your proposal is a good way to show editors and agents that you understand the academic buying market.

OUTLINE OF CHAPTERS

Introduction

The "Introduction" will give an overview of the book's contents and format. In addition it will include the text and ideas presented in the "Overview."

Chapter 1: Importance of Project Management

Why does a project need a project manager? The answer becomes obvious if the question is asked another way. Why does a car need a driver? The answer is: because someone has to steer. If no one steers, the car will not get where it is supposed to go. It may veer off course, go around in circles, or crash along the way.

A design project is like a car in that someone has to steer it, guide it in the right direction, and keep it from crashing. If the project crashes, a design firm's upper management usually looks for the reason why and often for someone to blame. Generally, it boils down to one reason: poor project management. Either nobody was steering, or not steering properly, or nobody was carefully reading the road signs along the way.

This chapter will discuss the importance of project management. It will give an overview of the fundamental project management objectives and tasks. It will discuss how to tailor the management strategy to the type and size of project. It will explain the difference between managing and micro-managing and how the latter can cause problems in certain types of projects.

Leading with a question that will be answered in the chapter is a clever way to start off. You can use any format you choose here, but be careful that you are staying true to the book. You need to convey what each chapter will cover in the tone that you will use in the book.

Chapter 2: Characteristics of a Good Project Manager

Nicolo Machiavelli (1469–1527) would have made a terrible project manager. In his book, *The Prince*, Machiavelli offered advice for a prince. He argued that since it is difficult to unite people into one like-minded person, "it is much safer to be feared than loved." He explained why by saying, "Because this is to be asserted in general of men, that they are ungrateful, fickle, false, cowardly, covetous, and as long as you [the prince] succeed they are yours entirely." Therefore, he concluded it is more practical to rule by fear than to spend time trying to win the love or respect of the subjects.

Whether this was good advice for a prince of the early Renaissance is hard to say. But it certainly is lousy advice for a project manager leading a multidisciplinary design team. The essential characteristics of a good project manager are something quite different than what Machiavelli had in mind.

This chapter will look at the important characteristics of a successful project manager. A good project manager is really a project leader, not just a manager, and there is difference between being a leader and a manager. This chapter will explain the difference.

Project managers must be good listeners. Good listening is the first step in developing good communication skills. Good listening is active, not passive. The difference will be explained and the chapter will suggest how the project manager can improve his/her active listening skills.

Since the main focus of this book is project management, it is essential that the book covers why that topic is so important. The author clearly explains project management in this chapter outline on this page and the next. Make sure your chapter information includes the core piece of your book. Show how important your topic is and bring it to agents and editors attention.

The project manager must be a good communicator. The chapter will explain why this is important and address ways of improving communication skills.

Additional characteristics of a good project manager are: cooperative, ethical, professional, and knowledgeable about the work. The project manger must be a creative problem-solver and not prone to panic. The chapter will discuss the importance of these characteristics and suggest ways of improving or developing these vital traits.

Chapter 3: Multidisciplinary Design Teams

This chapter will look at the characteristics of multidisciplinary design teams. It will discuss assembling the project team, defining roles and responsibilities. It will discuss the basic protocol for communication among design team disciplines and team members.

It will address the role of the project manager. It will discuss the rules of delegation and explain what the project manager can and cannot delegate.

The chapter will discuss the disciplines common to multidisciplinary design projects and the information they need in order to perform their work and the proper timing for this information. Typical disciplines that make up multidisciplinary design teams include: architecture; civil, structural, mechanical, and electrical engineering; surveying; landscape architecture; interior design; geotechnical engineering and construction cost estimating. Today's project teams

It is very important to lay out the scope of the project in your outline. You need to identify clearly what each chapter will cover without going overboard with too much text. Keep in mind that this is just an outline. This author created a succinct, yet thorough outline. A good rule of thumb is to treat your outline as if it is a pay-by-the-word ad. You want to pare everything down so that you get your point across without using any unnecessary verbiage.

may include a manager for the CADD (computer aided design and drafting), a project scheduler and a project controller. These team members assist the project manager in the set-up and monitoring of the computerized drafting, scheduling, and financial management tools common in many of today's design offices.

It will discuss the role of the project principal and the project quality assurance/quality manager (QA/QC manager). These two team members are generally part of the overall office management group and, consequently, are not under the direction of the project manager, both are important to a project's overall success. The chapter will explain why and discuss these two very important roles and the project manager's relationship and responsibilities to the project principal and QA/QC manager.

Chapter 4: Planning the Project
See Sample Chapter 4.*

If you are including a sample chapter in your proposal package, you can skip the summary of this chapter in your outline. The agent and editor will refer to the sample chapter for its content. It's always good to put a note in the space where your summary would have been to tell your reader where the information can be located.

In the original proposal, chapter summaries were included for all of the book's chapters.

Proposal 7
How to Raise Children You Want to Keep

Published in fall 2006 by Sourcebooks, Inc.

JERRY R. DAY, ED.D. Author

The idea for the book came from a parent who had used my techniques and liked the results. He asked a question that intrigued me and jump-started a restive search in my mind. This father said, "I know your techniques work because I have tried them, but what I want to know is why they work? So, could you explain to me, in plain English, why your methods work?" I was speechless. I had no answer, but the question made me wonder if there was a consistent theme that tied all of my techniques together. I pondered the question and discovered that all of my principles are grounded in one consistent theme. Each technique teaches this concept: The best thing a parent can teach a child is to learn to live willingly under parental authority. Before the "question" was asked, I had zero desire to write a book. I have thoroughly enjoyed developing this theme and writing about it in my book.

I wish I could take credit for the title of my book *How To Raise Children You Want To Keep,* but I can't. I was asked to lead a seminar at a Baptist Church in Winslow, Arizona. One of the seminar topics was about helping parents deal with difficult-to-raise children. The pastor and I were discussing some of the topics I planned to include in the seminar. After hearing about some of my techniques, the pastor grew pensive then brightened and said, "Let's entitle this section 'How To Raise Children You Want To Keep.'" I liked the title and the seminar was a great success. When I was searching for a book title years later, I remembered the pastor's suggested seminar title. The point of this story is: Pay attention, because a book title can come from surprising sources.

I have written one other book early in my psychology career. It was a professional book entitled *Counseling Techniques*. It was used for several years as a technical textbook for undergraduate students majoring in psychology.

Comprehensive research is critical in the presentation of a good proposal. The proposal writer must write with unwavering confidence. The best way to write with confidence is to do sound research. The proposal writer must know his competition and clearly present why his book can successfully compete with similar books in the field. I used Amazon.com to obtain a broad perspective of the competition. Research included reading a large variety of self-help books authored by established writers. I carefully pointed out why my book was not like any of my competitors' books. Using government statistics, I identified the buying audience as parents with young children and single mothers with young children. For my book, the buying audience was vast. Developing plausible methods of promotion was a prominent feature of my proposal. Quality research is the foundation of a convincing promotional proposal. For example, for my book I proposed that conducting professional seminars would be a viable promotion tool. My research revealed that about 70 to 80 percent of all professionals will purchase materials from the seminar presenter. I also found that professional psychologists will generate about ten to twenty book sales per professional through referrals of the book to their patients.

My proposal was forty-four pages in length and I invested four to six weeks in the writing phase. You have one shot at impressing an agent or editor so I do not think four to six weeks devoted to writing was excessive. My proposal generated a satisfying amount of interest among agents, so I think the extra care devoted to writing a comprehensive, readable proposal was worth the effort.

I purchased a book that listed the addresses of 200 agents who represented authors in my field of interest. I purchased several books that teach prospective authors how to write a query letter to agents. I wrote a pointed, punchy letter that presented the book concept, competition, and methods of promotion. The query letter was sent to 150 agents, and I received back thirty requests for my full proposal. Agents are inundated with query letters from many, many prospective authors. The query letter must be well done to get an agent's attention. I found it very difficult to condense my thoughts to one page. I must have written the letter fifteen times before I condensed it to one and one-eighth pages. I never could get it to fit on one page!

Agents are a funny lot, so a prospective author needs to have thick skin. A simple "no thank you" to my proposal would have been nice, but many seemed to feel compelled to offer unsolicited criticism of the proposal. Agent comments ranged from "great proposal" to "very boring" to "what you proposed is dangerous and you could be sued!" Agent evaluations seemed to me to be very subjective. In my opinion agent responses were exceedingly slow. I received representation offers a full six months after I submitted my proposal to the agent.

The agent I chose responded within two weeks after I mailed out my proposal. That impressed me very much. I also interviewed the agents who showed interest in representing me. I developed a list of twenty questions to ask the agent. For example, I asked my agent what she liked about my proposal. I reasoned that if she is going to represent me, she needs to have a variety of good reasons in the forefront of her mind why my proposal has merit. She did, and I was impressed. I wanted to know about her plans to promote my proposal to prospective publishers. I fully discussed commissions and extra charges, if any, that I could expect. Agent picking is an exciting but complex process.

PAM BRODOWSKY Agent

As soon as I saw the title to this, I had to laugh. Having young children myself I am well aware of the many hurdles one has to jump. I also handle a good deal of parenting projects, so the author was correct in targeting me for this title. I could relate both professionally and personally.

The parenting shelf is crowded but I had never yet seen a book with this approach, making this idea new and refreshing. I was intrigued.

Not only that, but Jerry comes loaded with the right credentials to author a book of this type. Jerry Day, Ed.D. has his doctorate in psychology, he has been in private practice for over thirty-seven years, and the proposed book is about his time-tested techniques. He is truly a delight to work with.

BETHANY BROWN Editor

Both the fact that the title was unique and catchy and the fact that the author really takes a different approach to discipline in getting the child involved in the process early on caught my eye. This is a crowded shelf, and the unique hook will make it stand out from the hundreds of books on discipline that are available.

We did request additional information as to how many children the author works with and what his success rate was with those children. This obviously gives the author more credibility both with publicity and with parents.

The author really had something new to say in a category that's really heavily published. This is really importan not only to sell in the category but also for a new author to have an impact in it.

Book Proposal

How To Raise Children You Want to Keep

By
Dr. Jerry R. Day

International Literary Arts, LLC
RR5 Box 5391 A
Moscow, PA 18444
(570) 689 2692

A fabulous title! This is one of the most critical elements of your proposal. In fact, at times it can make a difference as to the attention your proposal will receive. Even before your title needs to grab readers' attention in a bookstore, it needs to grab the attention of agents and editors.

Proposal Table of Contents

You'll notice in this proposal table of contents that the market analysis and promotional plan are combined. Many authors tend to combine these sections. This is perfectly acceptable as long as you do not intertwine the text. If you plan to use this format, your market section should come first followed by your promotional plan.

OVERVIEW
How To Raise Children You Want To Keep

I have counseled children and adolescents for over forty years. For thirty-seven of those forty years I had no interest in publishing a self-help book about my treatment methods until "the question" was asked. A dad said, "I know your techniques work because we have used them, but would you tell me in plain words why they work?" I was speechless. I too knew they worked because of years of application. What I didn't really understand was why uncooperative, hard-to-handle, miswired kids become cooperative, pleasant companions to their parents after only a few treatment sessions. I wondered, what does the More-Not-Less Technique teach children and is it different from what the Now or Later Technique teaches children? Pillow Talk seems to be totally different from the 30 Second Technique. I wondered, is there a golden thread that sews all of my child discipline techniques together? Is there one thing parents must teach their children? There is, and the idea for the book *How To Raise Children You Want to Keep* was born.

I call it "The Secret." My competitive literature review reveals that many writers write around "The Secret" and suggest methods and remedies that augment "The Secret" but none, to my knowledge, identify "The Secret." The ONE thing all parents must teach their children to do is WILLINGLY LIVE UNDER THEIR AUTHORITY. That is "The Secret." When this is successfully done, heaven opens up and happiness comes down for both parent and child. This is the one theme that ties all of my time tested, successful methods together.

The overview is a carefully crafted presentation of exactly what your book is about. It needs to grab its reader from the onset. Agents and editors are experts at analyzing proposals, and they will be able to tell from the first page if it is worth their time to keep reading. This author leads with information that proves his techniques have been used and work. That's a great way to substantiate his claim that the book should indeed exist.

Pillow Talk and the 30 Second Technique are alike in that they both effectively teach children to live comfortably under parental authority. When this is successfully done, children cooperate with their parents and become pleasant companions to their mom and dad. This happens only if they willingly give in to their parents' authority. Not only are children really easy to live with when they willingly live under their parents' authority, but they also become adults that can live under self-control in a society of order and rules. My desire is to stimulate a burning desire in parents to teach their child to willingly live under parental authority. To reinforce the importance of my theme, I skip to the end of child rearing in the first chapter and tell the parent about the seven adult benefits that are attributed to teaching a child to live willingly under parental authority. The benefits are awesome.

My book *How to Raise Children You Want to Keep* helps parents develop practical, easy-to-use methods that make it possible to teach children the one thing they must learn: how to live willingly under their authority. Everything in the book revolves around and supports this one essential learning. As the planets orderly revolve around the sun, my many child discipline techniques orderly orbit this one theme. Children must be taught to submit willingly to their parents' reasonable authority.

There are two distinct sections to my book. In section one, parents are taught methods about how to obtain a willingness from their children to live under their authority by forming a positive

The author clearly states what the book will do for its audience and how. You need to establish "why" your book is needed in the marketplace. Your editor is going to make the judgment as to whether your book is going to appeal to its target audience, and you need to provide him with enough information to make an informed decision.

relationship between parent and child. If a child does not behave because he wants to, then control is not enough. I take considerable time to teach parents how to form a close, bonded relationship with their children. I talk extensively about the four principles necessary to form a close relationship in which a child will want to cooperate with a parent's authority. Parents learn how to develop a workable, successful positive reinforcement program. Children will repeat anything that brings them reward and pleasure. Parents need to learn how to use positive manipulation in a way that works. My book tells them how to do that. I teach parents the essentials of a method I call The Talking Code. Communication is one of the most important tools a parent has to teach children how to live willingly under parental authority. My book teaches parents the method of Behavior Shaping. Behavior Shaping is an easy-to-learn technique that teaches a parent how to create cooperative, pleasant, useful behavior in their children that either does not presently exist or rarely occurs. Behavior Shaping firmly establishes a workable willingness to cooperate with a parent's goals and directives.

Section two is where my creative methods of child discipline become a very practical way of helping parents raise children worth keeping. The unique techniques I teach are centered on "escape" learning methods. Sometimes called negative reinforcement, most parents would refer to them as punishment learning. Negative reinforcement always works if a parent controls three things. I call it the Rule of Three. If a parent has all three, then punishment works every

---

Constructing the overview around the high points of your book allows you to condense a rather lengthy book project into a well-organized, powerful summary. You need to refine your focus and get to the essence of the project in this section. This author does this by explaining the two sections in his book: Section one explains the methods and section two shows parents how to put them to practical use. Editors want books that will have practical application to readers' lives, so this author is on the right track to creating a book that publishers want.

time. I teach parents how to obtain all those needed qualities. The methods described in my book create an ordeal for the child from which he can escape if he cooperates with parental directives, such as clean your room, go to bed, do your homework, or stop sassing me. My methods are strong but kind, moral, and ethical. Escape learning methods like Pillow Talk, Now or Later, More Not Less, Scarlet O'Hara, The Marks Assignment, The Holding Technique, The 30 Second Technique, and The Three Levels of Punishment are elaborately explained to the reading parent. Parents swear by them and kids respond well to them.

Many teaching stories are included in the content of the book to colorfully illustrate my main points and keep reader interest high. Parents will identify with the teaching stories because it seems like I have been living with them and the stories are straight out of their homes.

That's what my book is about. When both sections are applied non cooperative behavior stops and replacement positive behavior occurs. Then the replacement behavior is highly rewarded. It takes a balance between both positive and negative, but when successfully done it produces willingly cooperative children that parents want to keep.

Chapter Summaries

The book starts with a **Preface** that gives the reader hints about how to read my book so that the maximum benefit may be obtained. The theme is briefly introduced, but the main discussion of the one thing parents must teach their children is reserved until Chapter 1.

Explain to your agent or editor why your audience would be inclined to buy your book. Here the author stresses that parents will be able to identify with his project and why.

The author provides a clear, detailed outline stating how the book will benefit both the parent and child. The chapter summaries show that the author knows his subject inside and out. Convey your message for each chapter in a lucid fashion. Don't go overboard with details. Keep it simple and to the point.

In the Preface, I talk about my theoretical point of view and how I approach helping parents help children. The parent is instructed about the value of negative reinforcement, how it's done right, and why parental punishment methods often fail well-meaning parents. I tell the reader the three things that must be present for punishment to work and which one of the three most parents don't have. I conclude the Preface with a word of caution for abusive parents. The Preface is short, punchy, and powerful.

The following is a listing of chapter titles an d a brief narrative explaining each chapter.

Chapter I—How To Raise Children You Want to Keep. This chapter sets the table for what's to come. I carefully and in much detail explain the one thing all parents must teach their children and why. Immediately after explaining "The Secret," I tell a teaching story about "Fighting Freddie." This is a story that illustrates the positive outcome of using my strategies to teach a child to submit willingly to parental authority. From there I explain the long range benefits for adults whose parents taught them as children to live under their authority. The adult rewards are awesome. There are seven benefits that accrue to adults who learned, as a child, to live under self-control. I tell seven teaching stories to illustrate the seven benefits. The story I like best is "Doreen The Drama Queen." The summary section of this chapter brings it all together for easy remembering. By the time readers finish chapter one, they should be "frothing" to get at the main course of the book: the techniques.

Within this chapter summary there are interesting personal stories that bring the material to life. For each of the benefits the author introduces, he tells a story to illustrate that benefit. This is a wonderful way to freshen up your material. He even names each story with catchy titles, like "Fighting Freddie " and "Doreen the Drama Queen." This helps to create a picture in the reader's mind and helps him to remember this part of the proposal.

Chapter II—How to Create a Willingness to Live under Parental Authority. Parents are prone to skip the willingness part of what they must teach children and go straight to the living under authority part. They are anxious to stop non-cooperative behavior and get into negative reinforcement techniques, which do that. They are the most compelling. This chapter teaches a parent how to catch a child doing right and reinforce cooperative behavior with a variety of positive reinforcers. I illustrate the effective planning and execution of a workable, successful rewards program through the telling of the story of "Megan The Morning Killer." Megan's story is very powerful in terms of how to use positive reinforcement in a practical way. Now the parent reader is ready to learn the ten steps that guarantee a child will want to submit willingly to his parents' authority. I tell many other teaching stories to illustrate the concept that children will repeat any behavior that brings them reward and pleasure. Children will repeat cooperative behavior if properly and effectively rewarded. Most parents are aware of the benefits of rewarding a child for good behavior. However, most parent-directed rewards programs fail and parents lose interest. Rewards programs are sensitive and until all of the rules of learning are put in place, well-meaning rewards programs fail. This chapter teaches a parent how to do it right.

Chapter III—How to Create a Willingness to Live under Parental Authority, Part II. This chapter is about how to build a lasting, posi-

The titles for each of the chapters in this outline are powerful. They say something to the reader and tell what they are going to do. When creating your chapter titles be careful to construct them in this same powerful vein. You want your potential audience to be able to relate.

Closing your chapter summaries with a recap sentence is a good way to refocus your reader on the message you want. Each chapter summary should try to have a beginning, middle, and end so that the agent and editor can see you have a real structure to the material within the chapter.

tive relationship with a child. Children will cooperate with parental authority if they have a deep and abiding relationship with their parents. I fully discuss the four necessary characteristics of every successful relationship. These characteristics are discussed under the title, "The Four Principles:" 1. Tolerance/Acceptance; 2. Respect and Admiration (how to be positive with one another); 3. Fun; 4. Communication. Children actually want to cooperate with parental authority when they enjoy a positive rewarding relationship with their parents. I bring the points home by telling the teaching stories of "Mark the Communication Tester" and "Amanda Who Thought She Had Retarded Parents." This chapter concludes with a discussion of the Behavior Shaping Technique. Parents learn how to create any behavior they want from their children. Teaching stories are told to illustrate how to use this powerful technique in everyday family life. Story one, "The Professor" is about shaping the lecture methods of a college professor. Story two is about "Mariah the Morning Grump," and story three is entitled, "Kellie the Queen." These stories are full of examples that can be adapted to any family's needs. Behavior shaping is an easy-to-use technique that powerfully teaches children to want to cooperate with mom and dad's goals and directives.

Chapter IV—The 30 Second Technique. This is the simplest of the negative reinforcement techniques I use and the one I usually recommend first. If this one works, I know for sure we are going to soon have a child who will live happily under parental authority. It is an "escape"

The author uses easy-to-remember names for each of the techniques in his proposal. These names give the proposal a unique flair and show that the author is creative.

The fact that the author uses stories as a primary element in his book shows that he trying to engage the reader. He is writing with the reader in mind and has illustrative examples to back up his more theoretical points. This makes the book more accessible. Make sure you think about the reader as you develop a plan for your book, and any ideas you have for making the book accessible should be discussed in the proposal.

learning technique that settles the question of whether a child will follow a parent's directives right now. It prevents the parent from becoming
a nagger, and the child must immediately decide if he is going to comply
with the parent's directive or experience the unpleasant ordeal attached.
It's all over in thirty seconds. Most children comply. This technique is
effective for direct commands, such as get ready for bed, come to sup-
per, carry the trash out, set the table, do your homework, or apologize
for sassy words. Parents like this one. The child must comply with the
directive within thirty seconds or something of value is removed from
the child's room. Parents start with low priority items and move on to
items of ever-increasing value. Often children never lose even one item.
They just comply with the parent's order. Most children simply need
to know when their mother/father means business. I tell a story about
"The Last Call" to illustrate how children put off doing what they are
told to do until they hear "The Last Call." However, a few children are
tough. This technique works well for the toughies, too. The tough ones
rarely lose more than five items before they catch on that the more they
argue or delay, the more they lose of real value. Children thrive when
firm boundaries are set; they know the rules, and they are given choices.
Parents like this technique because they can step back and avoid getting
drawn into useless arguments.

Chapter V—Pillow Talk. This chapter is about training children
to put out-of-control behavior under better management. What is a
parent to do if a child:

It is clear that the author knows what he is talking about and has tried these methods with
real parents and their children. This gives his idea much more validity. He has already used
his ideas to help people. Now he is presenting a book to get the word out to more people. If
you can test your book's idea in the real world before proposing it, you should. It will help you
solidify your thoughts and give agents and editors some concrete evidence that you have put
time into this project and that it does have benefit.

- is afraid of the dark
- steals, lies, and cheats
- can't control his/her anger
- uses delay tactics
- is sassy
- ignores mother when she calls
- has superstition anxiety
- is forgetful
- freaks out at test time
- fights with brothers or sisters
- is argumentative
- throws temper tantrums
- uses rude, put-down language
- interrupts parents

I have developed a remarkable method of correction called Pillow Talk that addresses all of the problems above. There is one method but two versions of Pillow Talk. Version one is the statement technique and version two is the picture/statement technique. To successfully use Pillow Talk one must have a general idea of how the brain works. The hippocampus brain center sends messages either to short-term memory or long-term memory. Parents typically give their children many corrective suggestions (scoldings) that are simply sent into the short-term memory system of the child's brain. The messages are good, but the child forgets them (short-term memory) and

This chapter begins with a great hook. Then the author introduces a bulleted list of certain problems problems children may have. This helps to break up the text in an easy-to-read format. If an agent or editor is skimming the material, the list will immediately stand out and grab his attention.

repeats the naughty behavior. The statement version sends parental messages into long-term memory so the child can apply brakes to stop uncooperative behavior. The non-dominate, emotional brain is basically in charge of emotions and attitudes. The emotional brain responds very well to pictures. The parent can show the child what problem should be corrected through the picture/statement version of Pillow Talk. Either version works equally well.

Here is how Pillow Talk works using the statement version.

1. Decide what problem needs to be corrected.
2 Write out two to three corrective statements.
3. The child reads each statement five times at bed time.
4. The child puts the paper under his pillow and sleeps on what he needs to change. Research suggests that the thinking part of the brain will think about the statements periodically throughout the night.
5. After seven to ten nights of Pillow Talk, test the child.
6. If the child passes the test, then Pillow Talk is over, but if the child repeats the unwanted behavior, then go back to Pillow Talk for another seven to ten nights.

The picture version of Pillow Talk is done in a similar way, but the child draws a picture of himself with a speaking balloon coming out of the mouth. The picture version is usually reserved for more severe problems. The child writes in the speaking balloon exactly what he is doing wrong that is upsetting mom or dad.

To describe how this chapter's technique works, the author uses a numbered list. Again, this stands out on the page and also is a good way to sum up a process in a succinct way. The author also does a nice job of explaining his techniques. He doesn't just name them, but goes into detail. He gives a thorough review of the book's content. This is important. Proposals aren't meant to be a tease. Don't keep agents and editors in suspense; give them all the information they need to decide if your book is right for them.

Here is how it works using a practical example. Let's say Mark calls his mother "stupid," "idiot," and "bitch" when very angry. Using the statement version, mother might write out the following statements.

1. I will always remember and never forget (a reminder to send this statement into long-term memory) that calling my mother "stupid," "idiot," and "bitch" just makes mother mad, she digs in her heels, and I don't get what I want, so I won't do it anymore!
2. I will always remember and never forget that calling mother rude names is a really bad idea, so I won't do it anymore.

The child will be required to read these statements five times and put them under his pillow for further thinking. At the end of seven to ten nights, the test is given. If the child says any of the rude comments, even once, it's right back to Pillow Talk for seven to ten nights. The only way the child can escape this ordeal is to remember not to use the rude, put-down words.

The picture version requires the child to put the problem in the speaking balloon, but it is written in negative, harsh language. Mother directs the child to write, "I love to call mother 'stupid,' 'idiot,' and 'bitch.' It makes me feel better to make her feel bad. She never gives in, but that's okay. At least she has to hear me put her down!" The child is painfully aware of the error of his ways and the only way to escape this uncomfortable ordeal is to quit using these put-down words.

The results are dramatic. Bad, useless, uncooperative behavior is usually changed, using either version, in seven to ten days. Rarely

Throughout the proposal, the author is straightforward and serious, but he keeps his tone upbeat and positive. Since this is partly a motivational guide for parents, the tone throughout the proposal is very important. Remember to keep your tone and style consistent throughout your proposal as this author does so well.

does a child need a second dose of Pillow Talk. Many teaching stories are told in this chapter to illustrate the proper use of Pillow Talk. The technique seems so simple, but the power of Pillow Talk is dynamite!*

Chapter XVI—Conclusion. Everything in the book is briefly summarized and reviewed in this chapter.

MARKET ANALYSIS/PROMOTIONAL PLAN

At first blush the market seems flush with children's books in my field. When I did my due diligence research, I found, for example, that Amazon.com offered for sale 4,438 books under the topic of "children's self-help books." When I recovered from my initial shock of this discovery, I honed my research efforts to a sharper, more focused search. I found that there are 2,091 parenting books for children. I am now able to breathe. More research revealed that Amazon.com offers 2,056 therapy for children books and 1,815 books on the subject of family therapy for children. These later numbers, although better, still seem to indicate a crowded market. One more search revealed numbers that look much more encouraging. Under the topic of "child discipline," Amazon.com pulled up only 958 books. That number is much more manageable than the original 4,438 books on self-help for children.

When examining the list of 958 child discipline books, I found that many were five to eight years old so were no longer "fresh" competition. I also found a large number of books written to be read by children on such subjects as how to handle a bully, how to say

You always want to have a strong closer for you book, no matter what. There are different types of closing chapters. This author chose to summarize the contents of the entire book in one chapter. That's fine. Since there is a lot of information and techniques presented in this book, a summary chapter is a great way to tie up loose ends and give readers a strong wrap-up.

Here the author makes a powerful statement—parenting books abound. His research puts them into categorized numbers, which helps the agent or editor get a clearer picture of the market.

no to sexual overtures, and what to do when mom and dad divorce. When books like these are removed from the mix, the competitive field narrowed appreciably.

I researched the shelves of our local bookstores. I live in a city of half a million people so we have a variety of large national chain bookstores. When I perused the bookshelves of our larger stores, to my relief and delight I found that there were less than 15 self-help books on the subject of child discipline.

I believe my book will compete well with the 8–15 available books on child discipline because of the title of my book. The title, *How To Raise Children You Want To Keep* draws immediate attention, interest, and comments. I have tested the title with over 200 non-patient parents and in every case, the title draws a smile, positive comments about the title, and curiosity about what the book is about. The content was equally fetching to my test audience. When I told them that the book is about the one thing all children must learn from their parents, they all asked the obvious question, "And what is that?" My reply, "All parents must teach their children to live willingly under their authority so that they will grow into adults who can live under self-control in a society of rules and order," always drew immediate agreement. Parents intuitively know that the concept is correct. The title and theory of the book hold people's interest. Because the title of the book is fetching and arouses immediate curiosity, I believe my book will compete very well with the existing published books in my area. My book will stand out on the bookstore shelf.

The author shows that parenting is clearly a crowded shelf, but, even though his project will have competition, his unique approach to the topic opens up a slot for his project. You need to show you are filling a gap in the marketplace and that your book will be different from what is already available. Narrow your competition and tell your agent and editor why your book is going to work in the marketplace. Be realistic with your claims.

The general market is the 75 million parents who are searching for parenting tips on how to better raise their children. A very fertile market for my book are the 35 to 45 million busy single parents who are desperately seeking better child discipline techniques. My practice is filled with frustrated single moms who cannot control their children. These parents are actively looking for a better way. Newspaper articles, talk radio, and talk TV are excellent resources to reach these working moms. I expect the book will receive similar expressions of interest from popular TV and radio shows such as *The Dr. Phil Show*, *Dr. Laura*, and *The Oprah Winfrey Show*.

The strongest and most exciting book marketing methods available to me are the professional seminars I plan to offer in 2006 and 2007. I have an agreement with a professional seminar promotion agency to hold my first seminar in October 2005. There are over 600,000 professional psychologists, psychiatrists, social workers, counselors, and family therapists in the United States. I plan to market a seminar under the title "How To Help Parents Raise Children They Want To Keep" to the 600,000 professional therapists. The test seminar is already scheduled for October 2005. I plan to offer my seminar in 60 major cities per year and I anticipate reaching about six thousand professionals through the seminars. Research has indicated that about 60 to 70 percent of seminar attendees purchase materials from the lecturer during the course of the seminar. However, for my seminars the cost of the book will be included in the price of the seminar. So, I will have 100 percent sale of my book to professional

The author shows his wide target market by stating there are 75 million parents searching for parenting tips, a fertile market to say the least. You'll need to define your market into numbers for your agent and editor. It allows them too see the full potential for your proposed project.

The author cites a specific agreement he has for teaching professional seminars. This shows agents and editors that the author is committed to helping to market and promote the book. Any specific agreements or plans you can mention in your proposal help to make your case for a strong promotional platform.

therapists. Sales from seminars alone should range between 5,000 and 6,000 books depending on the attendance at the seminars.

However, the real power for book sales is not in selling books to seminar attendees. Therapists are always looking for good books to recommend to their clients. They call this therapy process bibliotherapy. After attending the seminar and hearing about the benefits associated with employing my creative therapy, I anticipate that each professional will be responsible for an average of 10 to 20 referral sales per year. This translates into some big numbers. If I touch the lives of 5,000 therapists and they sell 10 to 20 books per year, this means that yearly book sales will be 50,000 to 100,000 books

Of the 600,000 professional therapists, there will undoubtedly be considerable interest generated for my book through professional journals and magazine articles and advertisements. Newspaper articles, and radio, and TV talk shows should also generate interest in my book. Every purchase by a professional represents a potential 10 to 20 additional referral sales to their clients. The numbers are unknown but potentially powerful.

Another rich market for book sales is through pharmaceutical companies that produce drugs to treat ADD/ADHD. They organize brief lectures by professionals for M.D. doctors on the subject of ADD/ADHD in hopes of piggybacking on the lecture to promote drug sales. Children with ADD/ADHD have many behavior problems that interfere with home harmony and school performance. My book addresses these problems. I anticipate going to sixty cities to offer my seminar. A luncheon lecture could

Here the author defines what avenues are available to him for promotion and how he will utilize the same. Agents and editors want and need to know how you are planning to assist them in the promotion of your book.

Identifying the many readers that your book project reaches out to is always beneficial. Here the author clearly establishes that his book is *not* just for parents.

be arranged for M.D.s on the subject of ADD/ADHD. I have personally attended many lectures of this type sponsored by drug companies.

Parents have many pressing questions about what do to help their children with ADD/ADHD. It is natural to ask the doctor who diagnosed the disorder and prescribed the medication questions about how to handle behavioral problems. M.D.s have very little available time to discuss these matters. The doctors who attend the lecture will know something about my approach to treating ADD/ADHD. It would be a natural next step for these M.D.s to deflect the parents' questions by saying, "Dr. Day's book *How To Raise Children You Want To Keep* addresses these problems and I recommend you buy a copy of his book. It is an easy read." If each lecture draws 20 to 30 M.D.s, this means that 1,200 to 1,800 books will be sold. The drug company will purchase a book for each M.D., but the real sales power is in the referral sales of 10 to 20 books per year. If 20 to 30 M.D.s attend the lecture that number represents yearly sales of 12,000 to 18,000 books at 10 referral sales per M.D. If the 1,200 to 1,800 M.D.s stimulate 20 sales to patients per year that represents 24,000 to 36,000 book sales.

There is also a great opportunity to promote book sales through newspaper articles in the cities where I present my seminars. Talk radio interviews are also possible to arrange in the sixty cities I visit. The topic should be a popular topic for this media.

It would be a natural progression from a self-help book for parents to a second self-help book for adults. Many of the techniques

Even though this is a hypothetical marketing situation, the author cites strong statistics to back up his plan that referrals and word of mouth will help sell books. The scenario he describes is real and believable, so this will make sense to an agent and editor in understanding how additional books will be sold.

I teach in the children's book are applicable to adults. In addition, I have developed a number of original therapy techniques that address adult problems. A second book would be a natural promotional support for the children's book. The adult book will help to sell the parenting book. Parents have personal problems they seek help for. They also often have children they may need help with. If these parents are helped by the adult book, they would naturally refer themselves to my book for parents.

In conclusion, my book will also have strong appeal to the Christian audience. The Christian church strongly promotes family values and family harmony. I am very familiar with Christian values, the Christian faith, and the Christian position on the authority of the parent. While visiting the sixty cities in which I offer seminars, I plan to offer an evening lecture to Christian parents. I expect sales of my book to be brisk at these meetings. Again, the sales power is not in selling books to lecture attendees. The real sales power is in the referral sales from pastors who attend the lecture. They represent 10 to 20 referral sales per year. Pastors, assistant pastors, youth pastors, and educational pastors would be interested in learning new techniques to help parents raise more godly children. The premise of parental authority is definitely and clearly taught in the Bible. If 10 to 15 pastors attend my lecture, they will be prime candidates to become referral resources for my book. Using the figures of 10 to 20 book referral sales and 10 referring pastors then I would expect 600 pastors to sell 6,000 to 12,000 books per year.

The potential sales for my book are awesome.

The author addresses the issue of spin-off titles for the proposed project. If his first book does well, the publisher is likely to welcome this possibility.

The Christian market is very strong. If you can tie your book into any Christian organization or group, this is a great way to expand your market. Agents and editors are always looking for ways that your book can be introduced to a wide variety of readers.

THE AUTHOR

My most outstanding credential for writing a book about how to help parents raise children they want to keep is my many years of experience in the field of counseling psychology. I have been involved with helping children for forty-one years. I have been in private practice for thirty-seven years. In my private practice career, I have seen over twelve thousand patients.

I am a trained teacher. I began my secondary teaching career in 1961. I was known as a teacher who could also help parents manage the difficult behavioral problems of their children and my students. My professional counseling career started in 1964 after receiving my master's degree in counseling psychology. I was employed to develop a school counseling program for children in grades one through twelve. The counseling program involved parents as well as children. It was very successful. I realized that I needed more education, so I enrolled in the counseling psychology graduate program at Oklahoma State University. I received my doctorate (Ed.D.) in 1968. At the time, I thought that I wanted to teach graduate students in psychology for the rest of my career. I was wrong. I did teach graduate students for five years at Northern Arizona University beginning in 1967. Concurrently with my college teaching career, I started my private practice in clinical psychology. I soon realized that private practice was my real love and talent. I left the small college town of Flagstaff, Arizona, and moved to the larger city of Tucson, starting my clinical practice in 1976. I have been in continuous practice in Tucson for twenty-nine years.

By saying he has been in practice for thirty-seven years, helping children for forty-one, and that he has seen over twelve thousand patients clearly shows that this author has the expertise to write this book.

This author has very strong credentials—he is a teacher and a counselor and has developed his own school, all before starting his own practice. He is truly an expert in his area. Do all that you can to become an expert. Or, even better, propose a book that uses the expertise you have already gained in life.

Though I was officially licensed to practice psychology in 1968, but my counseling career actually began when I was six years old and in the first grade. My very first client was Ira. He probably had ADD, but in those days this disorder was not named. Ira was slow, chubby, and his mother dressed him funny. Ira was very unhappy and spent half of the day crying. I decided that it was my job to help Ira to be happier. I tried to cheer Ira up by talking to him and joking with him. One day I was exceedingly successful. Ira began to laugh uncontrollably. Ms. Johnson, my tall, thin first grade teacher came to my desk and loomed down on me. I realized, years later, that Ms. Johnson knew that Ira could not tolerate a good scolding so she lit into me. "Jerry Day, I have told you a thousand times to quit bothering Ira." Then she slapped me on my left cheek, knocking me right out of my little chair onto the floor. Teachers could do things like that in the "olden days." I remember lying on the floor looking at Ms. Johnson's long skinny legs and those practical brown shoes, rubbing my stinging cheek, and saying in my mind, "It was worth it; Ira laughed." Ira was my first client and I was very successful. I have a natural talent to help people in creative ways. Since Ira, I have better developed my counseling skills through excellent academic training. I still see fifty-five clients per week.

I believe I am exceedingly qualified to write a book designed to help parents raise children they want to keep.

I have put my teacher's training to good use by offering seminars to lay people and professional counselors, social workers, and

The author makes great use of an anecdote to personalize his bio. This story really shows agents and editors that the author has a personal stake in the proposal. It is not always appropriate to include anecdotes in your bio, but if your topic is about relationships with people, then you might want to consider it. Otherwise, just stick to the facts.

psychologists. I developed a series of lectures on the subjects of stress management and humor in the workplace. In the '80s, I presented these lectures to business groups, convention audiences, and professionals from New York City to Los Angeles. In the '90s, I developed a seminar presentation on the subject of biofeedback. I presented the biofeedback seminar to professionals.

I have publishing experience. I published a textbook called *Counseling Techniques* (1977). This book was used for several years as a supplemental training book for undergraduate students in psychology. I published a self-help manual on how to meditate. In 1976, I self-published a self-help book for parents called *How to Discipline the Hard to Handle Child*. I sold 7,000 of these books exclusively to my clients for five dollars per copy. I have been asked to write numerous psychological articles for Christian oriented magazines.

I have been married for forty-three years to Roena and we successfully raised a boy and a girl. Our children learned to live under parental authority and grew up to be adults who live under self-control. They are service oriented and have been very successful in their professional careers. We are family oriented, and, to this day, Roena and I enjoy a great relationship with our children, Amanda and Mark.

THE COMPETITION

There are two distinct divisions among writers in the area of child psychology. Division one books are academically oriented and basically written for professionals. For example, Michael L.

Self-published material is a great way to show agents and editors that you mean business and are willing and able to do your own marketing and promotion. Here the author describes a self-help book that sold seven thousand copies. If you have significant sales of previous books, you should definitely highlight that in your proposal.

The author has divided his competitive section into two divisions: academic and parent friendly. He has done so because his book has the ability to be a crossover title and apply to both of the stated markets. If your book has this type of potential you may want to follow this style of proposal.

Bloomquist, Ph.D., authored a book called *Helping Children with Aggression and Conduct Problems* that deals with some of the same issues addressed in my book. Dr. Bloomquist uses broad strokes to describe the anger and aggression problems children have. He writes elaborately about parent-child group training sessions with very good research references. He provides agenda outlines to describe the course content of the eight to thirty parent-child training sessions. It is a very academic presentation and not very friendly for parents who are dealing with their children's aggressive problems on a daily basis. He does not, in my opinion, offer to parents specific, understandable methods they can use to effectively correct their children. Although Dr. Bloomquist's book is on the shelf in a popular bookstore, it is clearly written primarily for professional readers.

The second division includes authors like Dr. Kevin Leman who writes parent-friendly books about correcting typical children's problems. At first look Dr. Leman's book appears to be similar to mine. The title, *Making Children Mind Without Losing Yours,* would suggest that the theme of his book is exactly like my theme, but in fact there are substantial differences. My emphasis is placed upon teaching children to submit willingly to their parents' authority. I am sure Dr. Leman would agree with my basic premise, but his approach to reaching this vital goal is substantially different. Dr. Leman identifies a variety of problems that are typical with children and suggests various remedies. His methods and my techniques are not the same. My philosophy is unique and most of my correction methods are original to me. Other

The author has done such a thorough competitive analysis that he can anticipate the questions an agent or editor might have. He realizes that, at first glance, his book may seem very similar to other people's books. He acknowledges this, then goes on to explain how it is untrue. By being so familiar with the competition, he is able to avoid a negative reaction that an agent or editor may initially have. Had he not addressed this issue, an agent may have tossed his proposal out as just another parenting book.

authors, in division two, also offer advice to parents that use methods like time out, distraction games, and removal of privileges. I have not read one book that duplicates my corrective techniques.

There are many good books in division two that truly help parents to increase their effectiveness. None approach the raising of children in the same way I do. None use the same methods I use, but all of the following books are useful and act as a supplement to my theme and child correction methods. The following is a general review of some of the books available to parents.

Division One: Academic/Professional

  A. *Cognitive Therapy with Children and Adolescents: A Casebook for Clinical Practice*, edited by Mack A. Reinecke, Frank M. Dattilio, & Arthur Freeman. The Guilford Press, 2003. This book emphasizes cognitive therapy applied to typical clinical problems associated with children. They discuss therapy and intervention for Oppositional Defiant Disorder (ODD), anxiety, depression, chemical dependency, Obsessive-Compulsive Disorder (OCD), low self-esteem, eating disorders, and academic problems of children. The authors teach a variety of cognitive-behavioral psychotherapy techniques a professional could use in the treatment of children. This is a well-written book focused on training the professional.

  B. *Treating Troubled Children and Their Families*, Ellen F. Wachtel, J.D., Ph.D. The Guilford Press, 1994. Dr. Wachtel is a

The way an agent or editor will determines whether your book is marketable is by thinking of other titles similar to it that have sold well. As this author has done, you will need to present a sharp analysis of the similar titles that you have researched. Comparable titles should not be more than five years old unless they are demonstrable perennials or classics.

family therapist trained in the Ackerman method of psychotherapy. Although motivated parents could benefit by studying her therapy methods, the professional therapist will derive much more benefit from her book. She advocates meeting with parents and children together. She discusses family dynamics such as family alliances and family systems. Dr. Wachtel discusses methods of family therapy that would be useful for boundary setting, anxiety, depression, and defiance.

C. *Your Defiant Child: Eight Steps to Better Behavior* by Russell A. Barkley and Christine Benton. Guilford Publication, 1998. Dr. Barkley is well known to professionals, especially in the area of diagnosing and treating ADHD. I have placed his book in division one because it is a blend of academic research on diagnosing ODD and general advice to parents about correcting defiance. He reminds us that one in twenty children display out of control behavior. He tells the reader what causes ODD and how to diagnose it. He presents to the parent an eight-step program to correct ODD. In his program he promotes the concepts of parental consistency and promoting change through a system of praise, rewards, and mild punishments, such as timeouts. He presents many charts, questionnaires, and checklists for parents. Although Dr. Barkley would agree with placing firm limits on out-of-control children, his approach is 180

These are very in-depth analyses of competitive titles. That shows that the author really did his homework. It's easy to do a quick Internet search and get information on competitive titles. But it is even better to go to a bookstore, look at the books, and flip through them. Or, as is probably the case here, the author is just familiar with these titles because they are directly related to his profession. You probably will have a good idea about competitive titles if you have used some of them yourself. If you have used them, and they don't meet all of your needs as a reader, then you have very strong evidence for why the market needs your book as well.

degrees from mine. There is no serious overlap between his book and my book.

D. *How Much Is Enough? Everything You Need to Know to Steer Clear of Overindulgence and Raise Likeable Responsible, and Respectful Children* by Jean Illsley Clarke, Ph.D., Connie Dawson, Ph.D., et al., Marlowe & Company 2004. The authors present scientific research to identify poor outcomes affecting children's lives that overindulgence brings. They include the presentation of assessment techniques to use in taking action steps to assist families. This work makes a significant contribution to social workers and other professionals who deal with children. Middle school teachers would be especially helped by reading Clarke and Dawson's book. However, it is not parent friendly. Parents are forced to read the entire book to obtain the necessary help they desire for a four year old. It is difficult to glean the necessary corrective information for age-specific problems.

This book is about parents who over coddle and over stimulate their children. The book graphically identifies the poor outcomes of overindulgence. The authors believe in positive love but also firm rules and boundaries. They give parents wise counsel about how to correct overindulgence such as:

1. How to figure out if you are being overindulgent and ways to act differently.
2. How to teach your children what enough means.

Keep your competitive analysis as positive as possible. Here the author points out that this book is excellent but that it does not address some of the techniques that his book offers. There is no need to make other books seem inadequate or poorly done. It is enough to show that your book will address different aspects of the topic.

3. Tips on establishing firm rules and structure.

4. How to instill responsibility and independence.

Any book that discusses the effects of overindulgence and what to do about it has some similarity to *How to Raise Children You Want to Keep*. Books of this nature promote the fixing of firm boundaries and sticking to them; however, there is little overlap with my approach. Most of my techniques are fresh and original, and I have never found them before in print.

E. *Too Much of a Good Thing: Raising Children of Character in an Indulgent Age,* Dan Kindlon, Ph.D. Cahners Business Information, 2001. Dr. Kindlon's book is a book that is recommended for healthcare professionals, especially psychologists, counselors, and social workers, who want to understand children raised in a self-indulgent world. He also speaks to parents about their role in the act of overindulgence. He gives many examples of dealing with the behavior problems of overindulged children. His suggested remedies are researched based. He uses natural consequences to help a child correct his misbehavior.

My techniques do not overlap his methods, and he does not approach the problem of effective child rearing with the same philosophy as mine.

Division Two: Parent Friendly

Division two books are more user friendly than division one books. In division two books, typical problems children have are

Breaking the competitive analysis into two clearly defined sections is a great idea if appropriate for your topic. This makes it even easier for an editor or agent to get a clear idea of the market and the types of books out there. It also helps them to see more clearly how your book would be positioned among the other titles.

addressed and practical suggestions are offered to help parents deal with the problems.

A. James A. Fogarty, Ed.D., has a typical division two book. His book, *Overindulged Children: A Parent's Guide to Mentoring*, addresses the problems that often develop when parents over-indulge their children. He discusses ineffective parenting styles and distorted parental beliefs such as, "I will correct my parents mistakes." He offers suggestions about how a parent can correct thier ineffectiveness and mistaken beliefs. The thrust of Dr. Fogarty's corrective strategies is to help the parent to coach or mentor the child to become less selfish, less demanding, and more cooperative with their well-meaning parents. Dr. Fogarty's goal, like mine, is to help parents to teach their children to live under self-control and cooperate with their parents. He just does not approach the goal in the same way I do.

Dr. Fogarty's book has a familiar ring to it. Like *How to Raise Children You Want to Keep*, he believes in setting firm boundaries, but after that similarities cease. My book teaches parents to put out-of-control child behavior back under the parent's control and put in place replacement behavior that is amply rewarded. My techniques to help a parent accomplish this are not addressed in his excellent book.

B. *Parenting the Strong Willed Child*, Revised 2nd Printing. Rex Forehand, Ph.D., Nicholas Long, Ph.D., NTC Publishing

Again, the author is very positive and compliments the other books, but then very simply states that his book addresses more. You don't have to go into detail about what your book covers. That's what you did in the overview. The author here does a great job of stating the fact that his book is different without repeating much of the information from the beginning of his proposal.

Group, 2002. Dr. Forehand presents a clinically proven five-week program for parents with strong-willed children. Based upon a forty-year review of the literature, he has developed a five-week program for parents. He discusses causes of defiance and how a parent can develop a positive atmosphere in the home. He presents strategies for managing specific behavior problems that oppositional children typically present. His program is designed to help children with defiance problems. He believes in setting limits for strong-willed children. He offers a prescription for parents. My book, unlike his, teaches the use of behavioral tools that can be creatively applied to hundreds of individual problems as well as OCD-type problems.

C. *Try and Make Me!*, Ray Levy, Ph.D., and Bill O'Hanlon, Roclate Inc., 2004. Dr. Levy informs parents how they may be unwittingly triggering their child's defiance. He presents a number of natural and logical consequences to help motivate children to change. Dr. Levy promotes positive rewards to correct bad behavior. The book presents a variety of problems children have and strategies to cope with these problems. His book is practical and readable but his approach does not overlap my presentation on similar problems.

D. *The New Dare to Discipline*, James Dobson, Tyndale House Publishers, 1996. Over twenty years ago, Dr. Dobson wrote *Dare to Discipline*. It was an instant best-seller. He sold sev-

The competitive analysis not only helps to establish that there is a market for the book, but it also helps agents and editors to see if there are any gaps in that market. This author clearly shows there is room for his unique ideas. His book will not just be more on the same topic. It will offer an approach that others don't. That's what makes his book truly valuable, and he isn't afraid to say it. Be confident that your book really does offer more.

eral million copies of his first book. Dr. Dobson was one of the first professional psychologists to advocate setting firm boundaries that defined the child's behavior. If the child did not adhere to these pre-set rules, a parent was to let natural consequences occur without protecting the child from them. His new updated book re-examines his early premise. His book is very reader friendly. He also advocates the use of logical consequences, which means that a parent devises an appropriate punishment for misbehavior and permits the child to experience this logical consequence.

Although his premise is similar to mine, which is that children should live under parental control, he does not develop in his book the same methods or even similar methods to my child control techniques. Dr. Dobson has written many other child parenting books, such as *The Strong Willed Child, Bringing Up Boys* and *Temper Your Child's Tantrums*. He promotes natural and logical consequences as well as other forms of practical advice in these books. I like Dr. Dobson's approach and books. He approaches the same problems I do but in ways that do not duplicate my child control methods. Our basic methods are not similar.

E. *Loving Without Spoiling*, Nancy Samalin, Catherine Whitney, McGraw-Hill 2003. Ms. Samalin's book offers 100 mini methods to help parents deal with many child discipline problems. She

Since there are so many competitive titles discussed in this proposal, the format in which they are presented is important. The information needs to be easy to navigate. The lettered list approach works well, and underlining the titles helps them to stand out. Always keep format in mind when working on your proposal. If it's hard to read, chances are agents and editors won't take the time to sort through it.

deals with issues such as whining, morning routines, encouraging honesty, and making uninterrupted phone calls. The information is not designed to be in-depth remedies, but she does offer useful tips. She offers new solutions to many age-old problems.

Ms. Samalin's book is very dissimilar to my approach.

F. *Setting Limits with Your Strong-Willed Child: Eliminating Conflict by Establishing Clear, Firm, and Respectful Boundaries*, Robert J. MacKenzie, Ed.D., Three Rivers Press, 2001. Dr. MacKenzie offers alternative solutions to ineffective extremes of punishment and permissiveness. He helps parents to motivate the strong-willed child into cooperative behavior. He advocates gentle methods like time outs for uncooperative children. He teaches parents to set firm limits and stick to them without being drawn into a power struggle with children. He frees parents from the feeling of guilt by pointing out that children are genetically pre-dispositioned to be strong willed. Parents may have little to do with the cause of this acting out. Parents should expect children to question parental directives and simply objectively answer the child's questions, tests, and challenges. Parents are to remind themselves that their child is strong willed, and the way strong-willed children learn about the world is to test limits. My theme and approach is not similar to Dr. MacKenzie's methodology.

End of Review

The author simply ends by stating "End of Review." It is not necessary to sum up the competitive analysis. It was thoroughly done book by book, so any sort of summary would just be redundant. Remember, your proposal should not be any longer than it needs to be to get your point across.

HOW TO RAISE CHILDREN YOU WANT TO KEEP
TABLE OF CONTENTS

The author clearly presents a well-formed book table of contents. The chapters have a powerful and natural flow to them. We can't emphasize enough the importance of the unique and clever chapter titles this author has created to really make this proposal pop.

Most books contain between seven and ten chapters, but you can have more if your idea warrants it. Each chapter should represent a major idea or topic in your book.

The Right Weigh

Published in January 2006 by Hay House Publishing

RENA GREENBERG Author

I have been conducting wellness seminars for weight loss for over seventeen years. The idea for the book came from the work I had done with over 100,000 people, to help them lose weight, using a mind-body-spirit approach, as opposed to a diet or exercise routine. The title idea came from a friend, and yes, it was my first book.

I actually wrote the draft for the book first on a ten-day cruise and then wrote the proposal shortly after that. It didn't take me long (maybe another week), since I already had the idea of what I wanted to share.

I e-mailed my query letter to about fifteen agents who I had found in a resource guide, in the library. Within a few days, I had seven responses from interested agents. I researched those agents and went with the one who I thought had the most experience and was recommended by a friend. I secured an agent within six weeks of writing the first draft of my book.

LINDA KONNER Agent

I liked the mix of practical self-help (i.e., the diet information) with the spiritual angle that Rena developed so effectively throughout the proposal. Rena writes clearly and well, and her ideas are immediately accessible to the reader. The proposal was well organized, and she covered such key areas as Competitive Books and Marketing & Promotion in detail, assuring me that she not only had studied and knew the marketplace but also could effectively promote the book once it was published.

Her platform is excellent. Rena has built up a large seminar workshop business, used in hospitals and large corporations around the country, and she was also able to generate her own publicity even before she had a book to promote, which publishers love to see. She had also sent me a DVD of her local TV appearances, which showed her to be attractive and articulate about her work.

JILL KRAMER Editor

I bought Rena's proposal because I liked the topic and the title was very catchy. Not only that, but also she had good credentials and great writing skills. When she first submitted the proposal, it was very complete and there was nothing more that was needed. Ultimately, Rena's credentials really stood out. She conducted a large number of speaking engagements and was a terrific networker so I knew I could really count on her to market the book. I also like working with her agent, so I knew material coming from Linda was going to be good.

THE RIGHT WEIGH:

The Wellness Seminar Program For Permanent Weight Loss Used
By Over 100,000 People

Overview

The Right Weigh is a unique approach to weight control that
balances the practical with the spiritual. There are a lot of books
about weight loss and diets and eating plans, and there are others
filled with psychological tools. There are also many books written
about the benefits of a regular spiritual practice. However, there is
no book to date that combines all of these necessary components to
weight loss in a comprehensive guide such as this one.

The author, Rena Greenberg, has taught these principles to over
100,000 people since 1989 at seminars she has conducted at over
70 hospitals throughout New York, Florida, Michigan, and Ohio.
She has had over two dozen media appearances including major
newspaper articles featuring her work and being a guest on network
television news and radio programs. She is a dynamic and heartfelt
motivational speaker who easily makes her audience feel comfortable and inspired.

This book is ultimately a road map that leads the reader from
being overweight and frustrated to achieving a life of health, slenderness, fitness, and inner peace. While Greenberg addresses the
importance of making physical changes in our diet and activity level,
and the necessity of using our minds to support us (by breaking

The author cites a powerful statistic of working with over 100,000 people at the top of her
proposal. This is a great way of hooking the agent and editor. A number like this shows the
agents and editors that you have a platform of readers already in place as potential buyers
of your book.

A key term here is "road map." This makes clear to editors and agents that the book will be
prescriptive and have take-away value for the reader.

unproductive habits, and changing our perceptions of pleasure and pain around food), the main component of her program is bringing a practice called the Remembrance into our lives. The Remembrance reconnects us to our vast spiritual nature, through the doorway of our own heart. When we re-connect with our Source of Divine Love in this way, the deepest internal shifts can occur for us. Through the practice of Remembrance, we can begin to recall our innate connection to the love, strength, beauty, wisdom, and peace that reside in the center of our being. These internal resources now become available to us. We learn to harness their power to help us achieve our deepest longing for our self, which is to live life healthy and fit, at our ideal weight, and to our fullest potential. Our own inner wisdom is now more accessible to us. Through deep communication with this wise part of ourselves, we stop listening to all the contradictory "advice" from the outer world, and tune in to those steps necessary to improve the quality of our life and live a life of health at every level of mind, body, heart, and spirit.

The other unique aspect of this book is that instead of proposing a "diet" with carbohydrate restriction, as is so popular today, the author, who stopped eating sugar in 1987 and at the same time ended her battle with weight, guides the reader through her own personal experience on how to face sugar addiction and be free from it. Because of her own life experience, she teaches the reader how sugar can be eliminated without being on a diet, or without feeling deprived. This book is not just an intellectual approach to finding

In the top paragraph, the author introduces some key concepts such as Remembrance and Source of Divine Love that are really attention grabbing. These words give the program a unique angle and twist.

The author gives a personal anecdote about how the topic of the book relates to her own life. This is a great way to engage the reader and show that you, the author, have a real personal investment in the proposal. Ultimately, editors and agents want to see real passion and commitment for your topic.

a dict that makes sense on paper. Instead, it is designed to help the reader discover for herself what foods and lifestyle changes are going to support health and desired weight, and how to stay motivated to stick with that sensible eating plan and increased activity level over the long term.

To support these changes, the reader is taught how to use the vast power of the mind to fulfill her deepest longing for slenderness. She is guided step by step on how to use tools such as self-hypnosis, neuro-linguistic programming, grounding, containment, opening awareness, and Remembrance to move from feeling out of control about her weight to living her life slender, healthy, and fit, making healthier choices naturally.

The Right Weigh is filled with practical suggestions from cover to cover. It is written in easy-to-understand language by someone who has been through the battle with food addiction and found her way through it to freedom. The tools the author shares are practical and easy to follow, and lead not only to weight loss but to a greater sense of peace and fulfillment in every area of life. The book is structured in two parts. The first part of the book outlines the six essential principles for success. In order to achieve lasting results, it is necessary to explore and address all six areas. The second part of the book is filled with exercises and suggestions that the reader can implement immediately in order to achieve the desired weight reduction. Every aspect of the reader is addressed—the mind, the body, the heart, and the spiritual. The author weaves these aspects

The author clearly states what techniques will make this book different. It is not only a step-by-step book but one that promotes weight loss through self-hypnosis, neuro-linguistic programming, grounding, containment, opening awareness, and Remembrance. These things grab your attention because they are different—maybe even unfamiliar. Always state the crux of your book; it should always be intriguing and unique.

The author gives a good overview of the structure and content of the book. She uses key words such as mind, body, heart, and spirit to organize the content. Organization is crucial for a book that's programmatic because the reader will be following a step-by-step plan.

of ourselves together, leading us to the result of health, fitness, and a deep sense of inner peace on every level of our being.

About The Author

Rena Greenberg has been the director of Wellness Seminars, Inc., since 1990. She has successfully conducted weight control (and smoking cessation) seminars for major corporations such as Walt Disney World, Busch Gardens, AT&T, and Home Depot, as well as in over 70 hospitals throughout New York, Florida, Michigan, and Ohio (see enclosed list). Since 1989, she has helped over 100,000 people to achieve their weight goals, using behavior modification and hypnotic conditioning.

She is a graduate of City University of New York at Brooklyn College with a degree in biopsychology. She is a certified hypnotherapist through the National Guild of Hypnotists and is a nationally certified biofeedback therapist. Prior to founding Wellness Seminars, Inc., Ms. Greenberg worked as a biofeedback therapist at the Hospital of Joint Diseases in New York City, and had a private biofeedback therapy practice in New York City and Bradenton, Florida.

Ms. Greenberg has had numerous radio and television appearances (see enclosed media lists). She continues to speak on a regular basis about weight loss to large audiences throughout Florida and Michigan.

She resides in Sarasota, Florida, in the winter and Ann Arbor, Michigan, in the summer, with her husband and two daughters.

The author states some powerful corporate connections. These connections show agents and editors you have potential resources to reach a very wide audience with your book.

Again, the author states her long-standing expertise in the field and the number of people she's helped. Those 100,000 people are not only potential buyers of the book but also can help to spread the word with personal testimonials once the book is published.

The author has a strong media platform to launch the book. Later in the proposal, she gives a list of media appearances. If you have a list of appearances, include them in your proposal.

Marketing for The Right Weigh:

The Wellness Seminar Program For Permanent Weight Loss

For the last decade, the media has been very interested in Rena Greenberg's unique approach to weight loss, even without any published book. Despite having no active public relations program currently in place, she receives media requests on a regular basis.

She continues to lecture frequently. In January 2004 alone Rena Greenberg's Wellness Seminar company conducted over 40 seminars for the public at Florida hospitals. She has an audiobook available that teaches self-hypnosis, and she has sold over 15,000 audiobooks sets at hospitals and corporate settings.

The audience at her existing weight loss (and smoking cessation) seminars would be a perfect market for her new book. With greater marketing efforts, the reader potential for this book is huge, as the market for new, innovative ways to lose weight is always expanding. In addition, more and more people, having exhausted all other possibilities, are open to a more spiritual, as well as practical, approach.

Her ongoing seminars would be a wonderful place to promote and sell the book. Aside from the participants of the seminars, the market for this book is enormous. Millions of people are actively trying to lose weight at any given time. People who want to achieve slenderness are always looking for new solutions. This book is extremely appealing because it is simple to understand and follow and

---

The author emphasizes she is a sought-after expert in the media. Editor and agents like to see that the media knows to come to you. From a publicity standpoint, that makes you and your book an easier "sell" to the media upon publication.

Citing the sales figures of her audiobook sets shows that the author has a proven track record and built-in audience for this book. If another project of yours has sold well, include the sales figures.

The author states that she will sell books through her seminars. This is a great way to show that you understand what it takes to sell books. If possible, project a number of titles you think you'll sell.

is filled with practical ideas on how to change our lives, our thoughts, and our eating behaviors. The heart-centered approach fills a need for many people who are looking for spiritual nourishment and guidance as well as an improved physical condition. The combination of these two concepts—weight loss and spirituality, in this type of format—is unique and refreshing. The fact that it is written by a woman who has been through the battle with her health, her weight, and sugar addiction and come out the other side gives the book a credibility that weight loss books sometimes lack. With a strong marketing effort, this book could potentially appeal to millions.

Competition

While there are many books on weight loss available today, there are none that offer such a comprehensive approach as *The Right Weigh: The Wellness Seminar Program for Permanent Weight Loss* does. There are a lot of books filled with diets, or even lengthy explanations about how our thoughts and emotions sabotage our efforts, but none that combine all aspects of ourselves in an integrative approach to losing weight. A variety of spiritual books have made it to the bestseller list in the last few years including *Conversations with God, The Power of Now, The Seat of the Soul,* and *The Four Agreements.* None of them are addressing the physical aspect of ourselves—our need to be healthy, fit, and in control of our life and our eating habits.

Greenberg's work uniquely discusses the physical addiction to sugar that must be admitted and addressed and our need to change

Mentioning that the ideas in this book have not only worked for other people but also for the author shows that this author is indeed the right person to write this book. She will be able to identify with her readers and her voice will ring true. Anything that demonstrates that you are the best possible author for a title is useful to include.

The author does a good job of distinguishing her book from the other weight loss books on the market by clearly explaining the conceptual framework of her book. You will need to explain your unique concept in the same detailed form.

our thinking to produce the results that we want. She gives us tools to clean our hearts and wash away the painful residue from stuck emotions. She also brings in the richness of our often untapped spiritual nature and teaches us how to access our deepest inner resources to lose weight and live our lives to the fullest.

- *The Ultimate Weight Solution – The 7 Keys to Weight Loss Freedom* by: Dr. Phil McGraw, Simon & Schuster 2003

  Dr. Phil is using a psychological approach to weight loss. Some similarities with Greenberg's work are the concepts of designing your life for success, being prepared, goal setting, being aware of and changing internal dialogue, and healing feelings. In Rena Greenberg's work, rather than simply presenting these obstacles, she offers a multitude of tools and techniques to make the required permanent and necessary shifts in thinking and behavior. Dr. Phil offers many self-tests to help a person determine their current way of thinking and behaving so that they can take self-responsibility. In contrast, rather than testing for the problem behavior, Rena Greenberg is offering solutions for change on all levels—our mind, physical body, heart, and spirit. Dr. Phil mentions the concept of relaxation and moves on, whereas Greenberg's whole orientation is the necessity of bringing all aspects of our being—including our deep innate spiritual nature, together in harmony for permanent results. *The Right Weigh: The Wellness Seminar*

The author gives excellent analysis of each competitive title by showing similarities and differences with the concepts presented in her book without being critical of others. The idea here is not to "bash" the titles that exist but rather state how yours is different or will complement the existing ones.

The author emphasizes the unique selling point of her proposal—the spiritual dimension to weight loss. This immediately shows agents and editors how her book will differ from the competition.

Program for Permanent Weight Loss puts its focus on teaching the reader how to accomplish this step by step.

Also, Greenberg uniquely addresses the issue of sugar addiction and treating our "food compulsions" as an addiction versus just an emotional problem. With this attitude, the necessary behavior changes can become automatic. There are similarities between these two books, but there are two major distinctions. Rena Greenberg deals with the concept of treating our tendency to overeat in an extreme way, as an addiction. She also teaches us a practical way to harness the enormous power of our own internal resources to help us lose weight, by connecting more strongly to the inner wisdom of our deeper mind and heart.

• *The South Beach Diet* by Arthur Agatston, M.D., Rodale 2003
Enter the Zone by Barry Sears, Ph.D., Harper Collins 1995

Like *The Right Weigh: The Wellness Seminar Program for Permanent Weight Loss,* these books explain the importance of eating in a balanced way and cutting our simple carbohydrates. The difference is that Greenberg's approach is to not follow any certain "diet." Instead we are encouraged to trust our bodies and listen to what our body needs. As we get healthier we naturally start to eat the way *The Zone* or *The South Beach Diet*, or even *Sugar Busters!* or *Dr. Atkins Diet Revolution* recommends, but we are not following any sort of diet.

The diet and weight loss market is a very crowded marketplace. When you're pitching a book in crowded market your competitive analysis section is extremely important. You must be very clear and precise as this author is in her proposal. In the top paragraph, she points out her view on addiction' which differentiates her book from the competition.

The author lists two major best-selling books. It's good to show that your title is competitive with a best-seller because it drives home the point that you consider your proposal to have similar selling potential. If you just compare your book to low selling titles then editors and agents might not believe your book has potential to hit the best-seller list.

The mindset of dieting is that it is a psychologically temporary situation. Therefore, it cannot work over the long run. Because Greenberg brings her readers to an understanding that they are suffering from sugar addiction, just like an alcoholic, it becomes easier for them to abstain from the obvious forms of sugar and change their lifestyle. Greenberg teaches how to more naturally gravitate to healthy foods and increased activity without engaging in the never-ending cycle of yo-yo dieting. Also *The Right Weigh* clarifies that the necessary component of a diet is the structure provided, but the downfall is the restriction. By maintaining the structure, but eliminating the tight restrictions, we extract the best and leave the rest.

- *How Much Does Your Soul Weigh? Diet-Free Solutions to Your Food, Weight, and Body Worries* by Dorie McCubbrey, M.S.Ed., Ph.D. Harper Collins 2002

    McCubbrey addresses many of the same concepts as Greenberg, e.g,. focusing inward for answers to our weight challenges vs. being guided by the outer world, and giving our soul the attention it requires. She, too, speaks about weight loss and eating disorders from personal experience. Both books focus on letting our intuition show us when to eat, what to eat, and why we are eating.

    The difference is that in *The Right Weigh*, rather than focusing on other people's personal histories as McCubbrey

To show how your project will differ from what is readily available, include the publication date of the book. If trends or research has changed since the publication, then your book can present newer information, which is good. If a book is out of print, then note that in your proposal. Make sure to explain why that book is out of print—if you know the reason. That will help agents and editors assess the competitive value of your book.

does, Greenberg is teaching the reader how to get in touch with his/her own intuition, and how to change the way we think about food subconsciously. With this guidance, our behavior changes naturally. *The Right Weigh* teaches in great detail many specific practices, step by step, e.g., through self-hypnosis, meditation, neuro-linguistic programming techniques, and Remembrance to get in touch with our highest qualities. The qualities we are connecting with internally are the attributes of our soul. The readers of *The Right Weigh* are actually being taught how to make the switch from being outwardly focused to being inwardly directed, and use this focus to lose weight.

Another major difference is that McCubbrey does not offer advice on the physical level of what to eat. *The Right Weigh* includes extensive information on how to construct a healthy lifestyle with positive eating habits and how to break free from sugar addiction permanently. Greenberg includes plenty of practical suggestions on foods to eat, foods to stay away from, and how to start naturally making healthier choices.

• *The Weigh Down Diet* by Gwen Shamblin, Doubleday 1997

The *The Weigh Down Diet* and *The Right Weigh* have one thing in common: They are both a spiritual approach to weight loss. Both authors agree about the necessity to turn to God to

The sentence structure of each of these two paragraphs is very good. The author states in her topic sentence exactly what the main difference is. She then goes on to elaborate on that idea. In the following paragraph she does the same thing. She introduces a "another major difference," then gives an excellent analysis.

end the battle with weight forever. However, there are many differences in the approaches of these two authors. *The Weigh Down Diet* focuses almost exclusively on biblical stories and quotes from scripture as a way to motivate people to eat less. The language Shamblin uses is Christian-based, with many references to sin, deliverance, and to Jesus Christ, our savior. She also encourages people to go outward to God through prayer and worship. Greenberg's focus instead is going inward to our Spiritual Source, which resides at the core of our being. Her teaching is to re-connect to this Divine Love and Wisdom through the heart by doing a practice called Remembrance. The Remembrance inherently connects us to all our higher qualities of love, patience, strength, determination, and joy. Shamblin recommends having a personal relationship with God through constant prayer. Greenberg's work teaches us how to create and strengthen this personal relationship on an ongoing basis. The language Greenberg uses would appeal to Christians and non-Christians alike. It is more spiritually based, as opposed to religious.

Another major difference in the philosophy of these two authors is their attitude towards food. Shamblin claims that when you turn to God fully, you will naturally start desiring and eating less food. Therefore, she recommends getting rid of any diet food, and eating anything you desire. *The Weigh Down Diet* advocates eating Fritos, blue-cheese salad dress-

The author provides a detailed explanation of the works she is analyzing. Don't immediately assume that the reader—the agent or editor—will be familiar with these competitive titles. It is better to assume that they do not know anything about the topic. That way you can make your analysis more pointed.

ing, and dessert as much as desired, with the expectation that when you are not deprived, you naturally choose what your body needs. She refers to "real food" as fried chicken and bread and butter. Shamblin asserts that all foods have some nutritional value and it doesn't really matter which foods one chooses. She also recommends "diet" soft drinks as a staple, or drinking orange juice prior to a meal to fill you up. Shamblin disputes the notion of food addiction, claiming that the problem lies in having a passion for food as opposed to a passion for God.

Greenberg agrees that it is a good idea to give up diet food and to listen to the body's natural hunger signals. That is where the similarity in their philosophy ends. Greenberg makes a strong case for the addictive nature of sugar (and sugar substitutes), regardless of one's relationship to her Creator. Her teaching is to eat small, nutritious meals regularly throughout the day, rather than waiting to be famished and having to cope with blood sugar that is plummeting. For those of us with sugar sensitivity, even diet soft drinks and drinking juice before a meal can stimulate strong cravings and binge-ing. She advocates eating mostly animal protein and lots of salads (with olive oil dressing) and vegetables as a way to keep the blood sugar stable. She recommends eating complex carbohydrates, proteins, and healthy fats in balance. While Greenberg acknowledges that some people can eat a variety of

Here the author describes more specifically than she has yet why her book is different not only from other diet books, but from other spiritual diet books. Within the diet-book market there are niches. It is important to distinguish your book from other books in your market and in the smaller niche. This clearly shows why this book is unique and how it will distinguish itself in the marketplace.

all foods, for many of us foods such as pizza and white bread are okay as a rare treat only, and sugar in obvious forms is to be avoided. Shamblin asserts that all food is equal and that this is the truth of God. *The Right Weigh* takes the position that there is no eating plan that will work for everyone across the board. Greenberg's program teaches us to turn inward and listen to our body to find out which foods will lead us to health, slenderness, and well being. Greenberg's takes a strong stand that all foods are not created equal and that many of us suffer from food addiction. Therefore she recommends abstaining from those offending foods so that we can achieve permanent weight loss and optimal health. Because *The Right Weigh* engages the power of the mind (as well as the heart), the reader is given tools such as self-hypnosis and neuro-linguistic programming to make the shift from "processed foods" to "healthy, nutritious foods" much easier and more natural.

Notice how throughout the analysis, the author uses third person to discuss her book. You can do whatever makes you feel most comfortable here. First person is fine, but third may make it easier for you to step back and truly compare your work to other books out there. It may help you to feel more analytical and do a better competitive analysis.

THE RIGHT WEIGH:

The Wellness Seminar Program For Permanent Weight Loss Used
By Over 100,000 People

TABLE OF CONTENTS (proposed)

This table of contents is broken down nicely into two parts. The first part explains what the program is all about and the second part helps readers to put it in action. The chapter titles are very clear and help readers to see exactly what will be covered and how the book has potential to benefit them.

Chapter 13: Changing Our Perceptions of Pleasure and Pain
Chapter 14: Breaking Unwanted Habits
Chapter 15: The Qualities That Transform Us
Chapter 16: Commit To Using the Techniques
Chapter 17: How To Live Your Life Sugar Free
Chapter 18: Closing

The book will be approximately 200–225 pages and will be delivered approximately three months after contract.

The author mentions here what she envisions the length of her book will be and when she'll have it completed. You can do this in a variety of places, but doing it here is fine. Hint: When thinking of your page count, remember that books are printed in signatures of eight or sixteen. An editor may be impressed if your page count reflects that, though it's not necessary.

Chapter Overviews

Chapter 1: The First Step

The book is described as a guide for a journey from being over-weight and out of control with our eating habits to gaining control and living a peaceful, balanced, harmonious life at our ideal weight. As with any journey, we expect curves, bumps, and turns, but we must stay steadfast and committed to the goal. The first step is creating a vision for ourselves. We do this by re-affirming why we want this so much for ourselves. What are our motivating factors? Health, comfort, looking better, and improving self-esteem are all important reasons to embark on this journey.

The second step on the journey is to stop "trying" and "hoping" we'll lose weight because these words imply failure. Instead, we need to make a decision for ourselves because when we make a decision, stay committed, and have faith that it is possible to succeed, our internal resources of strength, patience, determination, wisdom, and love become available to help us realize our deepest desires for ourselves. What is necessary is to have a road map, to know where we are going and to learn from our mistakes. That is the purpose of this book. In the first chapter, we take a look at the conscious mind, the subconscious mind, and the vast resources available to us through a deeper connection to our own innate spiritual nature.

Chapter 2: The Three Necessary Components

Consciously the reader already knows what physical actions need to be taken in order to lose weight permanently. In this chap-

The chapter overviews show that the author knows her material. Her detailed summaries show that she knows exactly what information is going to go into each chapter. This is of major importance for a new writer. Agents and editors want to see that you can clearly summarize your material and present a logical book. You must prove that you are capable of taking vast amounts of information and organizing it into a format that will interest and benefit readers.

ter, we explore the necessity of eating smaller portions, choosing healthier foods, and increasing activity.

There can be confusion in the reader's mind about what exactly are healthy foods since there is so much contradictory information. It is important to understand that no eating plan works for everybody. Some people do great with vegetarianism. For others eating this way leads to anemia, weight gain, or carbohydrate addiction. It is important for each of us to get in touch with our own body and discover which foods are best for us and which foods we need to cut back on or eliminate. Some tools for this are given here.

The reader is encouraged to learn to listen to his or her body and trust it. We talk about the pitfalls of being on a diet since dieting intrinsically is a psychologically temporary situation.

Instead of dreading the time of day when we need to exercise, we can start to look forward to the time of day when we get to move our body. When our mindset changes, we start to engage in the necessary behaviors for weight loss naturally. Weight loss does not have to be a struggle. We can find activities that we love to do—rollerblading, dancing, walking, jumping on a trampoline, tennis, bicycling, or golf—and incorporate them into our life naturally. This chapter is filled with practical suggestions on implementing the three necessary components for weight loss—eating less, choosing healthier foods, and increasing activity level.

When writing a proposal that consists of many chapters, as this one does, clearly written summaries make the writing and reading less tiresome. Editors and agents want to be able to move quickly through your text and onto the next chapter. Keep in mind when penning your chapter outline that you will want to thoroughly convey your message, but not to the point of excess. The length used in this proposal is perfect. It's kept short but detailed.

Chapter 3: Essential Principle #1—Transforming Old, Unproductive Eating Habits

Here we take a look at the old, deeply ingrained habits that are keeping us stuck. They are overeating, bingeing, snacking, and emotional eating. We explore the way we learned these habits in childhood. We were taught to comfort ourselves with food and to finish everything on our plate. Once we understand that our subconscious mind is like a computer and runs on programming, we can discover ways to reprogram this part of our mind with thoughts that will lead to the result we want for ourselves. It is our repetitive thoughts that lead to our consistent behaviors. In this chapter we look at the first Essential Principle—the need to transform these automatic behaviors into positive habits that serve us. When we break down our habits into a predictable stimulus-response mechanism, it is easier to stop the unwanted habits and replace them with the actions that will lead us to slenderness and happiness.*

In this chapter summary, the author makes a comparison between the human mind and computer programming. This is a great way to get a complex point across in a brief summary. It also creates a vivid image that readers can relate to. Condense complicated information into an easy-to-understand metaphor is great.

We've only included three samples from the chapter summaries to show you an example of how the author did a good job of summarizing the most pertinent information in each chapter.

Proposal 9
Powerwriting: The Hidden Skills You Need To Transform Your Business Writing

Published in February 2003 by Pearson.

SUZAN ST. MAUR Author

I had already published two books about business writing but felt there was a big gap in the market for DIY business writers. All the books on business writing in existence (my own included) were focused very much more on writing skills than on thinking skills. However, unless you get your thinking right—your strategy—whatever you write for business is likely to fail. As I saw it, there was a howling need for a book addressing that issue.

I chose the title because it had a good commercial ring to it and began with a term people would remember. The subtitle, "the hidden skills you need to transform your business writing," is truthful (people always underestimate the importance of getting writing strategy right) and also offers potential purchasers a key benefit.

It's difficult to measure how much time I spent researching, as I am always on the lookout for developments in this field and had been watching the business writing book market for some years. The proposals took me a couple of weeks to write, not 24/7, but using a slow editing process!

I had submitted the proposal to three other publishers, all of whom made offers. I was not overly impressed by those, though, so went on the Pearson Education/Prentice Hall Web site. I adapted the original proposal to fit their criteria and submitted that online. I heard back from Rachael Stock from Prentice Hall about a week later. We then went through a fairly short development phase. Rachael seemed fairly happy with the structure and nature of the book as it stood, so the contract was drawn up, signed, and off we went.

RACHAEL STOCK Editor

First, Suzan's proposal was well written and easy to read. If a proposal is hard work to read, it won't get very far. Beyond that, the concept seemed sound (it wasn't just another book on business writing). It had an angle and an edge in that it covered not just how to string a coherent sentence together but also how to put together your case/argument/sales pitch. In other words it wasn't just a "me too" book; it had something fresh about it.

She knew exactly the right level of information to include. It was pitched in a short, pithy, focused way instead of five pages of long-winded descriptive narrative. She could clearly write well and was adept at writing for a market. There was evidence throughout that she was thinking about and writing for the reader (rather than just writing what she knew/thought), which is absolutely vital in nonfiction. I felt very confident she was thinking about the market and had ideas for promoting the book in which she would be active. All these elements combined gave me a very positive impression.

Synopsis

As you know, now that written communications are so much easier and faster, increasingly business people are writing both screen- and paper-based communications themselves rather than delegating them to specialists.

However, writing—even writing well—is only half the story.

The other half is knowing how to approach the exercise in the first place—how to structure your message, how to understand your audience, and how to marry the two. To get that wrong is expensive, time-consuming, and professionally embarrassing. Yet millions are wasted every year on business communications that don't work, because the approach to the exercise (not the writing or design) is wrong.

Powerwriting will be the first book on business writing to give readers the tools they need to approach business writing properly: to define and develop their message and learn to understand target audiences. That way the writing craft skills that follow in the book can be learned in the light of an accurate, realistic, and positive background—the key to success in all forms of non-social communication.

Competition

None. All existing books on business writing focus on the craft. *Powerwriting* also teaches the craft of writing, but as the end product of effective research, planning, and thought, rather than the starting point. As such, *Powerwriting*'s content could even complement that of craft-focused books.

Note how the author hooks the agent and editor right from the start. She introduces something that we all commonly know and then shows how that common belief is only "half the story."

You should point out what is different in your project as early on in your proposal as possible in order to hook the agent or editor. This is very important to do when the topic is general, like writing.

If you plan to take the approach this author has and state that your book has no competition, make sure you have done your research and that your claim is true. Most books have competitive titles and, even with your unique approach, your book is still going to be competitive in its category.

Market/Audience

Powerwriting is *not* aimed at professional writers (copywriters, etc.) and is not aimed at other people wishing purely to write consumer advertising copy—that is an even more specialized discipline and there are several books out there already dealing with that.

However, contrary to popular belief, advertising forms only a relatively small part of the total business communication mix. Today, the role of advertising is purely to sell product/service through online or offline media to the customer. The remainder of business communication covers:

1. All the online and offline communications a business has with its customers other than upfront advertising (service, instructions, packaging, brochures, leaflets, catalogues, ongoing CRM, upselling, etc.)

2. All the online and offline communications a business has with other key groups/stakeholders, i.e., shareholders, potential/existing investors, internal managers/executives/ workers, suppliers, wholesalers/retailers/dealers, media, influencers, new recruits, trade associations, government bodies, etc.

In any case, *Powerwriting* will cover all forms of advertising not generally handled by "above-the-line" consumer advertising agencies. It will cover advertising often dealt with in-house or by other communications agencies and consultancies.

After discussing who her book would not apply to, the author then goes on to make the strong statement as to who her audience is. Your agent and editor need to know your market, and it's your job to define it in the best light possible.

There are many ways to show the size of your market. Obviously, hard facts like statistics work best since they give editors concrete numbers in their heads. But remember, there are other ways. While this author does not use statistics to show potential market size, she makes a strong case for the market for this book through her extensive knowledge of the industry.

Large organizations do use professional business writers to help them with communications aimed at these "non-advertising" categories sometimes, especially when they have a major problem to overcome. That's why professionals like Suzan St. Maur are in business.

However, in the vast majority of cases they attempt to do most of it in-house. In the main, they do it badly, and they know it. Hence the need for *Powerwriting*.

So, *Powerwriting*'s audience is:

Business: Corporate executives, management, SME owner/managers, sole traders/consultants, professionals. Of especial, but not exclusive, interest to sales and marketing personnel, HR personnel, corporate/public affairs staff, etc. All forms of marketing and business communications agencies and production companies with the possible exception of mainstream consumer advertising agencies (who think they know it all!). Public speakers, support staff of senior executives, etc. Companies selling by mail order/e-commerce, property developers/estate agents, businesses in the hospitality industry, etc.

Non business: voluntary organizations, charities, political bodies, government departments.

International market

Powerwriting is non-parochial, so it is suitable for all English language markets and also for translation into other languages rel-

To sum up the market, the author clearly states who this book will benefit and she even injects a little humor. A long list of specific types of people help gives to agents and editors a clear image of your book's potential. You should think through every possibility before you write your proposal.

Sales in international markets can give your proposal an edge. If you think your topic is appropriate for international sales, then by all means make that clear in your proposal.

evant to industrialized nations. It is also well suited to audiobook and online publication.

The Internet connection

Powerwriting, naturally, covers both online and offline communications. It is not an "Internet book" along the lines of the current vogue, but a book about writing, whatever the medium.

Powerwriting is, therefore, targeted for the marketplace as it will be from—let's say—2002 onwards, which experts predict will see a "settling" of the current online upheaval and which will put online writing into its rightful, important place within the overall communications mix.

Style and approach

Very informal, some humor, anecdotes where relevant to illustrate. Some short examples and exercises. Fun to read, *not* a boring textbook. The author sharing her skills and experience with the reader on a friendly one-to-one basis.

Illustrations not required, cartoons optional.

Endorsements

Suzan St. Maur works for a number of key international business leaders, all of whom fully appreciate her abilities as a writer. Endorsements and an appropriate foreword should be forthcoming with no problems.

Stating that this project works for online communications brings another audience into the picture. The author shows that her title will have value over time and is capitalizing on a growing trend.

Create a picture for your agent or editor by describing how you intend to approach your subject matter. Is it going to be funny? Technical? You will need to describe your style as is done here.

Endorsements show that experts and notable figures have put their stamp of approval on your book. If you can, include specific names of people who will endorse your book. Or you can simply note your connections to secure these endorsements once your manuscript is complete.

The 10-second and 30-second sell

10 seconds:

Powerwriting is the first book ever to give you the tools you need to approach business writing properly—the *real* key to success.

30 seconds:

Whether you work for a huge multinational corporation or a small community project ... this is the first-ever business book to reveal the real secrets of success in writing your online and offline communications.

Powerwriting teaches you how to think before you write—and get your message to work for the audience you need to address. Then, it shows you how to write that message so it gets the results you want—every time.

Delivery information

Length 60,000–80,000 words. Full MS within six to twelve months of contract. Full chapter breakdown/synopses and sample chapter available now.

The author

Canadian-born, UK-based Suzan St. Maur has twenty-five years of experience as a senior consultant and writer in business communications, working on projects for both external and internal audiences.

Her corporate clients include AXA Insurance Group, General Motors Europe, Norwich Union, The RAC, Clerical Medical Inter-

---

Giving the reader the down and dirty sell of your book—in 10 or 30 seconds—is a clever way to show that your proposed book is marketable. With so many books on the market, it's important to be able to pitch the concept of your book in a short period of time. By including this in your pitch, you are accomplishing two things: (1) you've proven that you have a succinct hook for your book, and (2) you've given an agent or editor the perfect tool they need to pitch your book to others.

Be realistic in your delivery date. If you're not sure about how long it will take, then leave that information out. If you decide to take the agent route, then your agent can help you figure this out and include the information when the proposal is ultimately submitted to a publisher.

national, and numerous others. She is also much sought after as a speechwriter for celebrities and business leaders.

Suzan has written six published books so far, including three previous business communication titles. In addition, she writes for various business and equestrian publications and Web sites.

She is a member of British MENSA, the Professional Speakers Association, the British Horse Society, and in 1997 was elected to Associate Membership of the Institute of the Motor Industry in recognition of her contribution to automotive communications and training projects.

Background to *Powerwriting*

As a professional business writer, Suzan has witnessed (and been called upon to correct) countless examples of both offline and online communications that have failed through inadequate and inappropriate thinking. Now that more and more business communication is written in-house by managers and executives, the problem is getting far worse.

Yet previous books on business writing—even, Suzan sheepishly admits, her own previous titles—do not address the "think before you write" requirements of business communication with anything like enough emphasis or detail. The result is that in-house managers and executives reading such books do not realize how and why they can go so disastrously wrong. Unwittingly, therefore, existing books on business writing merely help readers to craft well-structured words on poorly-structured foundations.

The author has great credentials in this area and includes some specific companies that make readers take note. As a previously published author she has a great track record for ultimately delivering a good book.

If you have an affiliation with a speakers association and a schedule of upcoming events, mention this. This shows what avenues you have available to create buzz and back-of-the-room sales.

The author's personal experience as a business writer shows she has a real connection to the topic. Always make sure to connect your experience and expertise to the material in the book.

Why do other books fail to address this "front end" issue—the foundations?

Presumably, all books on business writing are written by experts like Suzan. Expert business writers have lived with the ethos of "think before you write" all their working lives, to the extent that it has become a subconscious instinct. Consequently, if you are a professional writer teaching non-specialists how to do it, it is an understandable oversight to assume they understand the need to structure their messages on the basis of a thorough knowledge of the audience. The trouble is, as Suzan has discovered the hard way, they don't.

The objective of *Powerwriting* is to put that right. It will be the first book on business writing ever to do it well and is likely to attract a great deal of interest and comment as a result.

Suzan's previous books:

- *The Jewellery Book* (Magnum & St. Martins Press 1981) co-written with Norbert Streep
- *The Home Safety Book* (Jill Norman/Robert Hale 1984)
- *The A to Z of Video and AV Jargon* (Routledge 1986)
- *Writing Words That Sell* (Lennard/Musterlin 1989 & Mercury 1990) co-written with John Butman
- *Writing Your Own Scripts & Speeches* (McGraw-Hill 1991)
- *The Horse Lover's Joke Book* (The Kenilworth Press September 2001)

Explaining why other books fail to meet the "front end" issue shows that the author has given this a lot of thought and is prepared to make this book reader friendly. She is dedicated to making the book beneficial for the non-specialist, which is what her audience is. This is a great distinction.

If you have any previously published books, you will want to make a list of them for your agent and editor. They will want to know all you have done and to see sales records to back your claims. If this is your first book project but you have been published by a major magazine or newspaper, you will want to make note of that. All published articles, stories, etc., are working credentials for you.

Powerwriting
The hidden skills you need to transform your business writing

Chapters

Introduction

1. Think first, write later
How to think clearly and avoid being sidetracked

2. What do you need to communicate? (Really?)
The message brief—what you want your words to achieve

3. Who is your audience?
Who, where, how, when, and in what mood

4. How will the audience receive your message?
Different media and how your message will be seen/heard

5. Your final message
Putting the elements together into a good message structure

6. How to speak your audience's language
Approach, style, and words the audience will identify with

7. The nuts and bolts
Some tips on grammar, spelling, and other basics

8. Now start writing
Enough theory, let's see how it works

The chapter outline is concise and to the point. The author provides just enough information to give readers a sense of the overall concept. You need to decide for yourself if doing it this way works for your proposal. If an agent or author is not familiar with your work (remember this is a published author already), you may need flesh out the content of each chapter in a more detailed way as is done in some of the other sample proposals.

9. How to get the best from paper-based media
Some tips on how to write powerfully for print

10. How to get the best from electronic media
Some tips on how to write powerfully for online, video, and audio

11. How to get the best from "live" communication
Some tips on how to create powerful presentations

Outroduction

The author includes a good number of chapters—not too many that it is overwhelming, but enough to break the book into digestible pieces. Always keep that in mind as you are thinking about your book's organization.

Some excerpts from Chapter 3 ...

"Get to know your audience as well as you know yourself"

It's easy to fall into the trap of thinking you know who your readers or viewers are. Unless you're one of them, you usually don't. And that's the *Powerwriting* key: To get your message across effectively and to get the results you want, you have to know your audience as well as you know yourself.

+ + + + + + + + +

The point of getting to know your audience as well as you know yourself is to know how your message will be received in real life, and what it will really mean to the recipients. If you know that, you can structure your message so that it will be as effective as possible, whether it's intended to sell, motivate, inform, entertain, instruct, or whatever. The end product of this process is always the same, no matter what—your message has to do something real for the audience, especially if you want them to do something for you in return (like buy your product, or agree to support your proposals.)

Do yourself a favor. Take a felt-tip pen and a piece of white paper, and write this down:

Powerwriting = what's in it for them

Now pin the piece of paper up on the wall of your office or workspace. That's your motto whenever you write *anything* that's to be read by anyone other than you, or possibly your local laundry and dry cleaners.

These chapter excerpts are creative and give the reader a good sense of the style and format of the book. It shows that the author has a good grasp on the material to be covered in each chapter. We've included them to show you that there are many ways to present information in your proposal, and you don't always have to follow the same method or format as everyone else.

+ + + + + + + + +

Key question 1: What does it feel like to be in their shoes?
Okay, you don't need to be a Method actor and role-play for weeks, but you need to anticipate the audience's problems, the pressures they experience, the politics they may have to deal with, their financial circumstances, and how they view the world generally. **It's not enough to know that they're a pharmaceutical sales force or car drivers or bank employees or newspaper editors.** That tells you nothing other than their titles. Try to find out what really makes them tick. And don't worry if you can't take a few days off to work in a staff canteen or in a newspaper office. You can achieve a great deal by simply firing up your own imagination and empathy. And yes, we're *all* capable of doing that if we try hard enough.

Key question 2: Why should they care about your message? Unless it spells out what's in it for them they won't care, and they'll be right not to. So don't leave that until the end, no matter how much you may feel that you need to build up to it with preamble. Preamble is powerless, especially when it's being read or heard by a busy person. If you can grab their attention with what's in it for them right from the beginning, they are far more likely to give your message the attention it deserves.

Key question 3: Are these the people who will react to your message ultimately? Sometimes your immediate audience is not in a position to make a decision single-handedly to act on your message—they may be the monkey rather than the organ—grinder.

When providing sample excerpts such as these, you are killing two birds with one stone, per se. One, it got you out of having to write chapter summaries, and two, you didn't have to provide a full sample chapter to show your intended style and tone. This approach is okay if you are able to convey the full message of your book in this format, but if you think for even one minute that your agent or editor may not get the full picture, then maybe you should rethink your approach. Less is not always better.

There will be someone else in the background—a spouse, partner, colleague, several colleagues, superiors, financial controller, or other unseen third party—who may have some or even all of the say in the final decision. You should be able to determine if this is so as part of your research or even just by common sense. And you must ensure there's something in it for all them.

+ + + + + + + + + +

While we're on it, **let's have a look at the peculiarities of the main media in use today, and how we can use that knowledge to enhance our understanding of the audience involved with each.**

+ + + + + + + + + +

Brochures and leaflets. Brochures are not often read right away. Think back to the last time you picked up some travel or gardening or DIY brochures. Did you start reading at Page 1 and continue without stopping until you reached the end of the last page? No, and neither does your audience. **Nearly everyone will browse quite swiftly through a brochure and note the key points, if they can find any.** Later they will go back to sections that have caught their eye and read them in more detail. Assuming that the key points have already told them what's in it for them, of course.

+ + + + + + + + + +

Press releases (and the editors who receive them). Here you're dealing with a double audience with somewhat different but allied expectations. Before it even gets to the readers of the publication, your message will have to pass the test of appealing to an

The author uses boldface type to call out important parts of her book. It helps to draw attention to the tone and important topics that are covered. Any tool that helps ease of reading is a good one. In case an agent or editor decides to start skimming, these types of things draw their eyes back to the page.

editor or other journalist. These come from a breed of humans (some would even argue that!) with a very short attention span and, dare I say it, a certain sloth. Anything they receive either electronically or in print has to ring their chimes very quickly or it goes straight into the cylindrical filing tray. They haven't got the time or inclination to translate a dull and boring message into a story that will interest their audience. That's your job. And **these people make bloodhounds look incompetent when it comes to sniffing out camouflaged advertising in what purports to be editorial.** They will accept a plug or two for your product, service, or activity, but they are actually very good at judging what's in it for their audience. If they get it wrong and there isn't enough in it for their audience, they could lose their jobs.

+ + + + + + + + + +

Online communications. Although there are significant differences among the various types of online communication, they all have one critical thing in common: They're read off a screen. There are substantial benefits, too, in that while your message is on someone's screen, usually it has their undivided attention. You are genuinely "one-to-one" with them and that's something you must respect—you are literally "in their face" and encroaching on very personal territory. **The bad news about online communications is that your message can be "disappeared" faster from a screen than with any other medium.** If there's not enough "in it for them," it's a case of one click and it's gone forever.

This top part of this page shows are familiar the author is with the industry. This proves that her advice is going to be sound advice that will benefit readers. If you know an industry from the inside, make sure that is evident in your proposal.

The author highlights a good example here, since online is now the way most people communicate in business. Agents and editors will see the value of this book as it taps into a growing need and trend.

There are a few more stark facts about online communications that significantly influence how your message is received. One, **79 percent of online readers don't read—they scan.** That's a little like the way people browse through brochures. What it means is that your message must be delivered in a way that allows key points—and benefits, of course—to be picked up at the same speed as readers scroll and scan.

Secondly, **when people read from a screen they do so at a rate 25 percent slower than they read print on a paper page.** That's because, despite high-resolution screens and all the other technological wizardry, on-screen text is harder to read. For this reason, your messages have to be very much more concise than they do for printed media. Some experts say **screen text should be just half the length of its paper equivalent.** Let's now have a swift look at the circumstances in which people receive each of the main types of online communication.

E-mails. "This morning when I got into the office there were 73 e-mails waiting for me," said one of my clients recently, the CEO of a large organization. "And that's the same as most days," she continued. "My system has a feature which lets you read the first line of each one without opening it. If it doesn't grab my interest in the first line I go straight for the delete tab." **People are busy and e-mails take time to open, never mind read. And normally there are lots of others there surrounding yours, all shouting for attention.**

+ + + + + + + + + +

Her last paragraph of information sounds very similar to how agents and editors look at proposals! There are a lot of proposals fighting for attention, so make yours stand out or else it may never be read.

Published in 2003 by Broadway Books

AMY WEINTRAUB Author

The idea for this book arose as a result of my own healing from depression through daily yoga practice. I had been in therapy and on antidepressants for years and lived life as though I were moving through a dense fog with heavy weights on my arms and legs. When I took my first yoga class in 1989, the fog began to lift. I felt connected to my own feelings in a more direct way, which allowed me to begin to reconnect with others. I felt more hopeful and positive about my life. The immediate feel-good effect lasted for several days. And when it wore off, I practiced again.

Back then, there was little empirical data on the effects of yoga on managing mood, nor were there any books that included yoga as an adjunct treatment for depression and mood disorders like anxiety and post-traumatic stress disorder. But after years of psychotherapy and medication that did little to break through the numbness of depression, when I began to feel better, I knew that my yoga practice had something to do with it. I became a Kripalu Yoga teacher in 1992 because I was passionate about sharing the gifts of my recovery from depression. I began writing about yoga and its effect on the emotional body for national magazines like *Yoga Journal, Yoga International,* and *Psychology Today*. At first, my articles were based on anecdotal evidence—my own and that of the many practitioners and teachers I spoke with who had found an empowering way to manage their moods with their yoga practices. And then, as more and more studies that measured the effects of yoga practice on mood began showing up in medical journals, I was able to include solid empirical evidence for the shift in mood after yoga practice.

Yoga for Depression: A Compassionate Guide to Relieve Suffering Through Yoga. The title and subtitle arose naturally from the subject. I originally wanted to include the word "compassion" in the main title, but my editor, Kristine, encouraged me to be as direct as possible about the subject and include "compassion"—the heart of my practice and my title—in the subtitle.

I have written several novels that have been finalists in national contests, but none of them have been published. This is my first published book.

As a yoga teacher and reader, I had a fairly good idea about what was missing from the market. Most yoga books at that time focused on the physical postures and, therefore, the physiological effects. Some included yogic breathing and meditation techniques, but when I checked Books in Print to see what other titles had been published on the subject of yoga and mental health, I found nothing other than the book I had edited by my dear friend and colleague, Stephen Cope, *Yoga and the Quest for the True Self.* But not even Cope's book directly addressed depression, anxiety disorders, and other psychiatric imbalances.

After the proposal was accepted by Broadway Books, I finished the first draft in a year. More than half of the first draft was completed in the three months I was Scholar in Residence at Kripalu Center, where I could practice yoga and write all day long, knowing that nourishing vegetarian meals and a comfortable bed awaited me.

But in small ways, I have been writing this book all my life just by living for years with depression and then experiencing recovery through daily practice.

My book was a project whose time had come. I sent my proposal to three agents in New York and one in Boston, those whose work I respected because of their handling of other projects. I was also looking for agents who handled literary fiction, in the hope that they might also find a home for my novels. As it turned out, all were interested in the nonfiction book proposal and less interested in selling my fiction. I went with Deirdre Mullane in the Joseph Spieler Agency, because she was enthusiastic about the project and I liked her. It didn't hurt that the Joseph Spieler Agency is located in Carnegie Hall, and I love classical music. The first time I visited the office, I heard violins!

DIERDRE MULLANE Agent

The idea for a book is the first thing that captures my attention—and what a great idea this was. There was a clear need and demonstrably strong market for books for those who suffer from depression (who tend to buy books, and buy them all), and for books on yoga. And yet, despite the case that Amy makes for the usefulness of yoga to relieve depression, no one had brought these strands together. So, there was the exciting combination of both the tried and true and the cutting edge. But the idea is only the beginning. I was impressed as well by Amy's clear and beautiful writing. The better the writing, the stronger the proposal, and I knew immediately when I saw Amy's initial proposal that this was not only a book—this was a very big book.

Beyond the strength of the editorial concept, which combined a clear need for the book with the author's demonstrable writing skills, publishers must be convinced that they can really sell the book, often at aggressive levels, and they rely on the author to help them. There are so many books published today that even the best among them have to fight for attention. Amy was well connected in "yoga circles," and it was evident that she could get the significant figures in the areas of yoga, psychology, and even memoirists and literary figures, to support the book and provide endorsements, bringing the book to the widest possible audience. In addition, Amy's work on yoga and depression had been featured in several prominent magazines, demonstrating to the publisher the potential interest in the book and its fit with this readership.

Amy had, really, the perfect qualifications to write this book. She brought a strong voice and personal experience to the project, which would connect immediately with the reader. She writes beautifully, getting her message across with both precision and feeling; and, professionally, because of her work teaching and lecturing, she had the ability to promote the book, not simply for one season, but beyond. She's an immensely attractive, articulate, authentic spokesperson for the book—both on the page and off.

KRISTINE PUOPOLO Editor

This was one of the best proposals I'd seen for a work of practical nonfiction. It had everything: a fresh idea, a compelling promise, an exceptionally well-qualified author (her clips on the subject from many yoga magazines were included). And the writing in the sample material was both authoritative and beautiful. Amy is also a creative writer and novelist, and it really came across in the loveliness of her writing on the topic of depression, suffering, and the promise of relief through yoga.

I took the proposal to my acquisitions board, which includes people from our sales department, in order to make sure that the stores would welcome the book. They told me, amusingly, "Yoga is hot, depression is hot, what's the problem?" So we made a preemptive offer, which means we made our first offer our best offer in order to take the book off the table.

PROPOSAL
Yoga for Depression:
A Compassionate Guide to Relieve Suffering through Yoga
by Amy Weintraub

Table of Contents
Overview
About the Author
Supplementary Materials List

Chapter-by-Chapter Outline

Foreword by Stephen Cope
Preface: Empty Pockets

Part One: Exquisite Body Work—Yoga Postures that Help
Chapter One: A House on Fire—How We Suffer
Chapter Two: Why Yoga Works
Chapter Three: Lotus of Many Petals

Part Two: Healing Breath—Breathing Techniques that Help
Chapter Four: Putting Out the Fire—Breathing that Calms
Chapter Five: Fire in the Belly—Breathing that Energizes
Chapter Six: Art of Living—Breathing that Heals

Part Three: Meditation Techniques that Help
Chapter Seven: Relaaaax—Meditation that Calms
Chapter Eight: Wake Up! Meditation that Energizes

What a great title! This is an obvious tell-and-sell title. When an agent or editor sees this title they immediately know what the book does. Furthermore, the promise of the book is made clear through a powerful subtitle.

This author combines her proposal table of contents with her book's table of contents and puts them all on one page. There is nothing wrong with this as long as you format the list so that it is clear what comprises the actual book.

This author uses parts to break down her information. There are four distinct areas that readers will get help from. The part titles show this at a glance. It also shows that she has thought about the best way to organize her information and that it is not going to be one big jumble. Editors and agents like authors who have the ability to organize their own material logically to make it clear and reader friendly.

OVERVIEW

Estimates show that more than twenty-five million Americans are treated with antidepressants each year, at a cost of more than 50 billion dollars, and many more who suffer from depression go undiagnosed and untreated. Depression is a deadly disease. Even before the tragic events of September 11, 2001, depression was spreading in epidemic proportions. Several years ago, researchers at the Harvard School of Public Health and World Health Organization (WHO) cited depression as the fourth leading cause of death worldwide, and, by 2020, depression was expected to be the second leading cause of death. And since the attack on the World Trade Center, doctors are prescribing more antidepressants and anti-anxiety medications than ever before. According to a report published by the University of Washington's Kids Count just prior to September 11, mental health problems had already surpassed injuries as the single most common reason for hospitalizations among children, five to nineteen in the state of Washington. And currently, nationwide, suicide is the third biggest killer of young people between the ages of fifteen and twenty-four.

Millions who have found that their symptoms were alleviated with antidepressants are dissatisfied with the host of debilitating side effects like weight gain, lethargy, and sexual dysfunction that equal, and sometimes outweigh, the medication's obvious benefits. Many Americans are looking beyond biomedicine to Complementary and Alternative Medicine (CAM) for the alleviation of their symptoms, pursuing treatments that involve herbs, diet, megavitamins, essential

The author leads the proposals with very dramatic statistics that grab your attention. She also ties her subject matter into a trend that is growing and clearly states that with a variety of evidence. She also uses statistics from very credible sources. Agents and editors want to see that you are getting your information from sources that indicate that you have thoroughly researched your topic.

fatty acids, Chinese Medicine, acupuncture, and mind-body therapies. Books like Michael J. Norden's *Beyond Prozac* and others like
Listening to Prozac, Natural Prozac, and *Dealing with Depression
Naturally* that talk about treating depression, with or without medica
tion, become best-sellers as patients try to heal themselves and as their
families, friends, and doctors try to help them. Andrew Solomon's *The
Noonday Demon: An Atlas of Depression* has won critical attention
and high sales. William Styron's book about his own nightmare of
depressive illness, *Darkness Visible,* outstripped the combined sales of
all his other books. And there is a host of new books about depression
that offer natural remedies—*Undoing Depression, Change Your Brain,
Change Your Life, The Antidepressant Survival Guide, The Omega-3
Connection*—finding success in the marketplace.

At the same time, more than 15 million Americans are practicing yoga, which, according to the recent cover article in *Time* (April
23, 2001), is twice as many as practiced five years ago. No longer an
esoteric discipline followed only by men in loincloths seeking Nirva-
na, yoga is practiced by your grandmother at her senior center, your
neighbor at his health club, and your uncle at the nearby yoga studio.
A couple of years ago, a yoga mat was a specialty item, carried in
new age catalogs and yoga studios. Today, even the big box super
chains are carrying sticky mats and other props for yoga classes.
What's more, medical science is coming closer to establishing the
empirical evidence to support practitioners' claims that the practice
of Hatha yoga, including breathing techniques and meditation, has

The author mentions some books on this topic that have become best-sellers. Even though
you might include this information in your competitive analysis section, it's fine to hook agents
and editors early on in your proposal with some competitive data that makes clear why your
proposal has the elements to make the best-selling list, too.

Here the author cites a *Time* magazine article that provides evidence that yoga is a fast and
growing market—and is now reaching a mainstream audience. If you have read timely articles
on your subject matter that have been published by national magazines or newspapers, be
sure to shed light on the issue by noting the publications.

beneficial effects on their emotional well-being, their mental acuity, and in many cases has alleviated their depression.

Whether a new student signs up for his first yoga class to add a stretching component to his workout routine, or because Aunt Nancy lost fifteen pounds practicing in a heated room, or because Madonna looked good playing an Ashtanga Yoga teacher in *The Next Best Thing*, students claim the practice changes their lives. The specific techniques used in a yoga class—postures, pranayama breathing, meditation, and relaxation—have all been shown, independently and together, to create an immediate biochemical state that feels good. Many say that the immediate "feel good" effect of doing yoga and the awareness and equanimity that develop with long-term practice have helped them lighten their mood and even recover from depression.

For thirty years, major controlled studies at Harvard, conducted by Herbert Benson, M.D., and his colleagues, and duplicated at other research institutions, have documented the efficacy of relaxation techniques such as transcendental meditation in reducing anxiety-based depression, lowering levels of cortisol (the stress hormone), and promoting a state of emotional well-being. (Herbert Benson is the author of the best-selling 1976 book, *The Relaxation Response*, a new edition of which was released by William Morrow in 2000.) Since the early eighties, Jon Cabot-Zinn, Ph.D., the author of the best-selling *Full Catastrophe Living*, and his colleagues at the University of Massachusetts have documented the physiological and psychological benefits of the eight-week mindfulness-based training

The topic sentence of the first paragraph on this page is very engaging. The author connects the book to everyday life by referring to how yoga is part of the very fabric of our culture. You should always consider how your book connects to your reader's life. This will show agents and editors that your book can have personal meaning for people.

The author cites scientific evidence to back up the significance of her book. This is a good way to show that your proposed topic is a sound one. Any evidence you can use to back your theory is a good testimony to your claim.

they developed called the Stress Reduction and Relaxation Program (SRRP), which includes a yoga posture component.

The studies that have placed primary emphasis on yoga (but generally include a component of relaxation or meditation as well) have been smaller and less well funded. Even so, this research is demonstrating impressive results in the alleviation of depression.

This book will look at the current research linking yoga and meditation to recovery from depression and will include interviews with a wide range of mental health professionals, who are using aspects of yoga—postures, breathing, relaxation exercises—in treating their clients. The book will explore the different schools of yoga and yoga therapy being practiced in the United States, revealing what founders and senior teachers have discovered about how those systems may alleviate depression. Included will be excerpts from interviews with many real people who say their yoga practice has been essential in their recovery from depression.

Yoga experts interviewed for this book include the nationally known psychologist and yogi, Richard Miller, Ph.D.; the author, psychotherapist and yogi, Stephen Cope, M.S.W., L.I.C.S.W.; psychologist and longtime self-discovery program director at Kripalu, Deborah Orth, Ph.D.; author and Viniyoga therapist, Gary Kraftsow; international Iyengar yoga instructor, Patricia Walden; yoga doctor and founder of Prana Yoga, Jeff Migdow, M.D.; founder of Phoenix Rising Yoga Therapy, Michael Lee, M.A.; and many others. Medical experts and researchers interviewed will include Jon Cabot-Zinn,

The author gives specific examples of interviews to be included in the book. This shows that the author has thought out the material and is prepared to write the book. If you are planning to interview people for your project, it may be a good idea to cite them in your proposal. Agents and editors will want to know "who" you plan to get your information from.

Since the author is not a trained doctor or psychologist, she specifically describes how she will collaborate with other experts to make sure the book has credibility. Not having the necessary credibility and expertise on a topic can be a red flag to agents and editors. But here the author preempts that concern with excellent experts who will consult on the project.

M.D.; Zindel Segal, Ph.D.; Karl Goodkin, M.D., Ph.D., F.A.P.A.; Dean Ornish, M.D.; and others.

The book will look at real people's lives, including the author's, to talk about the various kinds of depressions and their treatments with yoga postures, yogic breathing, and meditation. Written in a lively prose style, each chapter will contain interesting cases and anecdotes about people with diagnoses that range from mild melancholia to severe bipolar disorder. The author will write the book in consultation with several clinical psychologists who work in the area of depression, including George Goldman, Ph.D.; clinical director of the Southern Arizona Center for Sexual Assault (SACASA); Rubin Naiman, Ph.D., a clinical and transpersonal psychologist who, in addition to his private practice, leads workshops at Canyon Ranch in Tucson and other locations around the country; and international yoga teacher and clinical psychologist Richard Miller, Ph.D., founder of the journal *Yoga Therapy*. Chapter Three will analyze the physical postures, both from the standpoint of practitioners' experiences and from the research pertaining to the physiological and psychological effects of the poses. Chapter Four will explore the psychological effect and the potential for emotional release in the practice of easy poses held for a longer period of time. Chapters Five and Six will explore the psychological benefits of the numerous breathing techniques, from evidence gleaned empirically and anecdotally, noting the differences in using the breath to treat anxiety-based depression and dysthymic, or chronic, depression. Chapter Seven will look at a particular breath that has proven to

It's nice that the author gives brief, one-sentence descriptions of each chapter. They give a nice overview of the book, and help the agent or editor see the project in its entire scope. It also shows that the author has a firm handle on what her book will include and how she plans to present it.

be as effective as ECT in recovery from a major depressive episode. Chapters Eight and Nine will consider the various relaxation and meditation techniques that have been documented to lessen psychological distress, including depression. Chapter Ten will examine the elements that make for a good yoga class and make recommendations about how to find the teacher and class that are most suited to you. Each chapter will include a "Practice" section with recommendations from yoga therapists, yoga teachers, and practitioners of techniques that alleviate depression. An appendix will include a compendium of resources—books, tapes, special programs, yoga schools, and yoga therapies that offer specific recommendations for depression.

Well-known author, therapist, and yogi Stephen Cope will write the foreword.

The market for this book is not only the millions of people who themselves or whose loved ones suffer from depression but also the additional millions who are practicing or are considering the practice of yoga at their gym, health club, church, neighborhood yoga studio, or, along with one of the popular yoga videos, in the privacy of their own homes. These people are already buying books on the practical and philosophical aspects of yoga and meditation, making books by nationally known yoga teachers like Donna Farhi, David Swenson, Dona Holleman, Beryl Bender Birch, and Stephen Cope popular. The author, herself a professional yoga teacher and writer, will be able to promote this book through her workshops, classes, media appearances, and articles in national magazines

The author has secured a well-known expert to write the foreword. This adds a lot of value and credibility to your project. Don't make any promises you can't keep here. If you are planning to get a foreword from a well-known expert or celebrity, make sure you have the okay upfront before giving this information to the agent or editor. There is nothing worse than falling back on your word as a writer.

The paragraph describing the huge potential market succeeds at pointing out that sales for this book could be great. The fact that the author is willing to promote her book at workshops, classes, and in the media is an additional bonus.

There are a number of successful books about the benefits of yoga and many on depression, some of which are mentioned above, but there are no books currently on the market that not only show the strong evidence, both anecdotal and empirical, that yoga can help alleviate depression, but can also offer insight, comfort, and practical advice on how to use yoga for relief. The one that comes closest is Stephen Cope's book, *Yoga and the Quest for the True Self* (Bantam, 1999), now in its fifteenth printing. This book examines yoga and yogic philosophy as it comes to us from India and compares it to Western adult psychological development. The author of this proposal was the developmental editor for Cope's book, acknowledged as "helping to build this book from the ground up."

About the Author

Twenty years ago, Amy Weintraub, M.F.A., R.Y.T., was an award-winning television producer and writer, suffering from depression. Throughout most of the '80s, she was treated for a depression so severe that she had trouble putting two shoes in a shoebox. Her own recovery from depression began in 1989, when she began a daily yoga practice. Within a year, she was no longer taking medication, and in 1992, she became a certified Kripalu Yoga Teacher. Today, she is certified by the Yoga Alliance as a Professional Yoga Teacher (500 hr) and a Kripalu Teacher Mentor. She leads workshops on yoga and depression and regularly writes on the subject for national magazines, including *Yoga Journal* and *Psychology Today*.

The author cites a competing book that is very successful, which she helped to develop, while at the same time indicating that there are no books that link yoga and depression. This says there is a market for her title, and her approach is unique to its category.

The author includes her own personal connection to the topic of the book in her bio. This is a great way to show you have personal expertise on the topic. The author also shows she has the credentials to be an expert on this topic. Make a list of your relevant credentials and include them in descending order of importance in your bio section. Your goal is to prove you are the best person to write your book.

Weintraub has done extensive yoga training in the United States and in India, including her basic certification at Kripalu Center in Lenox, Massachusetts, and advanced trainings at the Lakulish Institute in Gujarat, India, Vivekanandra Kendra in Mysore, India, and the Narayana Gurukala in Tamil Nadu, India.

She currently lives in Tucson, Arizona, where she teaches yoga at various locations and fiction writing at the University of Arizona Writing Works Center. She also teaches at Kripalu Center. Her feature articles and essays have appeared in a number of national magazines, including *Yoga Journal, Poets & Writers, Psychology Today, The Writer's Chronicle, Spirit of Change,* and *Healing Spas and Retreats.* She also edits books on spiritual psychology, including the much-praised *Yoga and the Quest for the True Self* by Stephen Cope (Bantam, 1999). She holds the master of fine arts degree in Writing and Literature from the Bennington Writing Seminars, Bennington College.

Her novel-in-progress, *Broken Strings,* was a semi-finalist in the 1999 James Jones Literary Society Award, the 1998 Pirate's Alley William Faulkner Award, and a finalist in the Heekin Group Foundation Fellowship for two years in a row. She has won numerous literary prizes for her short fiction, and her film documentaries have received awards from the National Academy of Television Arts and Sciences, San Francisco State University, and many other national competitions.

The author has experience as a teacher, which is always a plus in self-help or how-to books. It means that she knows how to successfully convey her knowledge to others. If you teach anything related to your topic, mention it. If you don't, consider teaching as a great platform for your book.

List any awards and recognition you have received as a result of any previous publications. It can't hurt to pat yourself on the back a bit. Your publisher may use this information later as a marketing tool for book buyers.

Author's Writing Samples Related to Subject

1. "The Natural Prozac"—*Yoga Journal*, (Nov/Dec, 1999) A 4,500 word feature article by Amy Weintraub on yoga and depression.
2. "Yoga: It's Not Just An Exercise"—*Psychology Today*, (Nov/Dec, 2000) A "Health Headlines" story by Amy Weintraub on yoga and depression.
3. "Depression Update"—*Yoga Journal* (July/August, 2001) A "Wellbeing" story by Amy Weintraub on yoga and depression.
4. "Living Out Loud"—*Yoga Journal* (March/April, 2000) A "Teacher to Teacher" column by Amy Weintraub about language and yoga.

Supporting Document

1. "Yoga as a Doorway to Mental Health"—KYTA Yoga Bulletin (Winter, 2001) An interview with Amy Weintraub.

This list of published articles related to the topic of the book shows the author already has a platform on this topic. The articles are in well-known magazines. Since these magazines, such as *Yoga Journal* and *Psychology Today,* have such large circulations, the author could have easily included circulation numbers.

Chapter-by-Chapter Outline

Foreword:

Internationally known yoga teacher, psychotherapist, and author, Stephen Cope will discuss the way Western psychotherapeutic theory and practice dovetail with Yogic philosophy and practice, particularly as they consider the treatment of depression.

Preface: Empty Pockets

I will discuss my own depression and how my life changed after I began a daily yoga practice in 1989. I will also summarize the general trends in depression research and yoga, and discuss why this book is important now.

Part One: Exquisite Body Work—Yoga Postures that Help

Chapter One: A House on Fire—How We Suffer

This chapter will explore the three main types of depressive illness, which include major depression, dysthymia, and manic depression, touching on related disorders such as Seasonal Affective Disorder (SAD), and anxiety-based depression. We will look at the lives of a number of yoga practitioners who suffered from these different forms of the illness to see how each of them found their depressions alleviated or better managed through the practice of yoga. I will suggest a specific beginning practice that the reader can follow at home.

The preface is a great place to include a personal story that connects to the topic of the book. Remember, the idea of the summary sections is not overkill but to be clear about what you are writing and how you plan to present it. It should be powerfully developed and consistent in format.

You'll notice that the author has made each title clever and descriptive to not only draw you into the subject matter but also to give you a clear sense of what the chapter is going to be about. Your job is to state your intentions clearly in a descriptive manner.

Chapter Two: Exquisite Body Work—Why Yoga Works

This chapter will look at why yoga postures create a "feel good" state. Material for this chapter will be derived from practitioners' stories, interviews with internationally known yoga doctors like Dean Ornish, M.D. and Jeff Migdow, M.D. The chapter will include current research that examines the endocrine, immune, and psychiatric effects of yoga postures. In the "Practice" section, I'll suggest, in language that the beginning yoga student can follow at home, a pose that calms and soothes the nervous system for anxiety-based depression and mania, and one that energizes the nervous system for dysthymia.

Chapter Three: Lotus of Many Petals—Postures that Help

This chapter will look at the various yoga systems such as Iyengar, Viniyoga, Kundalini, and Kripalu to find their recommendations for specific postures for depression. Internationally known yoga teachers from various traditions, including Iyengar Yoga teacher Patricia Walden and Kripalu Yoga teacher and psychotherapist Michael Kean, Ph.D., will offer a specific set of practices for people suffering from depression, both energizing and calming. This chapter will contain a "Practice" section, including techniques from the various traditions, and may be accompanied by instructional drawings or photos.*

It's fine to highlight key names and experts you'll be referring to in your chapter summaries. Citing specific sources, rather than just general information, makes clear to an agent or editor that you've really done your homework and that you have all the research tools to write a full manuscript.

The original proposal gave chapter summaries for each part of the book and the appendix, though not all are included here. The author specifically identified the types of material she planned to list in her appendix. It's a good idea to include more than just a list of Web sites if you are going to go this route in your proposal. Many of the resources you can list in your appendix will likely be the materials you used to research and write your book in the first place, so this should be very easy to do.

Published in May 2006 by McFarland

WILLIAM G. RAMROTH, JR. Author

I am an architect with over thirty years of experience. Also, I have had a strong interest in philosophy for most of my life. For many years I have noticed that architects, other design professionals, and I tend to make design decisions pragmatically. I decided to combine my interest in both architecture and philosophy and write about how modern architects and theorists use Pragmatism in developing their architectural designs and writing. The final title, *Pragmatism and Modern Architecture*, is not the title I originally chose. The working title I used in my book proposal was *Pragmatism and the Method of Modern Architecture*. After I had written the manuscript, the publisher, McFarland, suggested the shorter title to me. I liked it and readily agreed it was a better choice. *Pragmatism and Modern Architecture* is my first book or, I should say, my first book that has been published.

Throughout the years I have collected quite a number of books about architecture and philosophy. Once I decided to write the proposal, I used books I already had as reference. I supplemented these with Internet searches to fill in the missing pieces I needed in order to write the proposal. Researching to write the proposal was not the same as writing the book. Writing the book required much more extensive research than writing the proposal. It took approximately four weeks to write the proposal.

While *Pragmatism and Modern Architecture* is the first book I have had published, it is not the first book I have written. I first contacted my agent regarding another manuscript I had written—not about architecture, by the way. My first contact was a query letter along with a couple of sample chapters of my manuscript. The agent asked to read the manuscript, she did, accepted me as a client, and our relationship began. During the course of trying to sell my manuscript, my agent suggested that I try writing something about architecture. She suggested that I write down a few ideas, send them to her, and she'd let me know whether they sounded interesting or not. This is how I latched onto the idea of writing about Pragmatism and modern architecture. The agent sent me a copy of a proposal as a go-by for content and formatting purposes. I wrote the proposal. The most difficult thing about the process of getting a proposal accepted is the waiting.

PAM BRODOWSKY Agent

To put it simply Bill fascinated me with this combination. I've always been intrigued by philosophy and architecture, and the mix here was that much more intriguing. He is a talented writer who has the rare ability to write a book that will appeal to both an intellectual audience and the general public.

Book Proposal

PRAGMATISM AND THE METHOD OF
MODERN ARCHITECTURE
by
William G. Ramroth, Jr. AIA

International Literary Arts, LLC
RR 5 Box 5391 A
Moscow, PA 18444
(570) 689-2692

This is a good cover page sent by an agent to an editor. However, if you are the one sending your proposal, include your name and address at the bottom in place of the agent's. You can also include an e-mail address. You want to make it easy for agents or editors to contact you.

The format of your proposal table of contents can vary as much as your proposal itself. The idea of this section is to enable your prospective agent or editor to find the information he desires quickly.

OVERVIEW

Architecture is not origami. A drawing of a building cannot be folded in a clever way to make a real building. A picture of a building is no more architecture than a drawing for a sculpture *is* the sculpture. Architecture cannot be fully captured with pencil and paper. Confined to paper, it is only theoretical. To exist, it must be built. Architecture is a practical art, a product of theory and action.

Pragmatism is the philosophy that synthesizes theory and action. No other worldview stresses the relationship between the two with greater significance and clarity than Pragmatism. Pragmatism is not like origami either. A dry philosophical treatise on Pragmatism does not do justice to its subject. Words on paper do not embrace its spirit. Pragmatism is not just about words any more than architecture is just about pencil lines. Pragmatism is the philosophy of actions, and actions speak louder than both words and lines on paper.

This book is about the relationship between Modern Architecture and the philosophy of Pragmatism. In a nutshell, this book has three objectives: 1) to explain why Pragmatism is the predominant method or philosophy of Modern Architecture, 2) to show that both Pragmatism and Modern Architecture grew from common ideas and events of the mid-nineteenth century, and 3) to give examples of Pragmatism within the architectural work and writings of predominant practitioners and theorists of Modern Architecture.

A building does more than just enclose space and resist gravity and lateral loads. Its existence defines the very space it encloses, and

---

This is a fabulous opening sentence for a proposal because it makes you want to read more. When crafting your opening sentence, think about what's going to grab someone's attention.

Never assume an agent or editor is familiar with your material. The author gives a clear definition of "Pragmatism." It's better to define any terms you think your reader might not know.

The author clearly establishes what his book is about and what it will do for its audience. This is your first stab at getting the attention of an agent or editor. You'll want to be as focused on your content as you are persuasive in your ploy.

it defines the space around it as well. A successful building must respond to many needs. Its design and construction must respect the owner's budgetary constraints. It must meet the demands of the project schedule. It must comply with building code requirements and zoning ordinances. It must abide by the development plans of the city, community or region in which it is sited. Its appearance or façade must respect the aesthetic sensibilities of the jurisdictional architectural review board that will pass judgment on it. It must respond to the health and life safety needs of the fire code and local fire marshal.

Yet, when well executed, a building is a work of art. It can at once uplift the human spirit while enhancing the functional and spatial requirements of its program, its *raison d'etre*. Architecture is a juggling act of technical, financial, functional, and aesthetic parameters. It is Pragmatism that brings these diverse design requirements into balance.

Pragmatism is the philosophy that maintains there is a fundamental connection between ideas and actions. The meaning of an idea lies in the perceived action that the idea brings about. An idea, if it is to have any tangible meaning, must produce an action that is demonstrable, an outcome that is detectable by sense perceptions. The success of the idea can thus be judged by its outcome. Herein is a fundamental insight of Pragmatism: The outcome defines the idea. Look at the outcome. If the idea cannot be seen, there is no concrete idea.

Modern buildings are complicated. They are a homogeneous assemblage of structure; finishes; mechanical, plumbing, and fire protec-

This proposal is well written. The author is a good writer, which he demonstrates as he explains his book. Don't forget that in your proposal, not only do you want to explain your idea, your marketing plans, and your credentials, but you also want to show that you know how to write. You don't have to be showy; just pay attention to what you are writing and how you are writing it. Make sure the finished product is a good showcase of your talent.

tion systems; electrical power, lighting, and communications systems. They must satisfy the owners' spatial requirements, site context requirements, material and system technological requirements, aesthetic and financial requirements. Successful buildings must synthesize criteria that are often at odds with one another. Through their very being, buildings speak of the design ideas, theories, and compromises that brought them into existence. Their voices are heard in their arrangement of spaces, their composition of materials, their mechanical and electrical systems, and in their exterior and interior expressions.

Conscious of it or not, modern architects demonstrate the method of Pragmatism in their work. Architects may assert something else when explaining their work to clients. They may claim some other worldview when talking with colleagues or friends. But the overriding philosophical method that best explains the design process and actions of architects is Pragmatism. In the office or at the job site, architects don the clothes and habits of the pragmatist.

The philosophy of Pragmatism and Modern Architecture grew up together. They share common roots. Their genealogy can be traced to the 1870s, although some suggest that modern architecture began in 1750 at the end of the Baroque period (see the outline for chapter three). Several common ideas and events of the mid-nineteenth century led to their development. By the 1930s, within the span of a single lifetime, both had reached maturity. As Modern Architecture climbed skyward, it did so as a concrete example of Pragmatism, and one of glass and steel as well.

No matter how long, your overview needs to be focused on explaining the concept of your book. This is a tightly written overview, although somewhat lengthy compared to the other examples. However, it states exactly what it needs to in order for the agent or editor to get the full scope of this title.

This book will explore the overlapping histories of Modern Architecture and Pragmatism. It will discuss the conditions and intellectual environment of the nineteenth century that led to their formulation. It will discuss the development of Pragmatism through the ideas of its three American founding fathers: Charles Sanders Peirce, William James, and John Dewey. It will trace the rise of Modern Architecture from the Chicago Fire through the so-called Chicago School and discuss the pragmatic factors contributing to the buildings of that School. It will discuss Modern Architecture's setback with the Columbian Exposition of 1893. It will follow its subsequent development in Europe, in the Bauhaus School. It will discuss Modern Architecture's return to the United States in the form of the International Style and the factors that brought this about. It will discuss the mature stages of Modern Architecture and Pragmatism and address the continuing influence of Pragmatism on today's architecture.

Examples of Pragmatism abound in the writings and works of modern architects. The text will include examples of Pragmatism taken from the writings and buildings of modern architectural theorists and practitioners. These will include the writings of architectural theorists such as Eugene-Emmanuel Viollet-le-Duc, Henry-Russell Hitchcock, and John Ruskin. It will include the writings and works of modern architects such as Louis Sullivan, Frank Lloyd Wright, Le Corbusier, Walter Gropius, and Ludwig Mies van der Rohe. Photographs of buildings will be included when they contribute to the understanding of a particular discussion.

The author continues to explain what the book will cover. He simply spells it out in a series of sentences that start with "It will discuss." This is clear and to the point, no wasted words or time for the agent or editor. He manages to give a complete historical timeline in one paragraph.

MARKET ANALYSIS

Based on a 1999 survey by the National Council of Architectural Registration Boards (NCARB), there are approximately 100,000 practicing architects in the United States. Within the profession there are at least three times that many unlicensed practitioners made up of architectural apprentices, designers, and drafters. There are tens of thousands of university students studying architecture, aspiring to become architects. In addition, there are tens of thousands of practitioners in the related professions of interior design, and landscape architecture. There are hundreds of art and architectural critics throughout the United States writing newspaper columns and magazines articles about architecture. It is impossible to estimate the number of laypersons who have strong interests in architecture and/or philosophy, but it easily must run into the hundreds of thousands.

Most architects, architectural practitioners, and students of architecture have a passion for the theory and history of architecture. It is safe to say that all have a keen and personal interest in the practice of it. Architects read many books and magazine articles about their profession every year. As an architect and former student of architecture, the author attests to the voracious appetite architects and students have for learning more about the profession they love.

There is already a mature, rich, and fertile market for books about architecture. This is true for books about philosophy as well. Neither market is saturated. Books about architecture and philosophy are published every year. A subject search of Amazon.com

You will need to identify your market and put a number on it for your agent and editor as this author does in the first sentence of this section. You wouldn't open a newspaper stand without knowing how many people buy newspapers would you? No, of course not. The same goes for agents and editors. They are not going to attach themselves to a project that they don't see a projected audience for; it's just not feasible. It's your job to show them who the audience is and how many of them there are.

yields over 500 books that discuss "Pragmatism" in one form or another. For the subject of "architecture," there are over 40,000 books. A word search on Google.com brings a total of over 700,000 hits for "Pragmatism" and a staggering 55 million hits for "architecture." However, if the Amazon subject area is narrowed to the combination of "Pragmatism and architecture," there are no books listed. On Google, the number of hits drops to approximately 58,000, many of which use the word "architecture" in its newer context of computer science and the term "Pragmatism" not as a philosophy or method of inquiry, but as a synonym for the word "practical." A random and unscientific check of the Google hits yields a smattering of columns and magazine articles about Pragmatism in architecture, but no books on the subject.

There are, of course, many books about the history of architecture. There are books about the Chicago Fire and books about Modern Architecture. There are many books about philosophy and specifically about Pragmatism. But there are just a few magazine articles that discuss Pragmatism in architecture. The author is not aware of a single book that discusses the two in combination.

There is, however, an interest in Pragmatism as a decision-making tool for architects. In November of 2000, there was a symposium about Pragmatism and Architecture at the Museum of Modern Art in New York. Architects and philosophers attended, including the architect Peter Eisenman and the philosopher Richard Rorty. In debate fashion they, along with others, explored whether or not Pragmatism

In demonstrating the size of his audience, the author provides the agent or editor with the demographics of practicing architects, apprentices, and such. You'll want to list all that apply to your project as well as provide the agent or editor with those same numbers.

The author makes a clever use of online search engines to show a market need for his book. Since so many people now use the Internet to research and ultimately buy books, this is good anecdotal evidence to support the market value of this project. What makes this "test" so powerful is that the author details the exact steps he uses to conduct the search and what those searches yield.

is the decision-making method of architecture. The debate was inconclusive, but nevertheless, it was interesting and relevant to the subject of this book. It will be discussed in more detail in the final chapter of the book. See the outline for chapter twelve below.

COMPETITION

The author is aware of the following recently published, related books. None of the books, however, address the overall objective or subject of this book proposal. The books listed also illustrate the richness of the market area for a book that combines the two interesting subjects of architecture and philosophy.

- *Pragmatism: A Reader*, edited by Louis Menand, 1997, Vintage, paperback, list price $16.00, Amazon sales rank 30,857. A compilation of writings by various philosophers of Pragmatism, Peirce, James, Oliver Wendell Holmes, Dewey, Rorty and others.
- *The Devil in the White City: Murder, Magic and Madness at the Fair That Changed America*, Erik Larson, 2004, Vintage, hardcover or paperback, list price–$14.95, Amazon sales rank 147. An entertaining history about the building of the 1893 Columbian Exhibition.
- *Modern Architecture*, Vincent Scully, 2003, George Braziller, hardcover, list price–$45.00, Amazon sales rank 105,746. A recently published book about Modern Architecture.
- *The American Evasion of Philosophy: A Genealogy of Pragmatism*, Cornel West, 1989, University of Wisconsin Press,

Make sure you do your research for this section. Search online and visit your local bookstore. You need to know who you are up against. This analysis shows there is a market for this type of book and states how the proposed book is unique from what is readily available.

List as many competitive titles as you wish, but stick with current titles. Every book proposal should contain at least four titles that are either competitive or will complement your book.

paperback, list price–$19.95, Amazon sales rank 143,065. Discusses Pragmatism in American thought from Emerson through Dewey to the present.

- *Philosophy and Social Hope*, Richard Rorty, 1999, Penguin Books, paperback, list price–$15.00, Amazon sales rank 196,469. A collection of essays including a discussion of Rorty's philosophical move from the Rationalism of Plato to the Pragmatism of James and Dewey.
- *Louis Sullivan, Prophet of Modern Architecture*, Hugh Morrison, updated and reprinted 1998, W. W. Norton & Company, Inc., hardcover, list price–$25.00, Amazon sales rank 196,956. This is a reissue of Morrison's classic text about Louis Sullivan.

ABOUT THE AUTHOR

William G. Ramroth, Jr. is a practicing architect with over thirty years of experience in architectural design and construction. He has been involved in the management, design, and construction of dozens of building projects, ranging in size from small remodeling projects to multidisciplinary, large-scale building projects of over $100 million dollars in construction cost.

He has Bachelor's and Master's of Architecture degrees from the University of Oregon. He is a member of the American Institute of Architects (AIA) and is certified by the National Council of Architectural Registration Board (NCARB). He is LEED certified by the U.S. Green Building Council (USGBC) as a leader in the design

You need to realize that the competitive analysis has several missions. It is to show your agent and editor what type of similar books exist and hopefully that they have sold well; to show how your book differs from them, is unique, or will shed new light on your subject; and to show that you in fact have done your research homework. You need to prove you know what you're proposing.

The bio section of your proposal is where you are marketing yourself as an author, an expert, and a relentless promoter. You need to shine in the eyes of agents and editors, and here is your chance to do it. This author states his experience and shows he his an expert in his field. He also lists his professional memberships, which are great avenues for promoting a book of this sort.

of energy-efficient and environmentally sensitive "green" buildings. He is a member of MENSA.

He has been a guest lecturer at the University of Oregon where he lectured and participated in seminars regarding methods of synthesizing the aesthetic, structural, financial, and technology parameters that affect the design of buildings.

Publications include:

- "Upgrading the Great Hall Ceiling", *APT Bulletin*, Vol. XIX No. 3 1987, The Association for Preservation Technology, Washington DC.
- "Energy and Building: A Study of the Energy Consumption of Structural Systems", Thesis presented to the Graduate School of the University of Oregon, August 1974.

Mr. Ramroth has been a keen student of philosophy his entire life. Pragmatism is the philosophy he has found most relevant to the practice of architecture. In his continuous study of architectural history, theory, and philosophy, he has found the pragmatic method to be most beneficial in resolving the multifaceted factors at play in the real-world practice of architecture. Pragmatism is the philosopher's stone for understanding the theories of design, actions, and rhetoric of modern architectural theorists and practitioners alike.

This author already has some experience as a speaker. Even though he doesn't mention further engagements, at least the editor or agent will know that he isn't afraid to speak to groups of people and that universities think he is a qualified expert. Think back to any speaking experiences that you have had that are relevant and include them in your proposal.

PRAGMATISM AND THE METHOD
OF MODERN ARCHITECTURE

TABLE OF CONTENTS

Keeping within the range of ten to twelve chapters for your proposed project is most common, although some do vary in length from quite short to extremely long. The basic idea is to use as many chapters as you need to develop your book in full form. Every book is different and will require a different commitment on the part of the author.

OUTLINE OF CHAPTERS

Introduction

The "Introduction" is included in the "Sample Chapters" section of this book proposal. Note that some of the ideas and text presented in the "Introduction" were included in the "Overview" as well.

Chapter 1: A Clean Slate

The first chapter will start with the Great Chicago Fire of 1871. It will discuss how it produced a clean slate, or Locke's tabla rasa, the necessary conditions for a new approach to architecture. See Sample Chapter 1.

Chapter 2: Proto-Pragmatism—Nineteenth Century Philosophy in America

During the late eighteenth and early nineteenth centuries, Americans accepted Europe as the bastion of everything that was Culture with a capital "C." This included architecture and philosophy. Americans designed and built buildings in the style of Europeans. They thought like Europeans as well.

For most Americans thinking like Europeans was done without reflection, without any formal schooling. It was done by simply doing what came naturally—naturally, that is, for someone steeped in the culture of Western Civilization. For the more privileged, this fondness for everything European came about as a result of European-styled education. Designing buildings in the style of the Europeans

---

This is a very thorough outline detailing the chapter contents and doesn't leave the reader to guess what will be covered. Tell your agent or editor what insight she can expect to gain from each of your chapters. They will also be paying close attention to your organizational skills.

Describe each chapter in an easy-to-understand way. Your objective is to convey your idea to the readers, not to confuse them. The amount of text you apply is up to you and the project you are preparing to write.

was done so deliberately. It gave immediate cultural recognition and an air of significance and tradition to American architecture.

As Americans moved westward, they relied more and more heavily on their own abilities, wits, and skills of craftsmanship. By the 1870s, Americans had gained confidence in themselves and in their growing nation. Americans were beginning to develop their own ways of doing things, including their own way of building. Balloon framing, as discussed in Chapter 1, is one such example.

Americans were beginning to develop their own way of thinking, too. At the outset, this was not done consciously. Nevertheless, Americans slowly developed new attitudes towards problem solving and testing out ideas. Pragmatism, the only truly American major philosophical system, grew out of this uniquely American way of thinking and doing.

This chapter will discuss the prominent European philosophical systems of the early nineteenth century that factored into the formulation of the philosophy of Pragmatism, often called American Pragmatism. These philosophies will be discussed in enough detail to allow an understanding of their influence on the founding fathers of Pragmatism as discussed in the following chapter.

Following is a list of the major philosophical systems prevalent in mid-nineteenth century America that affected the development of Pragmatism. Each will be discussed in this chapter.

1. Rationalism: Truth and/or knowledge are arrived at intellectually, deductively.

The benefit of crafting these summaries helps both you as the writer and the agent and editors to which you will be proposing your book. The agents and editors can see how in-depth you have gone in the creation process and get a feel for what the book will contain. For you as the writer, it is essentially your road map for the book to follow. Because this author has put so much thought into creating detailed summaries, it will be easy for him to take this outline and flesh it out into a complete book.

2. Empiricism: The sole source of truth and/or knowledge is sensory experience.

3. Kantianism: Sometimes called Transcendentalism because Kant claimed his philosophy transcended Rationalism and Empiricism. Knowledge comes by way of the mind's processing of sensory experiences through its *a priori* categories of understanding.

4. Hegelianism: Both a philosophical doctrine and a method, called the dialectic. Knowledge and history spiral upward towards the ultimate truth through a triadic process of Thesis, Antithesis, and Synthesis.

5. Traditionalism: Truth is not discovered individually, or personally. It is to be found in societal traditions.

6. Utilitarianism: The greatest good is the act that brings the greatest pleasure to the greatest number of people.

7. Darwinism: The theory of evolution that holds that all plants and animals, including man, developed from earlier life forms. Darwinism employs the scientific method.

8. Social Darwinism: An application of Darwinism to human societal affairs. Its mantra was "the survival of the fittest."

Chapter 3: Peirce, James and Dewey—The Prophets of Pragmatism

This chapter will discuss the work of Charles Sanders Peirce, William James, and John Dewey, the founders of Pragmatism.

This author presents a list of what will be covered in this chapter. This is the perfect use of a list. Explaining terms that people may be unfamiliar with is easier to do in list form than in paragraph form. And since each of these things is covered in the chapter, the list allows the author to present a lot of information at a glance. Lists are a great way to get your message across quickly. Not only that, but it's a clean, easily read format, appreciated by both agents and editors.

Charles Sanders Peirce was thirty-two years old at the time of the Chicago Fire. An employee of the U.S. Coast and Geodetic Survey, he returned to the United States six months prior to the fire from an assignment in Europe where he observed solar eclipses. A mathematician, an astronomer, a geologist, a physicist, a chemist, and a self-taught philosopher, Charles Peirce was a Renaissance man of the nineteenth century. His mind was a busy, buzzing place, afire with contrasting, exciting, and new ideas. By the early 1870s he was already searching for a method of clarifying the many concepts in his head. In 1868 he published his first essay, "On a New List of Categories", in which he argued that the sole purpose of any concept was to bring unity to sense impressions. If the concept failed to do this or if the unity of impressions could be explained without applying the concept, then the concept was useless. His article, "How To Make Your Ideas Clear", which appeared in *Popular Science Monthly* in 1878, he suggested that the best method for clarifying ideas or concepts was to put them to an experimental test. The test would produce observable results. Analyze those results. The results would tell the actual meaning of the idea or concept. If no results were observable, there was no idea or concept. Peirce suggested this method without giving it a name. The name for the method came later from a lecture given by William James.

James chose the term "Pragmatism" for the method "invented" (James' word) by his friend because of James' familiarity with the work of Emmanuel Kant. Emmanuel Kant was the first to use the term "pragmatic" in a philosophical treatise, his *Critique of Pure*

The author covers a lot of ground in chapter three but does a good job of breaking down the information into clearly defined paragraphs. Each paragraph flows logically form one to the next, and the author is able to weave together three different key figures in the history of pragmatism. Overall, agents and editors will glean that the author is an excellent writer and has the skills to ultimately write a complete book.

Reason, published in 1781. Kant used the term to describe the reasoning method employed by the mind to give meaning to the phenomena it receives through sense perceptions. Kant saw this pragmatic technique in stark contrast to the other way that the mind gives meaning to the world, through *a priori* principles which he called categories of understanding.

William James was both a close friend and disciple of Peirce. It is James' lecture, given some twenty years after Peirce's *Popular Science Monthly* article first appeared, that presented the philosophy of Pragmatism to a worldwide and enthusiastic audience. In the lecture, James gave full credit to his friend, Peirce.

Later in their lives, Peirce and James had a bitter falling out, which led to tragic consequences for Peirce. There are subtle but significant differences between Peirce and James in their meaning of Pragmatism. For Peirce, Pragmatism is a method, which is basically scientific and empirical, used to attain the truth regarding an idea or concept. For James, Pragmatism was more than a method. It was a philosophy, a comprehensive worldview that offered an explanation for the beliefs and social interactions of man. It was not of much importance to James whether an idea or belief was true or not. What mattered was the practical consequence, the cash value, of the idea or belief. This difference led Peirce to eventually rename his brand of Pragmatism, "Pragmaticism," an awkward-sounding name that never caught on.

John Dewey arrived in Chicago one year after the Columbian Exposition, taking the position of Chairman of the Department of Phi-

You may find as you write your summaries that your book has begun to evolve. Writing is a process, and out of this process you can expect change. You may end up with an entirely different book in the end from the one you first had in mind. Or you may come up with several new book ideas that just magically came to mind while you were writing this one. If that is the case, write the titles down for future possible book projects.

losophy, Psychology, and Education at the University of Chicago. He spent the previous ten years as a professor at the University of Michigan. Prior to that, he received his doctorate from Johns Hopkins University. While at Johns Hopkins, he met and studied under Charles Peirce.

While strongly influenced by Peirce, Dewey preferred to call his brand of Pragmatism "Experimentalism" or "Instrumentalism" to distinguish his work from Peirce and James. Since Dewey's work offered only subtle differences from Peirce and James, the practical outcome is that Dewey is remembered today as a pragmatist.

Dewey was a professional philosopher in an era when philosophy was just becoming a true profession, one with an identifiable career path. With Dewey, Pragmatism reached maturity.*

Crafting your summaries is going to be hard work; don't let anyone tell you different. It will take an enormous amount of research, time commitment, and persistence to get the job done. But if you really work at it, your well-written summaries will speak for themselves and get the attention of an agent or editor.

Again, this author originally included chapter summaries for each chapter in the book.

Published in October 2000 by Aegis Publishing Group

SANDY TRUPP AND MAUREEN CHASE Authors

Maureen Chase and I were looking at some terrible emails that were sent to us including all caps, bad spelling and grammar, and no subject header, and we decided that someone should do a book on the subject. Ten minutes later Maureen came into my office and suggested that *we* do the book together.

Don't Stub Your Pinkie on the Spacebar (our original title) was a play on the "Oh-No Moment" when you realize that you just sent a really bad email and can't bring it back. We found though that it worked better as a subtitle and the final title for the book is *Office Emails That Really Click: Don't Stub Your Pinkie on the Spacebar*. It is the first book for both of us. However, we have both coached many authors.

We used the Internet and just couldn't find any books that approached the subject.

We wanted to make it different and brainstormed the concept. It took us a few days to write the proposal.

We decided to sell the book ourselves without an agent. We aren't recommending this at all. The rejection letters came to my house, and I thought I could "take it," but it was starting to get depressing after the fiftieth letter. Then we did a "re-spin" with a new title, and we received three offers.

ROBERT MASTIN Editor

The most compelling element in the proposal was the fact that the authors were already established experts in generating publicity for books. As professionals in public relations, they would be able to handle much of the publicity themselves with their expertise in PR, they could be immensely helpful with one of the most important chores of a publisher: generating publicity for the book. Knowing that much of this would be taken care of made me give their proposal a lot more attention.

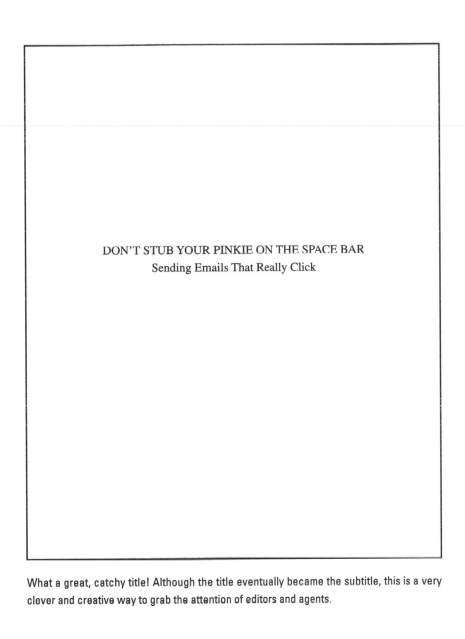

DON'T STUB YOUR PINKIE ON THE SPACE BAR
Sending Emails That Really Click

What a great, catchy title! Although the title eventually became the subtitle, this is a very clever and creative way to grab the attention of editors and agents.

TABLE OF CONTENTS

This table of contents is for the book and not the proposal. It is short, but contains a few explanatory notes for certain chapters. The authors give the information they feel is needed to grab someone's attention—and it worked. There are some intriguing items listed in this table of contents, like the EMQ quiz, and easy e-mail rules.

INTRODUCTION

Let us stop the madness before it proliferates! Electronic mail is a wonderful form of communication. We should not let our need for expedience interfere with the rules of English grammar and business etiquette.

(Electronic mail is commonly referred to as E-mail, Email, e-mail, or email. We prefer using "Email" in the beginning of a sentence or "email" within a sentence as a reference.)

This book will give you a good model of what emails in the workplace should look like. *Don't Stub Your Pinkie on the Space Bar: Sending Emails That Really Click* outlines a complete and standard format for emails. People spend too much time on email now to ignore the need for a guidebook. No more obsessing over what to say or how to say it: We have done that for you.

For example:

James gave a promotion to Lucy. What is the appropriate format for announcing her promotion on email?

The stock market has dropped hundreds of points this morning. Eric needs to hold an emergency meeting with his staff in thirty minutes in the conference room. What does he say in his email?

You need to ask a client to send you his bio. What is the best wording via email?

We have the answers to all of these questions.

After speaking with clients, friends, and relatives, we have found there is a need and demand for a book about sending suc-

This proposal begins with a great hook that everyone can relate to. After reading this paragraph, you want to read more and find out what the proposal is going to offer. Draw your reader in at the very top of your proposal. Your goal is to create interest.

cessful emails. In most offices today, there is no formal training session that covers the use of email. Between us, we receive 500 emails per day. We are communications experts and are internationally plugged into the world of business emails. We know what works and what flops—from experience. And, we advise our clients, who range from celebrities to corporations to politicians, on effective communication.

Don't Stub Your Pinkie on the Space Bar is for everyone at work who uses email or has even heard about email. We must ensure the preservation of our written language for a future that will rely heavily on email communication.

Our purpose is to raise questions about email, provide some answers through easy-to-follow guidelines, and to help people send successful emails that really "click."

CHAPTER I: ELECTRONIC MAIL QUOTIENT

No good book should start without a quiz! The following questions will test your Electronic Mail Quotient, or EMQ level!

QUIZ

1. When you receive an email message, at what point is it appropriate to reply?
   - a) immediately—I hate to keep people waiting!
   - b) within a week
   - c) do I have to reply?

Citing anecdotal evidence for the need for your book is fine. Here the authors connect their own anecdotal evidence to their expertise in the area of providing effective communication for the public.

Rather than writing a traditional chapter outline summary with a paragraph describing the content of the chapter, the authors have chosen a more creative approach. The material is funny and clever and shows they know how to write. If your proposal lends itself to this type of creative chapter outline, then give it a try. Ultimately, it may help your proposal to stand out from the crowd.

2. If you forward emails, how often do you send them out?

    a) only if it's a great or important message, like computer viruses

    b) sometimes—there are some pretty funny jokes out there

    c) all day long—I love all of those chain letters going around email!

3. Suppose you received a "joke" email that you think is funny. To how many people might you forward it?

    a) 1 person

    b) 5–10 people

    c) 50 people

4. Have you ever been guilty of spamming?

    a) no

    b) yes

    c) what is spamming?

5. When you send emails do you usually use a subject header?

    a) yes, of course, I label all of my emails

    b) no, why should I?

    d) what is a subject header?

6. How often do you check your email?

    a) every five minutes—I can't wait any longer!

    b) once or twice per day

    c) never—do I even have email?

A quiz is a great way to add interactivity to your proposal. Editors and agents are no different than the rest of us. A quiz will immediately get your readers hooked into the proposal and wanting to find out how they did.

7. When you compose emails do you usually use a greeting such as "Hello, Kathy"?
   a) yes
   b) it depends
   c) no

8. Do you spell check your emails?
   a) Yes
   b) No
   c) Is that possible?

9. How do you sign, or close, your emails?
   a) with my full name
   b) with my initials
   c) I don't sign my emails. People should know who the sender is!

10. Can I fulfill my business obligations through email, such as thanking someone for a gift or sending out company party invitations?
    a) always
    b) sometimes—depends on the particular situation
    c) never—email is not the right forum

11. Sometimes I like to write my emails in all capital letters, or even in all lowercase letters. Is this okay?

In addition to attracting the attention of the readers, a quiz has great publicity value. This part of the book could be pulled out and used in radio interviews, online, or in ads. Editors and agents like to see that the content of your book has direct tie-ins to the media.

a) never, unless you are intending to shout, or whisper, at someone!

b) sometimes

c) always

BONUS

Where can I find a comprehensive guide to sending successful emails?

a) right here in *Don't Stub Your Pinkie on the Space Bar: Sending Emails That Really Click*

TRACK YOUR EMQ!!!

If most or all of your answers were…

A—You are "EMAIL LITERATE"

Congratulations! You are Email Literate. Look through *Don't Stub Your Pinkie on the Space Bar* to perfect your skills!

B—You are "EMAIL FRIENDLY"

Not bad! You are getting there. Take a look through *Don't Stub Your Pinkie on the Space Bar* and brush up on your email skills!

C—You need "HELP!!!"

It's okay! We suggest you learn the tricks of the trade from *Don't Stub Your Pinkie on the Space Bar*! Really, it can turn your life around! Soon you'll be sending emails that really click!

A clever way of summing up the quiz is exemplified in the bonus question. It's a fun reminder of the value of the book. Any way you can keep mentioning your title and your book is good, but it can get redundant. Finding unique ways, such as this, are always a plus.

Again, the authors have chosen to highlight their own creativity rather than present information in a more traditional format as you've seen in the other proposals. If you decide to take this route, you need to be sure your subject matter lends itself to this type of creative presentation. Since the tone of this book is humorous, the authors have more leeway in creatively presenting the material.

EMAIL OUTREACH: DOS AND DON'TS

(Taking your EMQ skills to the next level)

Do you have virtual seizures when you arrive to work and discover you have 375 unread emails, not to mention mountains of other work for the day? (We won't begin to touch on voice mail messages!) Well, business email users are saying that there ARE unwritten rules for email etiquette, one of which is not to send too many emails out there. People don't have enough time to eat a square meal let alone read about 300 "junk" emails. Today, we are writing down the rules of etiquette, starting with DON'TS. Don't worry—for every "don't" we have a corresponding "do" below.

DON'TS

10. Forwarding jokes to a long list of your co-workers daily, especially without permission of those to whom you send the emails
9. Emails without greetings or closings
8. Emails without subject headers, or with improperly denoted headers
7. Sending urgent emails and expecting the receiver to have gotten the email
6. Writing private information over email
5. Spamming
4. Never replying to emails
3. Bad spelling and grammar in emails

The authors write their proposal in a light, breezy tone, which presumably will carry over into the finished book. They are conversational and engaging—a great thing to be when you are trying to engage a wide audience on a topic like e-mail. If your topic isn't serious, don't take yourself too seriously. You don't have to try to be comedic, but be as casual as you can while still getting your point across.

2. Using all capital or all lowercase letters in email

1. Sending junk email

DOS

10. Ask permission of your colleagues if they would like to be included in forwarded joke emails or any other type of email. And, when forwarding the email, please send it blind copy. You wouldn't want your email address being forwarded to strangers, would you?

9. Please use proper greetings and closings in your emails, such as "Hello, John!" or "Best wishes, Kathy." Sometimes, emails with nothing but the body of a letter come across as commands.

8. Please do not leave the subject header of your emails blank. If someone receives 300+ emails per day, how will he or she know what yours is about or how to prioritize it? When you respond to emails that were sent to you, remember to change the subject header if you are in fact changing the subject. A letter to your colleague with a subject header, "Eggnog and mistletoe" might look a bit silly in April. Although your last email with this colleague was at Christmas time, you are now replying to him or her about Easter vacation plans.

7. If you have an urgent email to send to someone, please write "URGENT" in the header, so the receiver knows it is to be

Dos and Don'ts lists help summarize your material in a fun and clever way. In the Dos section, the authors not only give the tip but also go on to explain it some. This gives a good taste of the content of the book and the advice that it will contain. Remember, you should give enough information to give an agent or editor the flavor of your book, but don't overload them in your proposal.

read immediately. Don't always expect the receiver to have gotten the email. He or she could be away on business or vacation. If you really need to get a hold of someone, call him or her. If you are going away on vacation or will be out of the office, use the "out of office assistant" (if available), which will notify everyone who emails you that you are out of the office until a date specified.

6. Remember email is not as private as we think, especially at work. Others have access to your email, so remember not to write personal things in your emails. And, if someone emails you personal information, ask this person kindly not to write anything personal in nature over the email.

5. If you receive a forwarded email, and the list of receivers is included on the email, please do not use this list for yourself. Do not be tempted to hit "reply all," and please do not use this list for soliciting. If you "spam" and reply to the list for another purpose, people will not be happy with you. The sender of the entire list should have been courteous to send a blind copied email to this list of recipients in the first place.

4. If you receive an email, a thank-you, or a question needing to be answered, then please reply. Granted, sometimes we don't have the time to email people. If that is the case, then reply to the sender that you are not able to respond quickly to emails, it might take up to three weeks. Give the sender an idea of how often you use your email. Not everyone is

The authors include some of the most fun and interesting material in the book in their proposal. That's important if you want to draw someone in. They give the information that may have the broadest appeal. That's not to say the rest of their book won't have that appeal, but they do a nice job at choosing effective material for their proposal. You can think of it like a movie preview: What will get people's attention and make them want to come back for more? On the other hand, we've all seen movies where all the good parts were in the preview and the rest of the movie was not good. Don't let that happen. Make sure your entire book will be interesting. Some parts are just better to use to attract attention to it.

online all day! Plus, if someone thanks you or asks you a question, it is only polite to acknowledge it!

3. Remember your spelling. Too many people stub their pinkie on the space bar. Bad spelling, poor grammar, and a host of other problems surface in emails that most of us would not do in normal letters. Email is not a forum for bad spelling. Use Spellcheck! If your system does not have it, then proofread your writing carefully, just like people did in the '80s.

2. WHAT THE HECK ARE YOU THINKING WHEN YOU USE ALL CAPS IN YOUR EMAILS? Basically, an email with all caps has the effect of shouting at someone. Plus, it is difficult to read all caps. And please do not write emails that are so small that people cannot even read them. Yes, it will get their attention, but really, it's very annoying. Plus, I need a magnifying glass to read this!

1. Do not send junk email advertisements to people without their permission. All that rubbish you receive in your mailbox outside the house will soon be replaced by rubbish in your virtual mailbox, if it isn't already. When someone sends you junk email, click on "reply to sender," and ask this person politely to take you off of his or her list. If the sender does not, then contact your email provider for information. Your email provider can often protect you against unsolicited email.

The authors use a typographical treatment that catches the eye but also serves a purpose. If your content lends itself to some visual treatment, don't be afraid to vary from standard type. However, don't do this unless it absolutely helps to make a point. Doing it just to be cute or to draw attention will just make an editor or agent think you are an amateur. But if it truly aids in meaning, then it can work.

CHAPTER II: GUIDELINES

Easy Email Rules that Everyone Can Follow

Have you received an email with a subject header that looks something like this?

FWD: FWD: FWD: FWD: FWD: FWD: FWD: FWD: FWD: No subject.

For sure you've gotten an email with no subject. What is this email about? After spending several minutes scrolling down the tangle of email addresses, did you wonder, "Where did this message originate? Is my name on some sort of list?" This may have happened to you. Or, you may have sent one just like it yourself!

Perhaps one of your colleagues has sent you an email like the following:

Outta here! Leavin' 2day @ 4 cos I need some zzzzzzs.

C Ya!

Are you flipping out yet? This email has no greeting or closing and uses incorrect spelling and words. Yes, it is cute and funny, but is this a professional way to communicate with colleagues? They might not even understand this! Do you?

Follow a few simple rules, and you can be understood in your emails. No confusion. No anarchy of the language.

Everyone can relate to this example of seeing the "FWD" repeated in the email. The idea here is to get the editor or agent to connect to the material.

The authors use clever examples to punctuate the proposal. You may want to sprinkle your proposal with some creative ways to get the agent or editor to stop reading and laugh to themselves. That's what's happening here.

GENERAL GUIDELINES FOR CREATING AN EMAIL

- Get your message across the right way.
- Use a subject header (e.g., Today's meeting, Urgent!, Happy Hour, etc.).
- Address the recipient with a greeting, such as "Hello, Rita!".
- Write the contents the way you would in a letter, adhering to the rules of English grammar.
- Sign off the email with a closing, and your name, or initials. (Some email programs have auto signature. That works well, too, for your name. Include your address and phone number in the auto signature, too, in case the recipient has questions.)
- If the email is urgent, address that in the subject header. Many people get dozens of emails daily; help them to decide which ones are most important. If the email is not urgent then do *not* label it as such.
- Attaching documents: When attaching documents, remember that not all computers can "talk" to each other. Your recipient might not be able to read your document. Always attach *and* cut and paste a document to be sure the recipient can read your email. Or ask first to determine if your computer can truly "speak" with that of your recipient.

Bulleted lists create a visually stimulating way to present this information. Each item on the list is a helpful tip that helps to flesh out the overall explanation of how to reply to an email. When creating a list bulleted list, make sure that each item is clearly connected to the overarching topic of the list.

REPLYING TO AN EMAIL

- Click on reply and email your message back to the recipient.
- Remember to follow the structure of a proper email: subject, greeting, contents, closing.
- Reply time—reply by the end of the day; if the email is urgent, then reply right away. If you only are able to check your email messages infrequently—for instance, once every other day—then let your recipient know that when replying. That goes for distribution of emails as well. When giving out your email address to people, let them know how often you check your messages. It is a more timely form of communication for some than others.

SENDING THE RIGHT SIGNALS

- Invite follow-through. Tell recipients how you would like them to respond to your email.
- Make no misunderstandings about what you expect from your recipient in sending this email.

GRAMMAR AND SPELLCHECK

- Remember to check your emails for correct grammar and spelling. Many email programs have built-in Spellcheck.
- Do not use all capital letters in your emails. That indicates you are shouting at your recipient. Likewise, do not use all lower-case letters either. That is the equivalent of whispering.

These are nice short lists with clear headings that make it easy to see what will be covered in the book. By reading the headings at first glance, an editor or agent already has a clue as to what will be addressed. Then, reading the lists gives more detail.

STYLE

- Remember who you are addressing
- Boss and clients command most formal language.
- Colleagues and staff can be a bit more relaxed.
- Format—use colors and other animation in your emails. This is one of the nice options in many email programs. You might not want to use this feature in your emailed annual general report, however. Use discretion. Colors might be best for invitations or happy hours.

TOOLS

- Address Lists: remember to create and use them with care. If sending out a group email, use the blind copy option in your email program in order to keep your recipients' email addresses private. Not everyone, especially fellow clients, like their emails to be distributed to others.
- Auto reply: when you are out of the office for several days, use the auto reply feature. When someone emails you, then they automatically will receive a pre-created message from you. Make sure to include your departure and arrival dates as well as emergency contacts in this email.
- Auto receipt: this is a nice feature to see when your recipient received his or her email from you. Don't always assume that the recipient has read the email carefully, though. Remember to label the email "urgent" if it is.

The authors do a good job of directly addressing the reader in their sample text. This shows that they know how self-help books should be written. Addressing the reader directly with imperative statements is much more engaging than saying "You should include ..." Simply saying "Include ..." makes for a much snappier book.

WHEN *NOT* TO USE EMAIL

- For confidential reports—Remember that confidentiality cannot be assured in email. Your system administrator has access to your files, for example, through back-up files.
- Personal emails—Each office has its own guidelines on the use of company email for personal use. If it is okay for you to use your company email, then just remember that anyone can read your emails. Don't be disparaging your boss on the email! And, keep in mind no love letter is sacred!

In general, make sure there are no misunderstandings in your emails. Sending the right "signals" is very important for emails that really click. If you don't hear back from your recipient by 12:00 noon and you sent an "extremely urgent" email at 8:30 A.M., then use the old-fashioned telephone and call. Remember, sometimes computers crash and your recipient might not have received your message. *

A list like this can also be turned into a great sidebar for a magazine article. You should always think about how your ideas can be turned into short pieces for newspapers or magazines. The authors of this proposal are two leading PR professionals, so their proposal contains a lot of "PR-friendly" material.

The authors included three more chapter samples that continue in this way. We believe these chapter summaries work effectively for a book of this nature. The authors took a chance in thinking outside the box in terms of the format and content of the proposal. But ultimately, the proposal sold, and this fresh approach helped to differentiate the proposal from the competition.

SANDRA TRUPP

Managing Director

Planned Television Arts Washington

As managing director of Planned Television Arts (PTA), a division of Ruder•Finn Washington, Sandra Trupp is responsible for the regional operations and creative strategies of the division. Her team develops media campaigns targeting national and local media for clients including spokespersons, celebrities, politicians, corporations and authors. Ms. Trupp also specializes in media training and publishing consultation.

Ms. Trupp has worked in the publishing field for over twenty years in the areas of publicity, marketing, and product development. She was also a producer at NBC. Ms. Trupp works with many best-selling authors, including Sophia Loren, Paul Reiser, Giselle Fernandez, Larry King, Harvey Mackay, Edward James Olmos, Jack Anderson, Rosemary Altea, Deidre Hall, Brad Meltzer, Letitia Baldrige, and Carole Jackson.

She developed the publicity strategy for *Color Me Beautiful*, which remained on *The New York Times* best seller list for three years and was reprinted in every country in the world. During her career, Ms. Trupp created joint promotions for major corporations and organizations, including Campbell's Soup Company, JC Penney, Proctor & Gamble, Clairol, The Insurance Information Institute, Kodak, Gannett Corporation, and Pepperidge Farms.

Her experience with book development includes coordinating projects with the Library of Congress, the Humane Society of the

The author has insider knowledge of the publishing industry. This is a great asset when it comes to publicity and marketing. Always make sure to show how your insider connections can lead to very specific publicity and marketing opportunities.

The author has ties to a best-selling book. This adds to her credibility as a successful public relations executive who knows how to publicize her own book.

United States, The Smithsonian Institution, the Brookings Institution, the National Museum of the American Indian, the American Academy of Facial and Plastic Reconstruction, and the National Wildlife Federation.

Ms. Trupp gives talks to writers and professional groups. She has produced several concerts at the Smithsonian's Baird Auditorium, Kennedy Center Terrace Theatre, University of the District of Columbia and George Washington University. She is a board member of the American News Women's Club and is also a member of many other organizations, including The Larry King Cardiac Foundation, The Women's National Book Association, and Women of Washington and Washington Women in PR (WWPR). She was honored by WWPR in 1997 for her PR achievements and mentoring efforts.

Ms. Trupp is a graduate of the University of Maryland and Peabody Conservatory of Music.

MAUREEN CHASE
Publicity Director
Planned Television Arts Washington
Maureen Chase is publicity director at Planned Television Arts (PTA), a division of Ruder•Finn Washington, and has worked with PTA and Ruder•Finn since 1995. Ms. Chase creates broadcast media campaigns targeting national and local media for a diverse client base, including celebrities, politicians, nonprofits, corporations, and publishing companies. Ms. Chase also specializes in media training.

Ms. Trupp has a strong platform which includes public speaking. This shows that the author can do her own promotion and publicity to sell the book. Any and all avenues you have to support your book and your publisher should be noted in your proposal.

Ms. Chase aslo has great media contacts, which are an essential part of her platform. As the editor mentioned at the start of this proposal, it was these kinds of contacts that ultimately sold the project for him.

Ms. Chase has extensive experience with book and magazine promotions for authors such as Jimmy Carter, Oprah Winfrey, William Bennett, Sophia Loren, Larry King, Giselle Fernandez, Tim Allen, Paul Reiser, Edward James Olmos, and Kitty Kelley. Ms. Chase has also provided media expertise for Johnson & Johnson, Procter & Gamble, Discovery Communications, Inc., the Brookings Institution, the Global Climate Coalition, National Clearing House Association, several U.S. representatives to Congress, and many others.

Ms. Chase is also a founder of PTA's Team Español, which specializes in Spanish media cultivation. She promotes the newly launched *People en Español* magazine series for *People* magazine on a bimonthly basis, and publicizes the Hispanic Heritage Awards at the Kennedy Center for the Hispanic Heritage Foundation. Ms. Chase promoted the company-wide multimedia campaign, Americanos, with Edward James Olmos, and clients Time Warner and the Smithsonian.

Ms. Chase is also a semiregular on Washington D.C.'s *Fox Morning News*, commenting on the image of public figures, including President Clinton. Ms. Chase has also been interviewed by many nationally syndicated media, including: *CNN*, *Bloomberg News*, *America's Voice*, and *Gannett News Service*.

Ms. Chase came to Planned Television Arts with international journalism and public relations experience. She has received fellowships for her writing, and she has been published in the *Tampa Tribune* as well as *The Stars and Stripes* newspapers. She has reported

---

The author has direct experience in promotion and cites specific authors she has worked with. Share your pertinent background information in your bio and throughout all other areas of the proposal where they may apply. Remember, you are selling yourself as well as your book project.

The author has experience with a variety of cultural organizations in other languages. This is a strong aspect of her bio because books are now marketed in many different languages and to a variety of different consumers. If you can help to reach a unique audience, then specify that in your proposal.

from many countries, including Kenya, Germany, Finland, Estonia, and Sweden. Ms. Chase graduated from Washington and Lee University with a B.A. in journalism, and attended Estudio Internacional Sampere in Madrid, Spain for studies in Spanish.

Ms. Chase is vice president of the Washington and Lee University Washington, DC, Alumni Board of Directors, publicity co-chair for the American New Women's Club Board, and a member of the Larry King Cardiac Foundation, Women of Washington, Washington Women in PR, and the Finlandia Foundation.

As an expert who already appears on television, the author already has a strong media platform from which to launch the book. If you have appeared on television, you should include these clips with your proposal or provide a Web site link for agents and editors where they can view them. This is a very strong asset for selling a proposal, and you don't want to underplay this in any way.

Appendix
Notable Web Sites to Visit

The best way to familiarize yourself with the industry is to visit publishing's most helpful Web sites. Here you will find tons of valuable information that will help you in your pursuit of becoming a published author.

The Authors Guild
www.authorsguild.org
The guild has been the voice of American writers for over eighty years. This comprehensive site features bulletins, contract advice, a listing of publishers, current articles concerning the industry, and much more.

Authorlink
www.authorlink.com
This is a connection service for agents, editors, and writers.

Literary Market Place
www.literarymarketplace.com
Literary Market Place offers a great deal of information on book publishers, small press organizations, and agents, including contact information.

The National Writers Union
www.nwu.org
The NWU is a union for writers providing various services to their members, such as health care benefits, contract assistance, and free resources.

291

R.R. Bowker

www.bowker.com

R.R. Bowker offers a listing of books in print and out of print. It is a directory of the industry and much, much more.

The Writers Guild

www.wga.org

Like the National Writers Union, the WGA provides a wealth of resources for its members, including health benefits, updates on industry news, contract guidance, and many other useful tools.

Endorsements Inc.

www.endorsementsinc.com

The industry leader in endorsement services for all your literary property needs, Endorsements Inc. is a major network that serves authors both before and after publication.

WritersMarket.com

www.writersmarket.com

This subscription-based service provides the most inclusive—and always current—market contact info for all your publishing needs

Writers Digest

www.writersdigest.com

A site hosted by *Writer's Digest* magazine, it offers writing instruction, conference schedules, competitions, and a variety of other resources that benefit writers.

Publishers Weekly Online

www.publishersweekly.com

A major news publication of the book industry, it provides up-to-date information on sales, marketing, production, and other aspects of the industry.

The Book Standard

www.thebookstandard.com

It contains publishing-related facts, figures, and charts, industry insights, and book reviews

Index